BUSINESS LENDING

Keith Checkley FCIB
and
Keith Dickinson FCIB

Financial World Publishing
IFS House
4-9 Burgate Lane
Canterbury
Kent
CT1 2XJ
United Kingdom

T   01227 818687

F   01227 479641

E   editorial@ifslearning.com

W   www.ifslearning.com

Financial World Publishing publications are published by The Chartered Institute of Bankers, a non-profit making registered educational charity.

The Chartered Institute of Bankers believes that the sources of information upon which the book is based are reliable and has made every effort to ensure the complete accuracy of the text. However, neither CIB, the author nor any contributor can accept any legal responsibility whatsoever for consequences that may arise from errors or omissions or any opinion or advice given.

Trademarks
Many words in this publication in which the author and publisher believe trademarks or other proprietary rights may exist have been designated as such by use of Initial Capital Letters. However, in so designating or failing to designate such words, neither the author nor the publisher intends to express any judgement on the validity or legal status of any proprietary right that may be claimed in the words.

Typeset by Kevin O'Connor

Printed by Ashford Colour Press, Gosport, Hants

© The Chartered Institute of Bankers 2001

ISBN 0-85297-603-8

CONTENTS

Contents

INTRODUCTION

The Concept of the Course

This study text has been written for students of The Chartered Institute of Bankers' ACIB/ BSc subject Business Lending, and also for practitioners in financial services who are looking for a practical refresher.

Each chapter is divided into sections and contains learning objectives and clear, concise topic-by-topic coverage.

Syllabus

The key sections of the Business Lending syllabus are:

● Risk management at portfolio level;

● The principles of business lending;

● Credit monitoring, control and recovery;

● An understanding of the borrowing requirements and credit risks associated with differing types of businesses;

● Outline knowledge of specialist services relevant to a lending situation.

Note: The syllabus is reviewed every year. Please make sure you have the most up-to-date version.

Your contribution

Although this study text is designed to stand alone, as with most topics, certain aspects of this subject are constantly changing. Therefore it is very important that you keep up-to-date with these key areas. For example, you should read the quality press and financial journals and look out for relevant websites.

We anticipate that you will study this course for one session (six months), reading through and studying approximately one chapter every week. However, note that because topics vary in size and as knowledge tends not to fall into uniform chunks, some chapters are unavoidably longer than others.

Study plan

If you are a distance learning student and have not received your study plan by the beginning of the session, please contact the *ifs* Student Learning Support team:

T   01227 818637

F   01227 453547

E   sls@ifslearning.com

Overview

As a starting point to our book on credit it is perhaps a good idea to start with the wider perspective of the risk management function and then we shall progress to examining the processes for business lending in detail as it applies to individual prospective borrowers.

Overview of the Risk Management Function

Risk may be defined as:

The exposure to present or future loss of profits and/or capital. It arises from:

a) Faulty analysis of current circumstances or probabilities.

b) Future change of a social, commercial, economic, environmental or political nature, the effect of which cannot be anticipated or hedged, or where reaction to such change is late or insufficient.

All banks have a need to spread overall lending risk as widely as possible to reduce exposure to any one trade or industry and thus reduce overall exposure risk and profit volatility. They reduce portfolio risk by making advances to a wide variety of industries, spreading the risk among a broad client base. Being very aware of the risk of overconcentration in any one sector, banks usually operate within industry thresholds, limiting credit exposure to achieve the best mix of individual and portfolio safety.

Although loans concentrated in one particular industry may appear sound and profitable, external factors may substantially affect some industries. In recent years cyclical economic forces have been manifest in the property market, transportation, the defence industry and electronics, as have changes in industry life cycles. Banks may impose internal limits on lending to restrict exposure to any one sector. Economic influences may well be caused by government fiscal policy.

Risk assessment and management are the key skills of any successful banking operation. Most banks have some sort of risk rating system in place. The risk management process usually falls into a centralized or decentralized system. Such systems allow banks to evaluate and track risks on an industry, individual, or portfolio basis.

The principles underlying a risk rating system include:

- A common framework for assessing risk.
- Uniformity throughout the bank.
- Compatibility with regulatory requirements.
- The ability to identify satisfactory levels of credit risk.

The principles underlying the risk rating process are:

- Common training through definition and risk rating assessment guides.

- Introduction and continuity of levels of achievement on a continuing basis.

- Regular reviews by senior bank officials to test for levels of accuracy and consistency.

Such a rating system is helpful in setting fee guidelines appropriate to the degree of risk involved. There is a need for banks' internal audit departments to test for accuracy, consistency and appropriateness.

Commercial lending exposes a bank to two major types of risk – borrower risks and operating/ transactional risks, which may be defined as:

Borrower Risks

Industry Economic Risk

These cover inflation and foreign exchange risk exposure.

Industry Structure Risk

These embrace the risk inherent in a company's business environment, including entry and exit barriers, the power of suppliers or customers, the impact of technology, regulatory requirements and capital requirements.

Operating Risks

These include inability to repay, receivership or liquidation, error or fraud.

Transaction Risks

These include the risk inherent in the lending itself. They embrace terms and conditions, tenor and maturity, the security/collateral implications.

Banks may give borrowers ratings based on historical, current and anticipated levels of performance. A borrower rating is likely to be based on the following criteria:

a) **The Industry and Operating Environment**

   Does the borrower operate in a strong and growing industry?

   Does the borrower hold a significant share of the market?

   Are legal and regulatory climates favourable?

b) **Earnings and Operating Cash Flow**

   Are earnings of high quality and growing?

   Are margins in line with others operating in the industry?

Is cash flow strong in relation to current and anticipated debt?

c) **Asset and Liability Structure**

Are asset values realistic?

Are assets and liabilities matched?

Have intangibles been discounted?

Are the assets available as security/collateral?

Is the bank avoiding a subordinated lending position?

d) **Debt Capacity**

Is gearing/leverage at acceptable levels?

What alternative sources of debt and capital exist?

e) **Management and Controls**

How competent is the management?

Are good reporting lines in place?

f) **Financial Reporting**

Are the auditors reputable?

Is financial information produced on time?

Is it accurate and complete?

Risk Rating

The risk rating is an index of risk intended to reflect the collectability of a specific advance in accordance with its terms. Each advance carries its own risk rating.

The risk rating is the risk of the particular advance or transaction to a particular borrower. There can possibly be positive and negative variables that may impact on an advance or credit facility. Some of the common factors include security/collateral, ownership, terms, subordinated position and country risk.

Industry Tier Position

A company's tier position should reflect its competitive position relative to its peers. The factors used to determine peer position may be qualitative or quantitative. They may include:

● **Market Share**
● **Pricing:**

Price leadership

Product differentiation/premium pricing

- **Cost Structure:**

    Labour cost

    Material costs

    Capital intensity

    Economies of scale

    Technological advantages/disadvantages

    Operating gearing/leverage

- **Managerial Skills**

    Industry reputation, expertise

    Marketing ability

    Long-term strategic focus

- **Financial Aspects**

    Cash flow measures

    Debt levels

    Profitability measures

    Comparable performance ratios

- **Miscellaneous**

    Diversification/concentration

    Divestiture/acquisitions

    Contingent liabilities and other off-balance sheet obligations

- **Credit Administration**

    It is often important for a bank's credit management functions to maintain an independent viewpoint. Senior management must ensure that:

    Credit policy is fully understood throughout the organization.

    Develop the training programmes needed to ensure that lenders have appropriate skills.

    Track credit documentation and decisions.

    Review policy decisions.

- **Statements on Advances Policies**

    Such a statement may include:

    Advances should have a sound funding capability and be predicted on sound lending principles.

Advances pricing should adequately reflect bank policy and requirements.

Rewards sought should be in line with risk assumed.

Advances must comply with laws and regulations.

Advances should not be of a speculative nature where the bank could be placed at risk.

All advances to be reviewed on an annual basis.

Credit decisions to be made as quickly as possible bearing in mind complexity and risk.

● **The Credit Review**

Lenders involved with the review and sanctioning of advances applications have a primary goal of minimizing loss. When reviewing advances applications, among the most important areas will be:

Business background, nature of business, management and control

Macroeconomic sensitivities/company problems

Quality of management

Product/service, market and trading outlook

Premises, machinery/vehicles – age and suitability

Trading performance

Conduct of account

Requirements

Ability to repay and source of repayment

Projections for the future and assumptions underlying them

Security/collateral available

Remuneration

Other business creative opportunities

Anticipatory Limits

The bank may agree that lending officers have authority to allow customers to anticipate their income streams to a limited degree.

To reduce the workload on lenders, many banks set up a system whereby a computer is programmed to allow an automatic anticipatory limit to be recorded on creditworthy accounts. It is crucial that such limits are set at appropriate and realistic levels. In a perfect system the limit should be linked to the customer's ability to repay.

Credit Scoring

Some banks allow loan applications to be assessed by a credit-scoring process, set in accordance with bank policy. Banks using the system have application forms for completion. Information submitted by customers may be checked against bank records. Non-customer applicants should be asked for proof of statements made.

Banks often provide for a manual override of decisions made by computerized credit scoring techniques.

Monitoring and Control – Spotting the Warning Signs of Trouble

Accountants often tell banks that they are between six and nine months too late in identifying problem lending. Part of the difficulty may be the anxiety of bankers to support a company as far as is possible through a difficult trading period, often maintaining that support longer than it should.

What Bankers can do, however, is to have regard for the warning signs of business failure that may be evident and are often ignored. Too often the monitoring of progress and the telltale signs of a downturn in the affairs of a customer are overlooked. In many cases the decline is gradual and an alert lender will see danger signals long before the situation becomes critical.

For example, Mark Homan, the Director of Corporate Reconstruction and Insolvency for Price Waterhouse U.K. wrote in a series of articles for *Banking World*, subsequently published in a useful publication entitled *A Banker's Guide to Survival*, that in his opinion root causes and danger signs can be analysed under four main headings:

- Weaknesses in Management and Proprietors
- Technical and Commercial Problems
- Financing Problems
- Faulty Accounting

Weaknesses in Management

Bad management is the most common cause of business failure and a proper appreciation of the capabilities of the company's management is therefore essential in any customer monitoring exercise.

In a family business the management of the company is frequently handed down from one generation to the next irrespective of whether management skills have been successfully inbred. Equally dangerous is the situation where a company's management is concentrated in the hands of a single executive. There is a limit as to what one man can do, but a dominant chief executive can be dangerous in many respects, not least when he dies. It is a common failing in such cases to find no management succession. There is also more likelihood of financial impropriety where there is a dominant chief executive.

A further situation that can give rise to problems is where the size or nature of a business is undergoing rapid change. An entrepreneur may be well suited to running a small, expanding business, but there comes a time when there is a requirement for other skills within the management team such as delegation and team building; such skills are not always inherent in the initial pioneer of a business. A well-run company will thrive on collective decisions and collective responsibility. If there is a lack of middle management it is hard to see how decisions can be implemented.

Apart from being alert to the factors described above, there are other indications of management weakness that the banker should look out for in monitoring his customers. These include:

● A high turnover rate among key employees may indicate that management is unable to motivate staff with a real sense of purpose.

● Extravagant spending on travel, entertainment and office accommodation may be an indication of irresponsible management. A reluctance to inject capital into the business indicates a management team lacking confidence in the business and may lead to a lack of commitment to it.

● Perhaps most important, a failure to take advantage of financial information (for example, by attending to variances) may indicate insufficient attention to planning and control which are so essential to good management.

Technical and Commercial Problems

Although weak management is still the prime cause of corporate failure, increasingly the pace of technical and political change is wrong-footing even generally competent management as it becomes more difficult to respond quickly to the changing environment. The banker needs to be alert to the implications of the environment in which his customer operates and to the implications of commercial decisions. A business with volatile products or markets, susceptible to changes in cost, fashion, technology, social attitudes, overseas competition or exchange rates, is clearly vulnerable. Such changes may be near impossible to foresee yet their impact can spread far beyond a particular business: they can spell doom for entire industries.

A business where sales are concentrated in a small number of customers may go into a rapid decline if one of its customers goes out of business or switches to another brand. Equally, a business whose prosperity depends on one large contract has a big question mark hanging over its future.

A business with sales volumes susceptible to sharp fluctuations is necessarily insecure unless its overheads can be easily controlled and flexed. If the business has a high level of fixed costs, there is an obvious cause for concern.

A business that bases its prices on marginal costing techniques can very easily get into trouble and the effect can multiply rapidly in the struggling company that seeks to 'buy' volume by paring its margins.

Financing Problems

Other possible indications that a business is heading for trouble lie in its financing.

Accountancy Systems

If the accounting system is inadequate, proper and corrective decisions cannot be made. Progress cannot be monitored if management has no information on which to work.

Creative accounting is almost invariably associated with corporate failure. It is seen, for example, in the revaluing of assets, changes in the bases of stock valuations and in expenditure being carried forward. Creative accounting improves profits and liquidity ratios, but remember that profit is merely an opinion whereas cash is fact.

Another sign of trouble is a deteriorating debt collection record, which may be caused by customer dissatisfaction with goods supplied or by more favourable credit terms offered so as to revive flagging sales.

As regards payments to creditors and collections from debtors – a successful company will demonstrate a reasonably steady pattern. As a company moves towards failure, this pattern will begin to deteriorate because the company will not release cash in the same regular way as before. Equally, it may simply be the result of poor credit control. The easiest debts to collect will be pressed for and difficult ones may be ignored. This symptom occurs late on the failure path.

A banker should be wary of a business that is overgeared or with a capital structure weighted to short-term maturities.

Other danger signs include the payment of dividends in the face of losses and the granting of increasing security interests to obtain credit.

A business that decides to diversify or expand its existing operations without sufficient capital to finance the high costs associated with such plans is courting trouble. Uncontrolled capital expenditure can give rise to serious problems in the short term, if the company's cash flow position cannot bear the cost, or in the longer term, if the return from the capital investment is inadequate. Equally, a failure to invest in the development of the production system can result in the business becoming uncompetitive.

An increase in the flow of status enquiries may give the observant banker advance warning that facilities are inadequate.

Faulty Accounting

No company can effectively monitor its progress (or lack of it) without accurate financial information. A qualified audit report is often an early warning. Other warnings may be changes in accounting policy (perhaps to mask losses) such as capitalizing research and development or advertising costs.

Even accurate information is of little value unless it is current and produced on a timely basis; late accounting should give as much cause for concern as faulty accounting. It is often the first telltale sign of trouble.

Without current and accurate financial information decisions are apt to be based on wrong assumptions while both favourable and unfavourable trends can go undetected. Hence, a lack of financial information or, equally, irrelevant or even excessive financial information, should be regarded as indicative of problems and as a possible root cause of them.

In a company that incorporates several different operations, the significance of this point is amplified: it may be possible to establish that problems exist but accurate and relevant reports are essential if the problem areas are to be isolated. Current financial information is essential to management.

It is (or should be) just as important to the banker for the purpose of any effective monitoring exercise. Too often the banker monitors his customer with last year's balance sheet rather than the projection of next year's profit and loss account. Bankers are busy people, but attention to the customer's current management accounts and future projections and an understanding of the commercial problems and assumptions, which underlie them, may save time in the long run.

Perhaps the most important overall feature is profitability: it may sound obvious to say that a company with a history of continuing losses is a serious risk but, especially where large and prestigious companies are concerned, this is sometimes overlooked. Lack of profitability soon turns into adverse cash flow and soon erodes the balance sheet. Obviously profit alone is not enough unless it can be turned into cash flow, but in reviewing financial projections it is worth remembering that a business without prospects of profit has lost its raison d'être.

The BIS Standards

The Bank for International Settlements (BIS) provides guidelines to commercial banks and bank regulators worldwide on the effective operation of banking institutions. Its sub-committee, the Basle Committee on Banking Supervision, Basle, is one that encourages banking supervisors globally to promote sound practices for managing risk. Their consultative document 'Principles for the Management of Credit Risk' discusses 17 principles applicable to the business of lending and which should be applied to all activities where credit risk is present.

The Committee recognizes that *'the major cause of banking problems continues to be directly related to lax credit standards for borrowers and counterparties, poor portfolio risk management, or a lack of attention to changes in economic or other circumstances that can lead to a deterioration in the credit standing of a bank's counterparties.'*

They define credit risk as the potential that a bank borrower or counterparty will fail to meet its obligations in accordance with agreed terms and point out that the objective of credit risk management is to maximize a bank's risk-adjusted rate of return by maintaining credit risk exposure within acceptable levels. They suggest that banks will need to manage the credit risk inherent in the entire portfolio, as well as the risk in individual loans. According to Basle: *'The effective management of credit risk is a critical component of a comprehensive approach to risk management and essential to the long-term success of any banking organization.'*

The sound practices set out in the document represent internationally acceptable standards, which should be instilled in all banks' credit risk management processes.

The principles, which fall under five main headings, are:

A. **Establishing an Appropriate Credit Risk Environment**

   1. The Board of Directors should have responsibility for approving and periodically (at least annually) reviewing the credit risk strategy and significant credit risk principles of the bank. The strategy should reflect the bank's tolerance and the level of profitability the bank expects to achieve for incurring various credit risks.

   2. Senior management should have responsibility for implementing the credit risk strategy approved by the Board of Directors and for developing policies and procedures for identifying, measuring, monitoring and controlling credit risk. Such policies and procedures should address credit risk in all of the bank's activities and at both the individual credit and portfolio levels.

   3. Banks should identify and manage credit risk inherent in all products, and ensure that activities new to them are subject to adequate risk management procedures and controls before being introduced and undertaken, and that they are approved in advance by the Board of Directors or its appropriate committee.

B. **Operating Under a Sound Credit-Granting Process**

   1. Banks must operate within sound, well-defined credit-granting criteria. These criteria should include a clear indication of the bank's target market and a thorough understanding of the borrower or counterparty, as well as the purpose and structure of the credit and its source of repayment.

   2. Banks should establish overall credit limits at the level of individual borrowers and counterparties, and groups of connected parties that aggregate in a comparable and meaningful manner, different types of exposure, both in the banking and trading book and on and off the balance sheet.

   3. Banks should have a clearly-established process in place for approving new credits as well as the amendment, renewal and refinancing of existing credits.

4. All extentions of credit must be made on an arm's length basis. In particular, credits related to companies and individuals must be authorized on an exceptional basis, monitored with particular care and other appropriate steps taken to control or mitigate the risks of non-arm's length lending.

C. Maintaing an Appropriate Credit Administration, Measurement and Monitoring Process

1. Banks should have in place a system for the on-going administration of their various credit risk-bearing portfolios.

2. Banks must have in place a system for monitoring the condition of individual credits, including determining the adequacy of provisions and reserves.

3. Banks are encouraged to develop and utilize an internal risk-rating system in managing credit risk. The rating system should be consistent with the nature, size and complexity of a bank's activities.

4. Banks must have information systems and analytical techniques that enable management to measure the credit risk inherent in all on- and off-balance sheet activities. The management information system should provide adequate information on the composition of the credit portfolio, including identification of any concentration risks.

5. Banks must have in place a system for monitoring the overall composition and quality of the credit portfolio.

6. Banks should take into consideration future changes in economic conditions when assessing individual credits and their credit portfolios, and should assess their credit risk exposures under stressful conditions.

D. Ensuring Adequate Controls over Credit Risk

1. Banks must establish a system of independent on-going assessment of the bank's credit risk management process and the results of such reviews should be communicated directly to the Board of Directors and senior management.

2. Banks must ensure that the credit-granting function is being properly managed and the credit exposures are within levels consistent with prudential standards and internal limits. Banks should establish and enforce internal controls and other practices to ensure that exceptions to policies procedures and limits are reported in a timely manner to the appropriate level of management for action.

3. Banks must have a system in place for early remedial action on deteriorating credits, managing problem credits and similar workout stations.

E. Role of Supervisors

1. Supervisors should require that banks have an effective system in place to identify, measure, monitor and control credit risk as part of an overall approach to risk

management. Supervisors should conduct an independent evaluation of a bank's strategies, policies, procedures and practices related to the granting of credit and the on-going management of the portfolio. Supervisors should consider setting prudential limits to restrict bank exposures to single borrowers or groups of connected counterparties.

Basle, however, makes the point that the above-mentioned principles should be applied in conjunction with sound practices related to the assessment of asset quality, the adequacy of provisions and reserves and the disclosure of credit risk, all of which have been addressed in other Committee documents.

Ref: Basle Committee on Banking Supervision, Principles for the Management of Credit Risk, publication No.75(2000)

1

GENERAL CONSIDERATIONS

Objectives

At the end of this chapter you should be able to:

- Be aware of general lending considerations;

- Understand a structured approach to risk assessment in business lending;

- Be aware of the more popular mnemonics of lending;

- Understand the basic component parts of financial statements;

- Know the basic terms used in business lending considerations.

When we agree to lend money to a business, be it large or small, we do so on the basis that we will get our money back on an agreed future date. To reach a decision to lend we have to make a prediction of the likely future trading performance of the business and its ability to repay borrowed monies at a future date in time. As we are unable to predict the future with any certainty, it is difficult to make any lending that is totally free from risk.

What we can do is endeavour to minimize the risk involved by a logical assessment of the available and requested information and then to evaluate it correctly. Because of these uncertainties many experienced lenders refer to lending as an 'art' rather than a 'science.'

We shall consider logical approaches to the analysis of lending opportunities and in this chapter consider some of the lending mnemonics that are popular with bank lenders.

Many lendings fail because of inadequate assessment, sometimes because we feel pressured by customers into reaching rapid decisions. Before we begin to consider lending opportunities, let us set out some general thoughts:

- Always try to obtain the relative financial information in advance of a meeting, in order that you may consider the questions you intend to ask. You cannot analyse financial information during the course of an interview. Usually this will be presented in the form of a business plan (discussed later). Sometimes smaller business customers will feel unable to provide the information in this form;

- Do not accept customer's statements at face value. Seek confirmation and clarification where appropriate;

- **Do not make assumptions or fill in gaps yourself.** It is the customer's responsibility to provide all the relative information you require;

- **Do be sure** that you fully **understand the risk** involved with the proposition before drawing a conclusion and stating your decision.

If you are still in doubt, discuss the proposal with a more experienced colleague.

Distinguish between fact, estimates and opinions when reaching a decision. That decision will be based on an appraisal of the financial and non-financial information that the customer provides.

Ideally the customer should provide the information in the form of a business plan which will address some of the following areas of the business:

A Business Plan Check List

Objectives	What are the customer's personal objectives?
	What are the customer's business objectives?
	Are they specific?
	Has he or she thought out the consequences?
The Business	History if already established.
	Accounts for previous years' trading.
	Present financial position.
Management	Experience of proprietors/managers.
	Responsibilities of managers.
	Is the team complete or is further recruitment necessary?
Market	How large is it?
	Is market research possible?
	What is the competition?
	What is the customer's competitive advantage?
	What advantages do competitors have?
	What are the distribution channels?
Products	Do they meet buyers' needs?
	Have they been tested, including production methods?
	How have costs been calculated?
Pricing	How have prices been arrived at?
	What are the gross margins?

Suppliers	Are adequate supplies available?
	Is quality known to be acceptable?
	What credit is available?
Physical Resources	What premises are available?
	Are they adequate?
	What is the cost?
	What machinery/vehicles are required?
	What is the cost?
	How are they to be financed?
Personnel	How many will be needed?
	What training will be required?
Profit and Cash Forecasts	Are they available?
	Are the assumptions valid and clearly stated?
	What are the risks?
	Can the business survive if it sells *20/40%* less than planned?
Outside Finance Required	What does the business need:
	for fixed assets?
	for working capital?
	How long is the money required for?
	What is the programme for repayment?
	Has the customer produced a monthly cash plan for the first year?
	What cash projections are there after the first year?

Aide-Mémoire Approach to Lending:

In lending appraisal it is very useful to use some form of aide-mémoire. There are a number of popular mnemonics, including:

CCCPARTS:

C   Character

C   Capability

C   Capital

P   Purpose

A   Amount

R   Repayment

T   Terms

S   Security/Collateral

PEST ANALYSIS

P   Political

E   Economic

S   Social/Regulatory

T   Technical

PARSER

P   Person

A   Amount

R   Repayment

S   Security/Collateral

E   Expediency

R   Remuneration

The most well known one is probably:

CAMPARI

CHARACTER   Integrity and honesty

                      Stability factors

                      Financial track record

                      Resources

                      Ability to repay if things go wrong

                      Liabilities

PC

	Assets
	Age
	Health
ABILITY	Earnings and prospects
	Professional qualifications and experience
	Business track record
MARGIN	Interest rate
	Commission
	Fees
PURPOSE	Reason for request
	Appropriateness of request
AMOUNT	Reasonable and correct in terms of purpose?
	What percentage will customer contribute?
REPAYMENT	Source. Analyse income, expenditure (and projections)
	Other sources of repayment available?
INSURANCE	Is security necessary?
	What is offered/available?
	Complete the security before making funds available

The use of a mnemonic ensures that many of the relative areas of a proposition are covered during interviews.

Key Assessment Areas

In taking a more structured approach to our lending topic, we can focus on the following key areas for risk assessment:

- The customer and his or her business;
- Asset cover for the advance (and security);
- Repayment ability/serviceability of debt;
- Monitoring of performance.

These areas are shown diagrammatically. This diagram should be studied carefully in order to avoid the pitfalls of lending to the applicant with little regard to the business, its net worth or serviceability; or lending to the applicant plus securing the debt, but with little regard to serviceability! If any of the key areas is ignored, problems will be encountered sooner or later. A full assessment must be made to reach a balanced judgement.

Figure 1.1: Key Assessment Areas

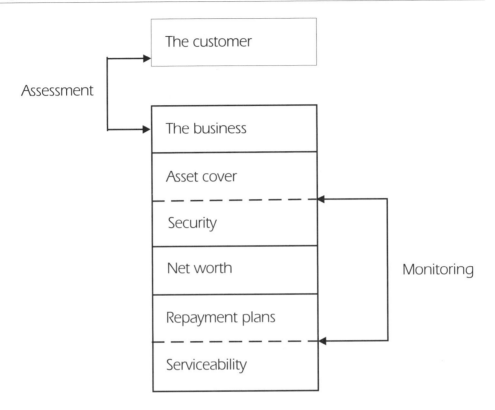

It is vitally important to remember that a business, no matter how strong its balance sheet, cannot carry a debt burden greater than can be serviced by the income-earning capacity of the business. It is for this reason that great emphasis will be placed on understanding the trading 'profile' of the business. This is displayed in the trading and profit and loss account and is projected in the profit budget.

Essential Requirements

The five basic points, which are frequently stated in lending texts and that need considering for any type of bank lending, are:

● How much is required?

● What is to be done with the money?

● What are the plans for repayment?

● What will be the bank's position if the plans for repayment go wrong?

● What is the experience and track record of the borrower?

In exploring these points, the following will help:

- The cash flow forecast will tell us what is to be done with the money and how much is required;

- The plans for repayment will be illustrated in the cash flow forecast and the feasibility of any repayments will be shown by looking at any margin available in the profit together with the record of past profits in the audited accounts;

- If things go wrong, the 'buffer' or net worth is illustrated in the past audited accounts.

The Technical Ability of the Customer

A key feature of the analysis of any lending proposition is the technical ability of the customer – can he (or she) perform the tasks required of him to make enough money for successful repayment? For example, can mechanics repair cars effectively, can plumbers install central heating appliances without having leaks, can builders lay bricks to the standards required by the surveyors from the local authority or the building society? There will be no source of repayment if the applicant does not have the skills to satisfy reasonable customers – they will simply refuse to pay.

The Integrity of Proprietors

A check-list approach will be helpful:

- How long has the borrower been known? What is the borrower's track record?

- If not known to the lender before, why is the borrower making the approach?

- Can evidence be shown of an acceptable track record elsewhere?

- Does the borrower have any business experience, especially in the area of trade that is the subject of the borrowing request?

- What is the borrower worth financially and how has personal worth been accumulated?

- What is the borrower's personal commitment to the business? Is a personal guarantee being offered where the borrowing will be by a limited company?

- Does the borrower have adequate life and health cover?

The Availability of Business Resources

Visiting the business, particularly when it is a small enterprise, will be essential and will yield a lot of information. Most people are receptive and only too willing to show you around. Observation and discussion will enable you to make a judgement as to technical and management ability.

- What is the customer's experience?

- How long has he been in business?

- Does he use modern techniques?

- Is he in full control or does he spend a lot of time away?

- What is his depth of management ability and who is there to help him?

- Does he delegate routine tasks?

- Who keeps the business records?

Also, you will see the business size and learn about the products, the state of the buildings and machinery. Does the place look well organized? Have the buildings and machinery the capacity to meet production plans? Look at any business plans and discuss them.

1.1   Financial Performance

Historical annual accounts should be available to be analysed for all businesses except new ventures. However, the standard of accounts can vary widely. The important thing which a lender wishes to establish is the true financial position of the business and its real cash-generating capacity to cover debt repayment.

Bank Records

This is where the banker is fortunate. He has all the usual bank records available to him. Examination of the bank statements will reveal:

- Business turnover;

- Average bank balance;

- Range of the account;

- Standing orders and direct debits and any unpaid cheques.

Comparison of these statistics with previous years will help to paint the financial picture, e.g. falling turnover coupled with an increasing debit balance will merit close investigation! This could indicate early warning signals of downturn business in performance.

Annual Audited Accounts Evaluation

The accounts could well be historic but they are well worth analysing. Most banks have forms for extracting ratios. What we are looking for is a 'reasonable' balance between net worth and debt; other ratios will give us indications of liquidity, debt serviceability and trading performance. We shall look at the interpretation of financial information in more detail using ratio analysis in Chapter 2.

Understanding the Figures

Let us commence an appreciation of the skill of a lender by asking ourselves to whom will we be lending. Let us consider the different forms that businesses take. The principal ones that we meet most frequently are:

Sole Traders

Partnerships

Private Limited Companies

Public Limited Companies

1.2　Business Types Summary

Features	Sole Trader	Partnership	Limited Company
Ownership	Owned by a single person.	Owned by two or or more people. No more than 20 partners (except for most types of professional partnership).	Owned by shareholders – must have at least two shareholders.
Income	Taken in the form of drawings from the net profit.	Taken in the form of salary and/or drawings from net profit.	Receive a salary from the company and will receive dividends when these are declared.
Taxation	Profits subject to income tax (including any salary paid).	Partner's share of profits and/or salary subject to income tax.	Company profits subject to corporation tax. Shareholder is subject to income tax on remuneration from company (if director or employee) and dividends.

Interpretation of the Figures

If you were to ask experienced lending bankers what they considered to be the most important aspects to consider when lending money to businesses you would receive a wide range of answers. The most important areas should include:

- The quality of the management
- Profitability
- Liquidity
- Gearing

- Interest cover
- Safety.

The Quality of the Management

It is difficult to place too much emphasis on this aspect of a business. The success of a business (and the lender) are very much in the hands of the management team. The areas that should be considered are:

- Ages – background and health?
- Expertise – sales, production, financial?
- Well-balanced or weak in some areas?
- Shareholdings/responsibilities?
- Track record?
- Succession?

(We shall discuss these in more detail later in the book).

Profitability

Is the business capable of generating profits? Where will they come from?

Liquidity

What are the cash flow implications? How will the money flow in and out of the business? Liquidity is the lifeblood of a business. The liquid position is important because it indicates whether liabilities could be met without recourse to the fixed assets of the business. The collapse of a business occurs primarily because it has run out of cash.

Gearing

Comparing the proprietors' stake in the business with the amount of borrowed money, which may be calculated on a gross basis or a net basis.

Gross Basis – compares the total borrowed from outsiders with the amount that the proprietors are providing to finance the business. An increasing trend would highlight greater reliance on outsiders. When we calculate gross gearing we include all borrowing, short term and long term (including directors' loan monies, but not trade creditors or taxation).

Net Basis – (net of cash held and quoted investments) – may be a more realistic view of gearing.

Interest Cover

This is the number of times that pre-tax, pre-interest profit covers the interest charged. It provides an indication of the margin of safety before profits fail to cover interest charges. The higher the figure the better. It should be not less than two.

Interest Cover (Cash Flow basis)

Because interest is paid out of cash rather than profits, it may be more relevant to consider how successful the business has been in generating sufficient cash surpluses to cover its interest payments.

Safety

How safe would the advance be if the business encountered problems?

(This will be discussed in more detail shortly).

The Importance of the Audited Accounts

When assessing any business lending proposition, one of the most important pieces of information available to a banker is the customer's audited accounts. The financial statements of the differing businesses will vary in detail enormously, from the small contractor filing self-assessment figures of sales and net profit to the rigorous disclosure requirements of a publicly quoted company.

We must be aware that these figures have limitations, namely:

- They are only a snapshot of one day in a year;

- It is possible to manipulate the figures to show a distorted position. This is known as window dressing;

- When received the figures will be out of date;

- Having said this, the audited accounts are usually the best source of financial information available, giving a clear indication of a customer's past trading record. These figures together with up-to-date management accounts, projections for the future, our knowledge of the business and the run of the bank account should enable us to ask relative questions with a view to quantifying future borrowing requirements;

- Past performance will not necessarily be a guide to the future, but the information that can be obtained from historical accounts provides a good starting point for assessing trends and future plans;

- Bank lenders usually extract the figures shown in audited accounts onto standardized spread sheets, allowing the trends revealed by several years' figures to be compared. The value of any individual year is limited and, ideally, no one year should be looked at in isolation.

Analysis involves examining the relationship between groups of figures and trends from one year to the next. A minimum of three years' accounts should be analysed, if available.

Before we go on to use several lending assessment frameworks, in the next chapter, it is, therefore, very important that we have an understanding of the figures that are presented to us in various formats.

1.3   Financial Statements Analysis

The Profit and Loss Account

The profit and loss account reports primarily the profits earned (or losses suffered) from normal operating activities; it also reports gains or losses in transactions that are not part of normal operations. All figures are accruals and do not reflect actual cash movements.

- Are profits being made and are these increasing in line with turnover?

- Are the profits from trading? This is preferable to profits generated by extraordinary activities, e.g. profit on sale of fixed assets.

- Are they being retained in the business? We would not expect all profits to be paid away in the form of drawings or dividends.

Sales

The main source of income for a business is its sales. Sales have two components – price and volume – and therefore the total sales figures may be increased either by an increased volume of goods sold, prices charged, or both. The ability to change one or both of these elements will depend on the demand for product(s) and the competitive position.

We would only expect to see a downward trend as a result of some form of rationalization, otherwise it may indicate an inability to sell the product or service.

Cost of Goods Sold

This reflects the costs associated with those goods sold during the period in question, e.g. the costs of material. The stock valuation method that the company adopts will have some influence on this figure. A comparison of profit performance between two businesses may be distorted where the businesses use different methods. Overpurchasing will be reflected in increased stock levels, and a deteriorating stock turnover period.

Gross Profit

Gross profit is calculated by deducting COGS from sales. Gross profit alone is of limited value unless we compare it year by year to the sales figures.

Gross Profit Margin

The gross profit margin allows us to consider the profitability being generated from sales. A declining gross profit margin may be one of the first signs of problems.

Depreciation

Depreciation is a charge made in the profit and loss account recognizing the fact that fixed assets decrease in value and are 'used up' over a period of time. It is an accrued or non-cash charge. The Companies Act requires that the amount of depreciation, and that the method of calculation of depreciation, is disclosed by a company. In normal circumstances the level of depreciation should vary proportionally with fixed assets.

Different calculation methods may be adopted, the most common being:

a) Straight-line/fixed instalment method: If a machine has a value of £10,000 and an anticipated life of 5 years, the depreciation charge would be 20% or £2,000 per annum in each of the five years it is owned by the business;

b) Declining/reducing-balance method: The percentage charged depends upon the expected useful life of the asset but the expense or charge is heavily weighted in the earlier years, e.g. a machine worth £10,000 depreciated at 40% per annum would have a charge of £4,000 in Year 1, 40% of the balance of £6,000 or £2,400 in Year 2, and so on.

A business may change its method of depreciation where this will more fairly represent the financial position, but the effect of the change must be disclosed in the annual report and accounts.

Directors' Remuneration/Drawings

Is it reasonable or are excessive amounts of remuneration being taken from the business? If excessive future trading may be affected.

Distribution Expenses/General and Administrative Expenses

This refers to those costs not directly attributable to the cost of the goods sold but incurred by the business in its sales effort and general administration, e.g. indirect overheads and advertising.

Operating Profit

Sometimes also referred to as trading profit, this gives the normalized profit of the company before financing costs.

Interest Expenses

These are the costs incurred by the business in borrowing money over the period (principal repayments are not included within the income statement). This figure is sometimes not shown in the P&L itself but can be found in the notes to the accounts.

Interest Income

This is the interest paid to the business on its deposits over the period.

Exceptional Items

Any exceptional item that is abnormally large and unusual and which would distort the operating profit is shown here. It would be incurred in the *normal trading* of the business, e.g. a large one-off provision for bad debts.

Profit Before Tax

These are the profits before deduction of tax liability

Taxation

This is the total amount of taxation being charged against the company's profits during the trading period in question.

Net Profit After Tax (Companies)

This is the profit available to shareholders before extraordinary items and dividends.

Extraordinary Items

These include any income, charge, profit or loss that is significant in size (i.e. material) but is derived from event or transactions *outside the company's normal activities*. Typical examples are profits from 'one-off' sales of fixed assets or redundancy costs.

Dividends

This is the amount of money that is to be paid out to shareholders

Net Profit

This is the net figure after deduction of all expenses and running costs.

Net Profit Margin

This represents the premium gained by the company for its products over the cost of production. By comparing the trend of this margin and the gross profit margin we can ascertain how closely the business is controlling its overhead costs.

The Balance Sheet

Current assets

These are assets that are expected to be converted into cash within a year.

Cash

Is this available immediately? Compare with previous years. Any substantial difference should be examined to ascertain what has been done with the money.

Short-Term Investments

Where investments are quoted on an established stock exchange they may be valued easily and should be saleable. They are therefore liquid but nonetheless can drop in value. What is the current value? Any difference between current market value and balance sheet value will have an effect on the net worth of the business.

Trade Debtors/Accounts Receivable

This is the amount a business is owed by customers to whom it has sold on credit terms. Are they collectable? Are they well spread? The danger of a dominating debtor is that should it fail it may precipitate the collapse of our customer.

Does the customer collect its debts efficiently? Are there any bad debts? If debts become doubtful or irrecoverable, adequate provision should be made. Consideration should therefore be given to the bad debt policy – what level of debt historically have they had to write-off? Is this level conservative or over-optimistic? Can the business provide an aged schedule of debtors? What are the terms of trade? What is the average length of credit given?

Stock/Inventory

This is valued in the balance sheet at the lower of cost or net realizable value. If the NRV. or best price obtainable in the market is below cost it must be written down and the loss taken in the P&L account.

Stock is often broken down to:

a) **Raw Materials** – Risks to consider relate to the reliability of supply and variability of price. Consider also whether any stock is subject to reservations as to title by the supplier until they are paid for;

b) **Work in Progress** – This is the amount of material tied up in manufacturing within the production process;

c) **Finished Goods** – A high level of finished goods may indicate stocking up for high seasonal sales, or that the company has a high level of obsolete stock.

Often the figures for the audit are provided by the proprietors/directors.

Let us consider an example of the calculation of gross profit:

ABC Company Ltd. 12-month Trading Period ended 31 December 19X9

	£	£
Sales		225,000
Less:		
Cost of Goods Sold		
Opening Stock 1 January 19X9	81,500	
Add		
Purchases in Year	135,000	
Sub-Total	216,500	
Less:		
Closing Stock at 31 December 19X9		
(Valued by the Directors)	85,000	
Total Cost of Goods Sold	131,500	131,500
Gross Profit		93,500
Gross Profit %		41.5%

If the closing stock is undervalued then this will understate gross profit, net profit and ultimately the net worth of the business. Conversely, if a customer wishes to show a better position, by overvaluing stock, this will increase both gross and net profit figures and the net worth.

An expanding business will have a need for additional stock levels. Stock should be compared with turnover and a rate of stock turnover calculated. This and other ratios will discussed in more detail in the next chapter.

An increase in the number of days could indicate:

- Out-of-date or unsaleable stock being held;
- Falling sales;
- Stock being built up for a large contract;
- Special purchase of stock made at an advantageous price;
- Special purchase of stock prior to a price increase;
- Special purchase of stock prior to a peak sales period, e.g. Bonfire Night, Christmas.

A decrease in the number of days could indicate:

- High demand for the product;
- The business is deliberately running down stock levels, e.g. change of fashion trend;

● Unavailability of stock.

The rate of frequency of stock turnover will depend on the type of business. Any substantial change in the stock turnover rate should be examined.

Prepaid Expenses

These are payment in advance. Although normally shown as a current asset in the case of a going concern, these items will usually be irrecoverable in the event of liquidation or winding up, e.g. rates, rent.

Fixed Assets

Fixed assets are those assets held permanently in the business that facilitate production or operation but are usually not for resale, i.e. it is generally not the company's intention to convert them into cash but rather to replace them on a continuing basis when they are worn out.

Land and Building – Balance sheet value will be the original cost less depreciation.

Are the premises adequate for the business as regards size and location? Does the figure shown disguise a hidden reserve? (e.g. balance sheet value £50,000 – realistic current market value £100,000.)

A revaluation of assets can be made by a qualified surveyor and if the value of a property has appreciated this can be shown on the balance sheet. The increase in value will be shown on the liability side of the balance sheet as a revaluation reserve.

Plant and Equipment – The machinery required in the manufacturing processes. Is the amount shown a true reflection of the asset's realizable value? In a liquidation the asset may have very little value. Are the assets adequately insured? Is depreciation adequate?

Fixtures, Fittings and Motor Vehicles – May be shown separately where substantial – check that depreciation is adequate.

Intangible Assets

Goodwill: This arises only on acquisition where a business is acquired for a price greater than its net asset value. Sometimes goodwill and intangible assets are written off over a period of years.

Patents, Licenses and Trademarks: These can have substantial value in that they may result in the accrual of future benefits to the company. They can be shown on a balance sheet only if purchased from or when acquiring another company.

1.4   Liabilities

Liabilities indicate amounts owed by the company and claims against the assets of the company.

Current Liabilities

These are amounts due to creditors of the company within one year.

Short-Term Debt

These are amounts due, e.g. overdrafts/short-term debt. They are facilities that must be repaid on demand or are committed for less than a year and consequently will be shown as current liabilities.

Long-Term Debt
Current

This is the element of long-term debt that is due for repayment within 12 months of the balance sheet date.

Dividends Payable

This is the amount of dividends declared by a company in the P&L statement and not yet distributed.

Trade Creditors/Accounts Payable/Bills Payable

This is the free credit granted of suppliers of goods and services required by the company's trading activities. It is important to know whether these creditors hold security either over goods supplied or other assets of the company.

Are creditors well spread? Can creditors be paid as they fall due? Compare with debtors. If there are no cash transactions, debtors should exceed creditors. What proportion of creditors are pay-as-you-earn/National Insurance/value added tax? The Inland Revenue/Customs and Excise are preferential creditors. Can an aged analysis of creditors be provided?

Sundry Taxes Payable

These are other taxes than those charged on the profit of the company.

Other Creditors

These are those to whom money is owed in the next 12 months other than creditors already specified.

Accruals

These are liabilities that correspond to and have arisen within the last financial period but have not yet been invoiced.

Corporation Tax Payable

This is the amount of tax payable on profits within the following 12 months.

Due to Group Companies

This may be included in the general creditor figure but should be noted separately. In addition even where it is stated as long term many consider it a current liability – in the event of difficulties this amount may well be paid off prior to the due date.

Due to Directors

This may appear in the accounts of smaller companies, either in the form of loans or undrawn remuneration; it is also often considered as current for similar reasons.

If the directors have no intention of withdrawing these monies, it is possible to look on these sums as quasi capital. If needs be a letter of postponement of the repayment of the loan monies may be completed.

Long-Term Liabilities

These are liabilities due in a period of over one year.

Shareholders' Funds/Net Worth/Equity

Equity represents the owners' share in the assets of the business and equates to the difference between total assets and total liabilities due to outsiders. Any surplus belongs to the proprietors of the business. Liabilities can generally be defined accurately but the valuation of assets requires careful analysis to determine the shareholders' actual equity.

Shares – Shares are generally referred to as 'risk capital' because the shareholders are the last to be repaid should the company fail. However, a company may have many different classes of shares, which will confer different rights to their owners and consequently to which different degrees of risk apply. Distribution of profits to shareholders may be made out of after-tax profits by way of dividend. The most common forms of shares are:

- **Ordinary Shares (common stock)** Ordinary shareholders usually represent the greater proportion of shareholders in a company. Within a company's balance sheet the figure for ordinary shares will represent the nominal value of shares issued to ordinary shareholders.

- **Preferred Shares** These confer some preferential rights above those applying to ordinary shares. The most common is the right to a fixed rate of dividend provided a dividend is declared and the right to be paid before ordinary shareholders in the event of liquidation.

- **Share Premium Account** This arises when shares have been issued at greater (a premium) to par value.

- **Revaluation Reserves** This arises where properties or other assets have been revalued. It is not available for distribution by way of dividends.

Retained Earnings

This is the profit earned as shown in the P&L of a business after payment of dividends and accumulated since the inception of the company.

The total shares and reserves represent the shareholders' equity or net worth of the company.

Contingent Liabilities

These are potential liabilities which may become due at some future time. Because of their nature no provision is made in the company's accounts; however an indication of their extent should normally be found in the notes to the accounts. Contingent liabilities include guarantees given, letters of credit opened and bills of exchange discounted.

These items should be analysed carefully because they may have significant impact on the company should they cease to be contingent and become actual liabilities.

Capital Commitments

These represent items of future expenditure and are consequently also off balance sheet but shown as a note to the balance sheet as:

(a)   Contracted: where the company is legally committed to purchase an item;

(b)   Authorized but not contracted: where the company has resolved to purchase an item, but has not as yet legally committed itself by entering into a contract.

Lease Obligations

Most accounting standards call for a reasonable amount of information to be provided but sometimes only current payments will be disclosed. In such cases some attempt should be made to discover future payments due and the length of the obligation.

Analysing the Information

In the next chapter we shall undertake a series of ratios but before this we can refresh our memories on what the accounts should reveal and what they generally do not reveal.

What We Can Get from Audited Accounts

Trend of Sales

Trend of Profits

Trend of Liquidity and Working Capital

Trend of Net Worth

Trend of Cost of Sales and Expenses

Trend of Various Key Ratios

Customer's Stake in the Business

Gearing

Composition of Assets; these are indicative of the quality of working capital and net worth

Extent of Directors' Drawings

Amount of the Company's Deferred Taxation Liability

Proportion of Long-Term Debt

Repayment Dates of Loans

Sources of Finance

Uses to which Finance and Earnings have been put

Revaluation of Assets; Acquisitions and Sales of Assets

Extent to which Expenditure on Intangibles has been Capitalized

Existence of Free Reserves available for Distribution

Deficiencies as Revealed by Auditor's Report – Read the Report carefully

Existence of an Acceptance Credit Facility

Evidence of Potential Foreign-Exchange Risk

Contingent Liabilities

Name of Subsidiary Companies

Name of Holding Company

Capital Expenditure Commitments

Method of Valuing Stock and Long-Term Contracts

Depreciation Policy

Gross Margins and Net Profit

Relative Proportions of Fixed and Variable Expenses

Bad Debts incurred and/or provided for

Interest on Loans, Bank Loans and Overdrafts

Investment Income

Rent Received from Property Lettings

Hire Purchase Interest

Leasing Payments, indicating existence of assets not shown on the balance sheet

Non-Recurring or Extraordinary Items of Revenue or Expenditure

Prior-Year Adjustments

Dividend Policy

Changes in Capital Structure

What Audited Accounts Generally Do not Tell Us

Inflation The effects of inflation on reported accounts are, as yet, not reflected in the vast majority of audited accounts.

Activities The precise nature of the company's activities and proportion of turnover derived from each.

Environment Government, fiscal, environmental, economic and social factors affecting the company.

Market The location, area, proportion of turnover in each area.

The number of customers, consumer or commercial, potential customer's accessibility:

Market share, competitors, number and their market share;

Dependence on one or a few large customers;

Export markets – current and potential;

Dependence on special contracts;

Seasonal fluctuations;

Is the market static, growing or declining in volume terms?

Products The proportion of business confined to established products.

The dependence on new, as yet untested, products.

Are they protected by patents; for how long?

The volume of each type of product sold (product mix), contribution from each, (gross margin of each).

Are units high value/low value, heavy/light, big/small and what are the implications for transport?

Have products a foreseeable demand pattern?

Is demand elastic or inelastic?

What are the likely product lives?

Are replacement products under development?

Management The quality of management, i.e. integrity, acumen, technical expertise.

One-man rule, non-participating board, depth, unbalanced top team.

Age, health and succession.

Other commitments, business connections.

Management

Information What is produced for the benefit of management, e.g. budgets, cash flow forecasts, periodic profit and loss reports, debtor ageing analysis, sales.

Quality of information available from the bookkeeping system.

What systems are in efficient operation in the company, e.g. costing, stock control, labour productivity control, purchasing, production, credit control, etc.

Labour Quality and number skilled/unskilled.

Turnover, absenteeism, availability in the area.

Relations between management and unions.

Fixed Assets Assets written off which are still, or may become, valuable; hidden reserves.

Premises and plant held on lease.

Condition of premises, adequacy for current expansion, location, access, size and value.

Existence of premises used by company.

Whether building specialized and therefore needing to be depreciated.

Premises; whether planning permission for current use held.

Plant; whether modern and competitive, current value, replacement cost, whether adequately depreciated, condition, whether regularly maintained, capacity, extent to which capacity utilized.

Contingents

Liabilities: Guarantee liabilities, warranties.

Purchase and construction commitments.

Law suits pending against the company.

Subsidiary indebtedness.

Exchange risk.

Liability for rentals under leasing agreement.

Intangible Assets Goodwill, patents, trade marks, etc.

Sales Volume as opposed to sterling value.

Discount policy.

How much of sales total relates to duty (e.g. tobacco) thereby distorting apparent gross margin?

Cash How typical is cash figure of normal day to day balance?

How much cash is actually available to meet liabilities and how much is held as a permanent float in cash registers, e.g. in retail outlets.

Debtors Spread of debtors, ageing.

Does the company factor debtors?

Export debtors, method of settlement, proportion due from high-risk countries.

Proportion of trade debtors, retentions, pre-payments.

Credit terms offered by the company.

Creditors Spread of creditors, ageing.

Credit terms allowed under pressure from creditors.

Proportion of expense creditors, trade creditors, VAT, PAYE.

Amount of preferential creditors.

Stock Proportion of raw materials, work-in-progress, finished goods etc., analysis, etc.

Detailed analysis of types of product and stock turn of each type.

Obsolescence.

Amount of overheads included in valuation.

Whether stock supplied is subject to reservation of title clause (ROMALPA).

Whether levels are matched to production needs.

Level of shrinkage.

Subsidiaries Extent of company's interest in subsidiaries.

Do subsidiaries have different year-end from parent?

Distribution Number and location of warehouses, retail outlets, agents. Methods of distribution.

Insurance What insurance cover does the company have, e.g. buildings, fixtures, and fittings, plant and machinery, loss of profits, consequential loss, employer's liability, public liability, key-man.

Other: What are the company's corporate strategy and objectives?

Amount of overdraft facilities, acceptance credit facilities etc.

Availability of raw materials, dependence on one supplier.

Timing and amount of cash requirements of customers, length of order book.

Pricing policy.

Method used in appraising capital investment projects.

Imminent change in technology.

Balance Sheets - Creative Accounting (Window Dressing)

We often say that a balance sheet is a snapshot, a moment in time in the company's life. We should remember that the balance sheet may be window dressed for the occasion. Some of the ways in which accounts may be manipulated – some ingenious, some fraudulent – are given below.

Debtors Fail to disclose those debts that are long overdue and almost certainly bad.

Stock and W.I.P. In very many cases these are shown at directors' valuation and accepted by the auditor without verification. Following the introduction of stock appreciation relief, conservative values cannot therefore be assumed.

Fail to disclose the slow-moving/obsolete lines of stock.

Change the basis of valuing stock and take the surplus into normal trading profit rather than disclose it as an 'extraordinary' item.

Fixed Assets Revalue fixed assets without noting the contingent liability for capital gains tax which may arise.

Surplus/deficit on asset sales may be shown as: an adjustment to depreciation; a separate disclosure or a direct transfer to or from reserves.

Maintenance Cut expenditure on routine maintenance until plant is in such poor condition that it must be replaced. This can then be treated as capital expenditure, which may attract tax allowances.

Revenue Expenditure Capitalize such expenditure as research and development or advertising and write it off over a number of years.

Investment Grants Credit them in full in year of receipt and not over the useful life of the asset.

Subsidiaries Avoid consolidating unprofitable offshoots.

Reclassify an associate company as an investment, then its losses need not be disclosed.

Instruct subsidiaries to increase dividend to parent company.

Each year progressively bring in more results from subsidiaries to the consolidated accounts — first subsidiaries 100% owned, then 75% owned, then 50% owned.

Run part of your business in the form of a partnership; there is then no need to reveal any information other than the share of partnership profits in the 'parent' accounts.

Gearing   Use leasing to improve the apparent gearing.

Directors'   Inject money on the final day of the financial year — and withdraw on the
Loans   first day of the next year. Most people will assume it has been there all year round.

Sales   Fail to record some cash transactions.

Carry forward sales invoices into the next accounting period (thereby depressing profit) or bring them back from a subsequent period into the current year (thereby inflating profit).

Include unenforceable sales agreements or goods on sale or return basis.

Ratio   Take in short-term funds overnight to improve liquidity at the balance sheet
Juggling   date.

Liquidate stock a few days before the year end to improve stock-turn.

Squeeze debtors and delay paying creditors immediately prior to the year end to improve liquidity.

Delay purchases and speed up submission of invoices prior to the year end.

Using the above methods, working capital and quick asset (acid test) positions can be manipulated.

A glossary of frequently used terms can be found at the end of this book.

Summary

After having studied this chapter, you should be able to:

- Be aware of general lending considerations;
- Understand a structured approach to risk assessment in business lending;
- Be aware of the more popular mnemonics of lending;
- Understand the basic component parts of financial statements;
- Know the basic terms used in business lending considerations.

2

SMALL BUSINESS LENDING

Objectives

Within this chapter we shall give guidance on how to:

● Assess lending propositions from small or relatively unsophisticated business customers;

● Understand the fundamentals of ratio analysis;

● Manage the lending risk in business start-up situations.

Based on our earlier comments in Chapter 1, bankers lending to businesses should always have three thoughts in mind:

● Has the business traded successfully in the past?

● How is the business trading at the present time?

● Will the business trade successfully in the future, and what will be the business's borrowing requirement?

The first question can, of course, be answered by consideration of the business's financial accounts, usually a profit and loss report for the period under review and a balance sheet as at the audit date. Ratios can be calculated and trends analysed.

The second question can be answered by the preparation of management accounts, either by the directors/principals of the business or their accountants, for the period from the last audit date to the present time.

The final question is answered by the preparation of projections for the future. These will be discussed in more detail in the next chapter.

The lending banker will be keenly interested in not only the profitability of a business, but also its liquidity, because cash flow is the lifeblood of any business.

Introduction

As an introduction to the topic of lending to small businesses, it is worthwhile beginning with some background to this sector. Statistics in the UK show that the sole trader or partnership is still the most popular business structure and that 'small businesses' continue to dominate, in terms of the number of business units in the overall business scene.

The first major business study of small businesses was published in 1971. This report of the Committee of Inquiry on Small Firms was chaired by J.E. Bolton. Many significant points were made in the report as to the structure and financial needs of small businesses.

The Bolton Report (as it is commonly known) found that defining a small business was difficult, in that employment of assets, turnover, output, employees or whatever measure used, might not be applicable to each and every sector of small businesses. However, an adoption had to be made for each sector and was as shown in the table below.

It is worth noting the high percentage figures revealed but the low number of average employees. In formulating these sector definitions the Committee of Inquiry had the following business characteristics in mind:

● In economic terms the definition of a small firm is that it is managed by its owners in a personalized way;

● It is independent in the sense that it does not form part of a larger enterprise that can provide a financial umbrella;

● The owner-managers should be free from outside control in taking their principal decisions.

Figure 2.1: Small Firm Sector as Defined by the Bolton Committee

Industry classification	Statistical definition of small firms used by the Committee	Small firms defined as a % of all firms in the industry 1962	Average employees per small firm 1963
Manufacturing	200 employees or less	94	25
Retailing	Turnover £50,000 p.a. or less (1963 prices)	96	3
Wholesale trades	Turnover £200,000 p.a. or less (1963 prices)	77	7
Construction	25 employees or less	89	6
Mining/quarrying	25 employees or less	77	11
Motor trades	Turnover £100,000 p.a. or less (1963 prices)	87	3
Miscellaneous services	Turnover £50,000 p.a. or less (1963 prices)	90	4
Road transport	5 vehicles or less	85	4
Catering	All except multiples and brewery-managed public houses	96	3

A broad definition of a small business that would probably be acceptable for our purposes is: 'A small business is one employing fewer than 200 people and having an annual turnover of less than £3 million'.

The Importance of the Small Business Sector

The Bolton Report indicated the principal functions of the sector as:

- Providing outlets for large numbers of individualistic people who preferred to work in small units;

- Providing an essential source of suppliers to large firms;

- Performing a highly economic role in those areas where a large variety of products and where customer service were of key importance;

- Providing variety of choice for the consumer;

- Contributing towards a balanced and stable industrial structure;

- Offering an essential source of innovation, and a seedbed for large firms of the future;

- Furnishing a source of entirely new industries;

- Maintaining a means of entry to business for new entrepreneurial talent.

Some Bolton Report Conclusions of Interest to Lenders

Ample information is readily available about sources of finance, but surprisingly enough there does seem to be an 'information gap'. Although small firms suffer a number of genuine disabilities by comparison with large firms in seeking finance from external sources, most of these disabilities reflect the higher costs of lending in small amounts or the higher risk of lending to small borrowers. They do not result from imperfections in the supply of finance – indeed, the ability and readiness of the financial institutions to exploit every new legitimate demand for funds is one of the greatest strengths of our financial system. Some 93 per cent of small firms approached the clearing banks as their only source of external finance.

Bolton concluded that the main areas in which small businesses could improve their performances were:

- Finance – Small firms frequently lack knowledge of the appropriate sources of development finance and working capital. They are also unskilled in presenting a financial case to potential investors and lenders;

- Costing and control information – Cost control is often so poor that management frequently learns of an impending crisis only with the appearance of annual accounts or following an urgent call from the bank manager. Credit control and stock control information is often inadequate;

- Other reasons of weakness were organization, marketing, information use and retrieval, personnel management, technological change, production scheduling and purchase control.

The most frequent ways, therefore, in which distinctions are drawn between large and small businesses are number of employees, size of sales turnover, size of capital base, etc. For the lender these distinctions are not as important as the fact that many 'small' businesses may not be able to produce good-quality management information or projections, which are generally available from 'larger' businesses. The lender, therefore, needs to adopt a different approach to risk assessment for these two categories of business.

Taking decisions as to whether to lend to small businesses when there is inadequate information can be a demanding task for even the most experienced of lenders. In those situations where you still have doubts about the viability of a proposition, then seek a second opinion from a colleague! The canons of good lending and the CAMPARI approach set out in Chapter 1 can usefully form the basis for a structured appraisal method.

Other Studies and Surveys

Following on from the very useful Bolton Report in terms of numbers of small businesses and classification; there has been a number of more recent studies. Below we give some data extracts. Also readers will note the changes in terminology that are applicable to differing sizes of businesses.

Business Types - Market Share By Industry Sector

In August 1996, The Chartered Institute of Bankers magazine, *Chartered Banker* included the following statistics by grouping customers into 16 industrial sectors, showing the volume of businesses within sectors. These showed:

Sector	Total Number of Businesses
Construction	13,383
Contracting	17,881
Capital manufacturing	14,288
Intermediate manufacturing	27,637
Consumer manufacturing	23,405
Utilities & transport	15,257
Durable goods wholesalers	35,339
Non-durable goods wholesalers	18,408
Durable goods retailers	17,537
Other retailers	21,842
Financial services	9,684
Property services	6,665
Accommodation & leisure services	5,006
Personal services	13,134
Management & public relations	7,722
Business services	17,263
Total	**264,451**

Source: UK Corporate Banking: Annual Market Share Review.
Part 3: Market Share by Industry Sector, *Chartered Banker* August 1996, p 24

In August 1999, The Chartered Institute of Bankers Magazine, *Financial World*, included an article by Grahame Boocock, Senior Lecturer, Banking and Finance, Loughborough University Business School, on the changes in the way that Banks and SMEs do business since the recession of the early 1990's.

The article includes:

'It is important to clarify the terminology used when referring to SMEs and to set the analysis in its theoretical context. The 'small' and 'medium 'bands are usually defined in relation to number of employees, fewer than 50 and 250 employees respectively, or an annual turnover, maximum £2.8m and £11.2m respectively.

However, other reliable statistics in this field (produced by the British Bankers Association) classify 'small' businesses as those with an annual turnover not exceeding £1m.

Lending figures for 1990-91 have to be treated with caution, because they include a number of larger firms, as well as some Clubs and Charities. Nevertheless, the total lending shows a downward trend, and there is a clear switch away from overdrafts towards term lending.

Major Banks' Assistance to Small Businesses – £bn**.

	1990*	1991*	1992	1993	1994	1995	1996	1997	1998
Overdrafts	27.1	27.4	19.4	16.6	13.9	12.3	11.7	11.4	10.8
Term Lending	18.2	19.3	20.1	21.6	22.4	22.9	22.4	22.7	25.2
Total Lending	45.3	46.7	39.5	38.2	36.3	35.2	34.1	34.1	36.0
Deposits	23.4	25.2	22.3	23.5	24.8	26.2	27.8	31.6	31.7

*   *The 1990 and 1991 Figures are not produced on the same basis as subsequent years, and are given for indicative purposes only.*

**   *Figures not adjusted for inflation.*

There is increased evidence that SMEs are making use of a wider range of funding options, including asset-based finance, venture capital (both institutional and via business angels) and corporate lending. The Government has also played a part in filling the financial spectrum, complementing private sector finance with, for example, a revamped Loan Guarantee Scheme and measures to help high-tech firms.'

Source: Learning to live together, *Financial World* August 1999 p12

2.1 Business Start-Ups

This is a difficult area for lending evaluation because often there will be no track record and the banker will need to closely scrutinize both the business proprietors in terms of their personal history and the future potential for the business.

We all want to help to encourage the successful development of businesses, but start-ups do have a high failure rate. Problems frequently occur through overoptimism and a lack of managerial skills. Also it is essential that there is a reasonable level of capital to be introduced into the new business both as evidence of the borrower's commitment and as a buffer against loss. If a borrower is able to contribute a significant capital stake, it may give the lender confidence that future plans can prove successful.

Some lenders consider that a director's guarantee supported by a charge over personal assets can be regarded as a substitute for capital. Although such a guarantee is evidence of commitment, it does not represent capital resources.

Inadequate proprietor's capital can result in a business having a significant borrowing requirement, the interest cost of which will raise the business's breakeven point. A business with a low capital base will have to generate higher levels of sales and profits than one that is adequately capitalized.

Projections of future profitability and borrowing requirements should be closely analysed.

A business plan should be obtained, as outlined in Chapter 1.

Businesses Already Trading

Many businesses seeking finance will have a track record and will, therefore, be able to produce financial statements. We should seek audited accounts for the last three years, if available, with a view to evaluating the trends of the business.

Annual Audited Accounts Evaluation

The accounts could well be historic but will be well worth analysing. Most banks have forms for extracting ratios. What we are looking for is a 'reasonable' balance between net worth and debt; other ratios will give us indications of liquidity, debt serviceability and trading performance.

There are numerous ratios that can be used, but it is sufficient for the purposes of the examination to consider only the main ones. The following two case studies, **Clothing Imports Ltd** and **Light Engineering Ltd,** will take us into ratio analysis and the interpretation of this financial information.

Case Studies: Using Ratios

The banking facilities available from XYZ Bank for two companies trading from very modest industrial premises in the North of England as at the end of 19X6 were as follows:

Light Engineering Ltd

	£	Security:
Overdraft	60,000	
Loan	18,000	
	78,000	1st charge company premises:
		Freehold value £55,000
		Debenture

Clothing Imports Ltd

	£	Security:
Overdraft and/or irrevocable documentary credits	200,000	1st charge company premises:
	200,000	Freehold value £60,000
		Debenture

The following comprise extracts from the financial accounts of these two typical, private limited company customers. As the names suggest, Light Engineering Ltd is engaged in the manufacture of light machinery mainly against firm orders. Clothing Imports Ltd is a merchant engaged in the import and subsequent wholesale of ready made-up fashion clothing from the Far East.

Profit and Loss Reports

	Light Engineering Ltd			Clothing Imports Ltd		
	19X4 £	19X5 £	19X6 £	19X4 £	19X5 £	19X6 £
Sales	200,000	220,000	210,000	900,000	1,050,000	1,300,000
Materials consumed	55,000	66,000	59,000	810,000	956,000	1,209,000
Direct labour	75,000	81,000	80,000	-	-	-
Cost of Goods Sold	130,000	147,000	139,000	810,000	956,000	1,209,000
Gross Profit	**70,000**	**73,000**	**71,000**	**90,000**	**94,000**	**91,000**
Admin & distribution Expenses	59,000	60,500	59,500	57,000	59,500	78,000
Operating profit	11,000	12,500	11,500	33,000	34,500	13,000
Interest paid	5,000	5,500	6,500	8,000	8,500	11,000
Profit before Tax	6,000	7,000	5,000	25,000	26,000	2,000
Tax	2,000	2,200	1,000	8,000	10,000	-
Attributable Profit after Tax	**4,000**	**4,800**	**4,000**	**17,000**	**16,000**	**2,000**

Balance Sheets

	Light Engineering Ltd			Clothing Imports Ltd		
	19X4 £	19X5 £	19X6 £	19X4 £	19X5 £	19X6 £
Current Assets						
Cash	1,000	1,000	-	-	-	-
Debtors	44,000	51,000	46,000	150,000	170,000	230,000
Quick Assets	45,000	52,000	46,000	150,000	170,000	230,000
Stock	10,000	15,000	15,000	135,000	190,000	257,000
Work in Progress	25,000	29,000	25,000	-	-	-
Total Current Assets	80,000	96,000	86,000	285,000	360,000	487,000
Current Liabilities						
Creditors	9,000	13,000	11,000	140,000	180,000	280,000
Hire Purchase	1,000	1,000	1,000	2,000	2,000	2,000
Bank	38,000	47,000	43,000	90,000	105,000	138,000
Tax	1,500	1,700	500	8,000	10,000	10,000
Directors' Loans	4,500	6,500	5,000	10,000	10,000	10,000
Total Current Liabilities	54,000	69,200	60,500	250,000	307,000	435,000
Net Current Assets	26,000	26,800	25,500	35,000	53,000	52,000
Fixed Assets						
Property at Cost	35,000	35,000	35,000	36,000	36,000	36,000
Net Current Value	(45,000)	(50,000)	(55,000)	(60,000)	(60,000)	(60,000)
Plant and Machinery	47,000	45,000	55,000	5,000	4,000	3,000
Fixtures and Fittings	2,500	3,000	2,200	2,000	2,000	4,000
Motor Vehicles	8,000	7,000	5,000	8,000	6,000	10,000
Total Fixed Assets	92,500	90,000	97,200	51,000	48,000	53,000
Deferred Liabilities:						
Bank Loans	20,000	19,000	18,000	-	-	-
Long-term H.P.	13,500	8,000	10,900	6,000	5,000	7,000
Total Deferred Liabilities	33,500	27,000	28,900	6,000	5,000	7,000
Net Tangible Assets	85,000	89,800	93,800	80,000	96,000	98,000
Share Capital	40,000	40,000	40,000	20,000	20,000	20,000
P. & L. Account	45,000	49,800	53,800	60,000	76,000	78,000
Shareholders' Funds	85,000	89,800	93,800	80,000	96,000	98,000

Source and Application of Funds Statements*

	Light Engineering Ltd		Clothing Imports Ltd	
	19X5	19X6	19X5	19X6
Source of funds:				
Profit before tax	7,000	5,000	26,000	2,000
Depreciation	8,200	10,000	2,000	2,000
Funds generated by operations (A)	15,200	15,000	28,000	4,000
Application of funds:				
Purchase of fixed assets	5,700	17,200	Sale (1,000)	7,000
Tax paid	2,000	2,200	8,000	5,000
(B)	7,700	19,400	7,000	12,000
Net funds generated(absorbed) (A-B) (C)	7,500	(4,400)	21,000	(8,000)
Working capital change* (D)	(10,000)	5,500	(35,000)	(27,000)
Funds available for repayment of bank and H.P. liabilities (C-D)	(2,500)	1,100	(14,000)	(35,000)
Increase(decrease) in long- term debt	(6,500)	1,900	(1,000)	2,000
Increase(decrease) in net short-term debt	9,000	(3,000)	15,000	33,000
	2,500	(1,100)	14,000	35,000
*Working capital change:				
Increase(decrease in creditors	6,000	(3,500)	40,000	100,000
Less:				
Increase(decrease) in debtors	7,000	(5,000)	20,000	60,000
Less:				
Increase(decrease in stock	9,000	(4,000)	55,000	67,000
	(10,000)	5,500	(35,000)	(27,000)

* Authors' Note – Cash flow analysis and the new cash flow statement (Financial Reporting Standard 1) are explained in more detail in a future chapter.

The extracts are not from complex financial accounts, but they do contain a good deal of information. Three years' figures are shown, in order to form an assessment of the quality of the customer's business performance and underlying strength. Three years is considered the minimum from which to glean meaningful trends.

2.2   Capital Gearing

The most common ratio extracted by bankers is the capital gearing ratio. To simplify comparison of trends we will calculate this as a percentage. It is defined as:

$$\frac{\text{Actual borrowed money}}{\text{Net worth}} = \frac{\text{Actual usage of lines of credit}}{\text{Shareholders' funds}} \times 100$$

i.e. borrowed money expressed as a % of net worth

	19X4 £	19X5 £	19X6 £
Light Engineering Ltd			
Actual borrowed money:			
Bank overdraft	38,000	47,000	43,000
Bank loan	20,000	19,000	18,000
Current and deferred HP	14,500	9,000	11,900
Directors' loans	4,500	6,500	5,000
	77,000	81,500	77,900
Net worth	85,000	89,800	93,800
Capital gearing ratio	91 %	91 %	83%
Clothing Imports Ltd			
Actual borrowed money:			
Bank overdraft	90,000	105,000	138,000
Current and deferred HP	8,000	7,000	9,000
Directors' loans	10,000	10,000	10,000
	08,000	122,000	157,000
Net worth	80,000	96,000	98,000
Capital gearing ratio	135%	127%	160%

Having arrived at these capital gearing ratios it is now necessary to consider qualifying our calculations.

Capital Gearing Adjusted for Directors' Loans

The above calculations include directors' loans as actual borrowed money – in the numerator of the ratio. Such loans may or may not be interest-bearing. If they are not interest-bearing, it could be argued that they are a form of shareholders' funds, in which case they could be subtracted from the borrowed money side of the ratio, and added on to the shareholders' funds or net worth side of the ratio. If we amend the ratios for the two companies to reflect this, the situation will be as follows:

Light Engineering Ltd

	19X4	19X5	19X6
	£	£	£
Actual borrowed money (as above)	77,000	81,500	77,900
Less: Directors' loans	4,500	6,500	5,000
Revised actual borrowed money	72,500	75,000	72,900
Net worth (as above)	85,000	89,800	93,800
Add: Directors' loans	4,500	6,500	5,000
Revised net worth	89,500	96,300	98,800
Revised capital gearing	81 %	78%	74%

Clothing Imports Ltd

	19X4	19X5	19X6
Actual borrowed money (as above)	108,000	122,000	157,000
Less: Directors' loans	10,000	10,000	10,000
Revised actual borrowed money	98,000	112,000	147,000
Net worth as above	80,000	96,000	98,000
Add: Directors' loans	10,000	10,000	10,000
Revised net worth	90,000	106,000	108,000
Revised capital gearing	109%	105%	136%

As can be seen, this amendment has had the effect of reducing the capital gearing ratio.

There is no straight answer as to whether directors' loans (or indeed other forms of quasi-capital, such as family loans which often occur in private companies) should be put on one side of the ratio or the other. It is down to a banker's judgement. That judgement, however, should be influenced by the stability of the loans. In the case of Clothing Imports Ltd, where the loan has been stable for three years, it would seem appropriate to regard the loan as supplementing shareholders' funds and, as such, including it in the net worth side of the equation.

Capital Gearing Adjusted for 'Hidden Reserves'

In calculating the capital gearing ratio we have taken the book value of the balance sheet assets. These, for balance sheet purposes, are valued on a going-concern basis. Break-up valuations are considered later in this book, but we shall consider at this point assets which we know have a different 'market' value.

In the case of companies where the bank has a first charge over the company's properties, the banker will have specific knowledge of the current value of these properties. For each of the two above companies, it is shown that the current value of the properties significantly exceeds the book value and, therefore, you could if you wish adjust the net worth side of the ratio properly to reflect these 'hidden balance sheet reserves':

Light Engineering Ltd

	19X4 £	19X5 £	19X6 £
Revised actual borrowed money (as (a) above)	72,500	75,000	72,900
Revised net worth (as (a) above)	89,500	96,300	98,800
Add: Current value less book value of property	10,000	15,000	20,000
Revised net worth	99,500	111,300	118,800
Revised capital gearing ratio	73%	67%	61 %

Clothing Imports Ltd

	19X4	19X5	19X6
Revised actual borrowed money (as (a) above)	98,000	112,000	147,000
Revised net worth (as (a) above)	90,000	106,000	108,000
Add: Current value less book value of property	24,000	24,000	24,000
Revised net worth	14,000	130,000	132,000
Revised capital gearing ratio	86%	86%	111%

If current valuation is less than book value then the difference should be deducted from net worth, which would increase the capital gearing ratio.

Hidden reserves may also occur in stock and work in progress but caution should be used in these circumstances, because such items are generally more difficult for a banker to value than freehold property.

Capital Gearing Adjusted for Contingent Liabilities

The capital gearing ratio definition referred on the one side to actual borrowed money or actual usage of lines of credit. The two may not be identical. Actual borrowed money as revealed in a company's balance sheet will not include any usage of contingent liability facilities the company may have. Such contingent liabilities may include documentary credits, indemnities, negotiated bills, forward exchange contracts, etc.

Whether these contingent liabilities should be included in the gearing ratio is open to question. On the one hand it could be argued that only interest-bearing liabilities should be included, in which case contingents could be ignored. On the other hand, before marking a contingent liability facility, a banker will certainly want to justify it against balance sheet strength, in which case it would seem appropriate to include contingents in the gearing ratio.

Many bankers adopt a sort of compromise. While they include them as a liability in the ratio, they regard contingents as 'soft' liability and, as a generality, will often be prepared to countenance higher gearing levels if the make-up of the ratio is substantially comprised of 'soft' liabilities.

By way of illustration let us assume that Light Engineering Ltd had no contingent liabilities outstanding, but that Clothing Imports Ltd had the following outstanding at its year ends.

	19X4	19X5	19X6
	£	£	£
Irrevocable documentary credits	40,000	50,000	60,000

Clothing Imports Ltd's capital gearing ratio could therefore be further adjusted as follows:

	19X4	19X5	19X6
	£	£	£
Revised actual borrowed money as (a) above)	98,000	112,000	147,000
Add: IDCs	40,000	50,000	60,000
Revised net worth (as (b) above)	14,000	130,000	132,000
Revised capital gearing ratio	121 %	124%	156%

Potential Capital Gearing

So far we have been calculating actual gearing. A banker will also need to consider the gearing position assuming full utilization of whatever lines of credit are available, i.e., full potential gearing, in order to assess the full exposure to net worth.

The information given at the very beginning of the case study shows that total facilities marked by XYZ Bank as at end 19X6 for the two companies are:

Light Engineering Ltd   £78,000

Clothing Imports Ltd   £200,000

To this must be added hire-purchase commitments (it is assumed there are no undrawn hire-purchase credit lines) at 19X6 balance sheet date, i.e.:

Light Engineering Ltd   £78,000 + £11,900 = £89,900

Clothing Imports Ltd   £200,000 + £9,000 = £209,000

Revised net worth 19X6 (as (b) above)

Light Engineering Ltd   £118,800

Clothing Imports Ltd   £132,000

Potential gearing is thus:

Light Engineering Ltd $\dfrac{89,900}{118,800}$ x 100 = 76%

Clothing Imports Ltd $\dfrac{209,000}{132,000}$ x 100 = 158%

Caution, it has been assumed that XYZ Bank are the sole bankers to both companies here. In considering potential gearing a banker must make himself fully aware of any additional lines of credit that may be marked by other institutions, as such lines (even if undrawn) would have an impact on potential capital gearing. Even small companies can have contingent liability lines, such as IDCs, with banks other than their main bankers.

Capital Gearing Ratio Summary

	19X4 %	19X5 %	19X6 %
Light Engineering Ltd			
Actual capital gearing	91	91	83
Adjusted for directors' loans (a)	81	78	74
Further adjusted for 'hidden property reserve' (b)	73	67	61
(Contingent liabilities (c))	Not applicable		
Potential capital gearing (d)	Not available		76
Clothing Imports Ltd			
Actual capital gearing	135	127	160
Adjusted for directors' loans (a)	109	105	136
Further adjusted for 'hidden property reserve' (b)	86	86	111
Yet further adjusted for contingent liabilities (c)	121	124	156
Potential capital gearing (d)	Not available		158

The next ratio is an extension of the capital gearing ratio.

Total Liabilities/Net Worth Ratio (Leverage)

Before going on to comment on the interpretation of the trends seen so far, we need to consider this second ratio, which is defined as:

$$\frac{\text{Total liabilities (current + deferred)}}{\text{Net worth}} \times 100$$

For both companies we shall use the net worth adjusted for directors' loans and hidden property reserves. The contingent liabilities outstanding for Clothing Imports Ltd will be included.

	19X4 £	19X5 £	19X6 £
Light Engineering Ltd			
Current Liabilities	54,000	69,200	60,500
Less: Directors' loans	4,500	6,500	5,000
	49,500	62,700	55,500
Add: Deferred liability	33,500	27,000	28,900
Total liabilities	83,000	89,700	84,400
Net worth (as (b) above)	99,500	111,300	118,800
Total liability/Net worth x 100	83%	81%	71%
Clothing Imports Ltd			
Current liabilities	50,000	30 7,000	435,000
Less: Directors' loans	10,000	10,000	10,000
	240,000	297,000	425,000
Add: Deferred liability	6,000	5,000	7,000
	246,000	302,000	432,000
Contingent liabilities (as (c) above)	40,000	50,000	60,000
Total liabilities	286,000	352,000	492,000
Net worth (as (b) above)	114,000	130,000	132,000
Total liability/Net worth x 100	251%	271%	372%

Interpretation of the Capital Gearing and Leverage Ratios

We have calculated different measures of capital gearing and in addition the leverage ratio (total liabilities to net worth). We must now consider what these ratios reveal. We have demonstrated that gearing ratios can be calculated in several different ways, and that the results can vary considerably. Before considering whether a ratio points to problems the banker must be fully aware of what is (or is not) included in each side of the ratios.

Ultimately the capacity of a company to service its debt from cash flow is a truer test than any capital gearing ratio. However, the higher the level of gearing based on balance sheet calculations, the less, proportionately, is the cushion of net worth before the lender's money is placed at risk.

The first thing to notice is the trend. Light Engineering Ltd's gearing ratios reveal a falling trend, suggesting that it is increasingly able to finance its operations. This is also revealed by the leverage ratio. In contrast, Clothing Imports Ltd shows a rising capital gearing trend, particularly in 19X6, implying greater reliance on borrowed funds to finance its increasing level of operations. Even more revealing is the huge rise in the leverage ratio. This latter ratio is really an extension of capital gearing. It can, and in this case does, reveal that, apart from borrowed money, the company is relying heavily on its creditors to finance its turnover. A steeply rising trend in this ratio can indicate that a company is undercapitalized and could be vulnerable if external liabilities are reduced due to factors beyond its control (e.g. creditors reducing terms of trade).

As mentioned earlier there is no simple mathematical formula to give a satisfactory gearing level; it is a matter of judgement. However, the banker will find it useful to bear the following points in mind:

(a) His judgement will be assisted by further ratio analysis, and a banker will generally feel happier with a highly-geared situation if the customer has a long and profitable track record than if it is a new business or an old-established one with a poor recent history of profit performance.

(b) Whether or not the banker is lending secured and what that security comprises are two important questions. Generally, the higher the gearing ratio, the more crucial becomes the quantity and quality of the security!

(c) What the gearing ratio comprises will be significant. If much of the borrowed money side of the ratio includes 'soft' contingent liabilities, high gearing levels are likely to be acceptable. Similarly with net worth – what is the asset structure? If the bulk of net worth is dependent upon stock or plant and machinery, the banker may feel less happy than if it comprised readily saleable freehold property. Also, is net worth heavily dependent on directors' loans which could easily be withdrawn? Overall, the banker must judge just how strong a buffer is that net worth before the bank's own money is placed at risk.

(d) The type of business – this is crucial when assessing gearing levels. Generally speaking a wholesaler with a quicker cash flow profile (such as Clothing Imports Ltd) can be expected to maintain and manage higher gearing levels than a manufacturer with a slow working capital process, such as Light Engineering Ltd. Because of this a banker will often be more generous in lending (in gearing terms) to a wholesaler than to a manufacturer.

(e) The structure of the business – the banker may feel more comfortable in lending to a sole trader or partnership where there will be the addition of personal covenant, as opposed to a limited liability company.

Light Engineering Ltd is quite highly geared for a manufacturer. Clothing Imports Ltd is certainly highly geared and the adverse trends are of concern. Although the security position suggests no immediate risk to the bank we shall need to look at other ratios carefully to build up a more complete picture.

2.3   Interest Cover

Interest cover can be measured on a historic profit basis by the ratio:

$$\frac{\text{Profit before interest and tax (PBIT)}}{\text{Interest paid}}$$

	19X4 £	19X5 £	19X6 £
Light Engineering Ltd			
PBIT	11,000	12,500	11,500
Interest paid	5,000	5,500	6,500
Interest cover			
(Historic profit basis)	2.2:1	2.3:1	1.8:1
Clothing Imports Ltd			
PBIT	33,000	34,500	13,000
Interest paid	8,000	8,500	11,000
Interest cover			
(Historic profit basis)	4.1:1	4:1	1.2:1

The interest cover ratio tells us how many times interest paid is covered by profits before interest and tax. Obviously the higher the ratio the better. A ratio of 2:1 or less is considered low and can make a business vulnerable to fluctuations in interest rates. Also low cover has implications concerning the ability of a company to finance other areas of its business from retained profits and its ability to provide repayment of its debt from profits.

The interest cover ratios for Light Engineering Ltd look fairly tight for 19X4 and 19X5 and tight for 19X6. During 19X6 operating profits fell, while at the same time the company incurred higher interest charges.

As regards Clothing Imports Ltd, the interest cover ratio looked quite healthy up to and including 19X5. However, the decline in 19X6 gives cause for concern and if the trend were to continue the company would be unable to cover the interest on its debt for 19X7, let alone provide any repayment of its debt. Clearly the company has borrowed heavily in

19X6 to finance its increased turnover, but has failed to maintain its former profitability and former cash generation.

2.4   Control Ratios

Debtor Recovery Rate

This is defined as: $\dfrac{\text{Debtors}}{\text{Sales}} \times 365$

This ratio calculates the number of days taken to collect debts (debtor turnover).

	19X4 £	19X5 £	19X6 £
Light Engineering Ltd			
Debtor / Sales	$\dfrac{44{,}000 \times 365}{200{,}000}$	$\dfrac{51{,}000 \times 365}{220{,}000}$	$\dfrac{46{,}000 \times 365}{210{,}000}$
Debtor recovery rate	80 days	85 days	80 days
Clothing Imports Ltd			
Debtors / Sales	$\dfrac{150{,}000 \times 365}{900{,}000}$	$\dfrac{170{,}000 \times 365}{1{,}050{,}000}$	$\dfrac{230{,}000 \times 365}{1{,}300{,}000}$
Debtor recovery rate	60 days	59 days	65 days

Interpretation

This ratio provides an approximate indication of the efficiency of a company's credit control procedures. The length in days of the debtor recovery rate needs to be considered in the light of the company's terms of trade and those common for the sector in which the company operates. Obviously the debtor recovery rate should bear some resemblance to agreed terms of trade. The quicker the debt recovery rate the better, in so far as this will have a beneficial cash impact. Debtors are generally financed by bank overdraft and so minimizing debtors by improving the debtor recovery rate will save interest charges and thus improve profits.

Perhaps more important than the absolute values of this ratio, is the trend that is revealed. A falling debtor recovery rate, i.e., a lengthening of credit given, could indicate:

- lax control by the invoicing department of the company;

- market competition which has forced a company to extend its terms of trade in order to maintain its sales outlets;

- slow paying and potential bad debts that may be included in the company's debtor book.

The above comments may lead you to believe that a trend that reveals a more rapid debtor recovery rate, i.e., a shortening of credit given, is always a good thing! A word of caution –

although a rapid recovery rate will have a beneficial effect on cash flow, it may have been caused by the company having to put pressure on its debtors because of cash flow problems. Too much pressure could result in a loss of future sales!

The golden rule is: ascertain by enquiry of the directors just what is causing a particular trend in the debtor recovery rate. Obtaining a full age analysis of debtors is worthwhile to give the full spread of debts. This will be examined later.

As regards the two companies, in both cases the trends do not indicate any extreme variations.

Stock Turnover Rate

This is defined as: $\dfrac{\text{Stock}}{\text{Cost of goods sold}} \times 365$

This ratio indicates the number of days stock is held. (For simplicity's sake, in the following calculations, stock has been taken to include work in progress. However, it is often advisable to break the stock figure down into raw materials, finished goods and work in progress, and obtain separate ratios for each element in order to ascertain the stock component that underlies any particular trend.)

	19X4 £	19X5 £	19X6 £
Light Engineering Ltd			
Stock and WIP / Cost of goods sold	$\dfrac{35,000 \times 365}{130,000}$	$\dfrac{44,000 \times 365}{147,000}$	$\dfrac{40,000 \times 365}{139,000}$
Stock turnover rate	98	109	105
Clothing Imports Ltd			
Stock / Cost of goods sold	$\dfrac{135,000 \times 365}{810,000}$	$\dfrac{190,000 \times 365}{956,000}$	$\dfrac{257,000 \times 365}{1,209,000}$
Stock turnover rate	61	72	77

Interpretation

Ideally a rapid turnover is beneficial in that cash is tied up in stock for a shorter period. However, the optimum period of stock turnover will depend on the nature of that stock and the type of business concerned.

Again, trends are the thing to watch. A lengthening of the stock turnover rate may indicate obsolete items or damaged stocks that may ultimately be unsaleable. Also it is important to remember that stockholdings may be seasonal.

For Light Engineering Ltd, the ratio is reasonably static. A stock turnover of 100 days, i.e., over 3 months, should be considered, bearing in mind the greater proportion of stock lies in work in progress as opposed to 'items on the shelf'. As with all manufacturing companies, work in progress will depend on the length of time it takes to make an end product. This will vary depending on the type of product being manufactured.

The stock turnover for Clothing Imports Ltd is in many ways easier to comprehend, because all stock held will be finished goods awaiting a buyer or awaiting call-off from a firm order. A definite trend is being revealed here, and enquiry of the directors as to what underlies the trend is warranted. It may be that the stock includes unsaleable items caused by changes in fashion or stock that is out of season. Or it may merely represent the fact that the company is carrying more lines as a deliberate policy to back up increased sales.

Creditor Repayment Rate

This is defined as: $\dfrac{\text{Creditors}}{\text{Cost of goods sold}} \text{ x } 365$

This ratio indicates the number of days taken to pay creditors.

Some banks use: $\dfrac{\text{Creditors}}{\text{Purchases}}$

	19X4 £	19X5 £	19X6 £
Light Engineering Ltd			
Creditors / Cost of good sold	$\dfrac{9{,}000 \text{ x } 365}{130{,}000}$	$\dfrac{13{,}000 \text{ x } 365}{147{,}000}$	$\dfrac{11{,}000 \text{ x } 365}{139{,}000}$
Creditor repayment rate	25 days	32 days	29 days
Clothing Imports Ltd			
Creditors / Cost of goods sold	$\dfrac{140{,}000 \text{ x } 365}{810{,}000}$	$\dfrac{180{,}000 \text{ x } 365}{956{,}000}$	$\dfrac{280{,}000 \text{ x } 365}{1{,}209{,}000}$
Creditor repayment rate	63 days	69 days	84 days

Interpretation

As with debtor recovery rate, this ratio should be considered in the light of the terms of trade enjoyed by a business from its suppliers.

Again, it is trends that need to be analysed. While lengthening this ratio will have a beneficial impact on cash flow, an escalating trend will usually imply problems – a company may be delaying payment to creditors because of cash flow problems. On the other hand, a shortening of this ratio may indicate concern on the part of creditors or a change in terms of trade from suppliers.

As regards Light Engineering Ltd, credit taken does not particularly indicate anything. Turning to Clothing Imports Ltd, the rising trend, particularly from 19X5 to 19X6, can be seen. Enquiry of the directors is appropriate here, to be supported by an age analysis of creditors. It appears the company has financed its expanding sales in part by taking longer credit. The bank facility of overdraft £138K + IDC usage £60K, against the agreed composite facility of £200K, may well mean that to maintain the overdraft usage within the agreed limit, the company has had no alternative but to delay paying creditors. By obtaining an age analysis of creditors the bank will be able to assess the problem more fully.

As a final comment under this ratio, care should be taken to establish just what the creditor figure comprises. Only trade creditors are relative to cost of goods sold. If possible, expense creditors (i.e. rates, power, PAYE and other sundry and tax creditors) should not be included in this ratio.

2.5   Liquidity Ratios

Current Ratio and Quick Asset Ratio

The current ratio is defined as $\dfrac{\text{Current assets}}{\text{Current liabilities}}$

The quick asset ratio is defined as $\dfrac{\text{Quick assets (= Current assets less stock)}}{\text{Current liabilities}}$

By their nature these two ratios can be looked at together.

- The current ratio provides a measure of the ability of a business to meet its short-term liabilities from funds generated by current assets.
- The quick asset ratio, by excluding stock from the comparison between current assets and current liabilities, expresses the cover for current liabilities in terms of cash or near cash (i.e. debtors). To that extent the quick asset ratio provides the more immediate measure of short-term liquidity.

	19X4 £	19X5 £	19X6 £
Light Engineering Ltd			
Current assets	80,000	96,000	86,000
Current liabilities	54,000	69,200	60,500
Current ratio	1.48:1	1.39:1	1.42:1
Quick assets	45,000	52,000	46,000
Current liabilities	54,000	69,200	60,500
Quick asset ratio	0.83:1	0.75:1	0.76:1

Clothing Imports Ltd

Current assets	285,000	360,000	487,000
Current liabilities	250,000	307,000	435,000
Current ratio	1.14:1	1.17:1	1.12:1
Quick assets	150,000	170,000	230,000
Current liabilities	250,000	307,000	435,000
Quick asset ratio	0.6:1	0.55:1	0.52:1

Interpretation

Again the trend of the ratios needs to be examined. A falling trend in the current ratio, besides indicating a reducing ability to meet payments for current liabilities from current assets, may indicate reducing profit margins or losses. Also a reducing current ratio may arise from investment of liquid funds in fixed assets or alternatively borrowing on overdraft to finance fixed asset purchases.

Generally, the current and quick asset ratio should move in line. A static or increasing current ratio together with a falling quick ratio would indicate an increasing amount of money tied up in stockholding. A surplus of current assets over current liabilities is usually a sign of good business liquidity.

Turning to the example case study, the ratios for Light Engineering Ltd have held up well. The quick asset ratio is less than 1:1 and so the company would be reliant on quickly translating work in progress into finished goods and then its debtors into cash in order to meet all its current liabilities.

While the current ratio for Clothing Imports Ltd shows little movement, the quick asset ratio is revealing a declining trend. It should be recalled that both the stock turnover ratio and creditor repayment ratio were showing adverse trends – and the effect of this is borne out in the falling quick asset ratio. A picture is emerging of declining liquidity when measured by the quick asset ratio and lengthening of the creditor repayment and stock turnover ratios. Also in monetary values the gap is now considerable:

Quick assets	£230,000
Current liabilities	£435,000

Working Capital Turnover

This is defined as $\dfrac{\text{Sales}}{\text{Net current assets (working capital)}}$

This ratio determines the relationship between sales and working capital.

	19X4 £	19X5 £	19X6 £
Light Engineering Ltd			
Sales	200,000	220,000	210,000
Net current assets	26,000	26,800	25,500
Working capital turnover	7.69:1	8.20:1	8.23:1
Clothing Imports Ltd			
Sales	900,000	1,050,000	1,300,000
Net current assets	35,000	53,000	52,000
Working capital turnover	25.71:1	19.81:1	25.00:1

Interpretation

Again it is the trend that is important. A rising trend may indicate possible overtrading, whereby sales are increasing without the necessary additional working capital. Although a degree of overtrading can be often managed in the short term by good control over debtors, stock and creditors, over a period there will be increasing pressure on liquidity and the bank overdraft. Because the ratio provides an indication of the working capital needed to finance a given level of sales, it can be used to calculate approximately the additional level of working capital required to finance a projected increase in sales.

The ratios for Light Engineering Ltd show a modest rising trend, but nothing significant.

Turning to Clothing Imports Ltd – the company increased its sales by 17% from 19X4 to 19X5. It can be seen that the ratio fell across this period. This has been possible by investing the retained profit into working capital to finance the sales expansion. From 19X5 to 19X6 sales expanded more rapidly, by 24%. This time the ratio has fallen back to its former level of 25:1. The nominal profit retention has not enabled the company to match its increased turnover.

This clearly has a bearing on liquidity, particularly if sales are projected to increase still further in 19X7. The company has already extended its credit taken, and unless stock turnover or credit given can be shortened, increased sales will necessitate still further reliance on creditors (which may not be possible) or increased bank borrowing (which may not be agreed).

By way of example, let us project forward on a further increase of 24%. The following ratios for 19X6 were applicable for Clothing Imports Ltd:

Debtor recovery rate	65 days
Stock turnover rate	77 days

Creditor repayment rate   84 days

Sales   £1,300,000 x 24% = £312,000 = increased sales

Total sales for 1987   £1,612,000

- If we further assume that the gross profit margin (see next section) for 19X7 will remain at 7%, gross profit = £113,000. Therefore cost of goods sold = £1,499,000.

- So applying a debtor recovery rate of 65 days to sales, projected debtors at 19X7 balance sheet date = (1,612,000/365) x 65 = £287,000.

- And applying a stock turnover rate of 77 days to cost of goods sold, projected stock = (1,499,000/365) x 77 = £316,000.

- Total projected current assets = £603,000.

- How can this be financed?

- Applying a creditor repayment rate of 84 days, projected creditors = (1,499,000 x 84/365 = 344,000.

- Assume other current liabilities, i.e., hire-purchase, tax and directors' loans, remain the same: total £17,000.

- Applying the 19X6 working capital

Turnover ratio to the projected sales level: $\dfrac{£1,612,000}{\text{Net current assets}} = 25$

Net Current Assets: $\dfrac{£1,612,000}{25} = £64,000$

- Therefore projected bank overdraft at 19X7 year end is:

	£
Total projected current assets	603,000
Less: Projected creditors	344,000
Less: Other creditors	17,000
	242,000
Less: Projected net current assets	64,000
Projected bank overdraft	178,000

With this type of approximated calculation, the bank overdraft then represents the 'balancing item' and this means a sizeable increased borrowing requirement which the bank may not be prepared to finance.

Second method

This time we take out the bank balance from the working capital cycle and calculate:

Debtors + Stock – Trade creditors

	19X4 £	19X5 £	19X6 £
Debtors	150,000	170,000	230,000
Stock	135,000	190,000	257,000
	285,000	360,000	487,000
Trade creditors	140,000	180,000	280,000
Net balance	145,000	180,000	207,000
Sales	900,000	1,050,000	1,300,000
Net balance/sales	16%	17%	16%

This alternative capital measurement therefore equates to approximately 16% of sales. The 19X7 sales are projected to increase by £312,000.

Therefore, the projected extra capital required is: £312,000 x 16% = £49,920

Although a gradual rise in profits will improve liquidity, this will not suffice and the bank will be needed as the 'balancing' item to fund the increased sales turnover.

2.6 Profitability Ratios

Gross Profit Margin

This is defined as $\dfrac{\text{Gross profit}}{\text{Sales}}$ x 100

This ratio is calculated to show gross profit as a percentage of sales.

	19X4 £	19X5 £	19X6 £
Light Engineering Ltd			
Gross profit	70,000 x 100	73,000 x 100	71,000 x 100
Sales	200,000	220,000	210,000
Gross profit margin	35%	33%	34%
Clothing Imports Ltd			
Gross profit	90,000 x 100	94,000 x 100	91,000 x 100
Sales	900,000	1,050,000	1,300,000
Gross profit margin	10%	8.95%	7.0%

Interpretation

This ratio will vary from business to business, e.g., a manufacturer with a high fixed cost structure will have a higher gross profit margin than a merchanting-type business (high volume – fine margin).

Trends in the gross profit margin should be noted carefully and the underlying reasons ascertained. A declining trend could indicate one or a combination of the following:

- The business is becoming less profitable due to competition in the marketplace forcing it to reduce its pricing policy.

- Similarly, it could be due to an increase in costs of one or more of the components of cost of goods sold, which the business cannot, due to competition, pass on to its customers.

- A deliberate policy by the business proprietors to reduce prices in order to increase sales volume.

Looking at Light Engineering Ltd, the gross profit margin fell from 35% to 33% from 19X4 to 19X5. Further analysis of the components of the cost of goods sold figures will show why:

	19X4 £	19X5 £
Materials consumed	55,000 x 100	66,000 x 100
Sales	200,000	220,000
Margin	27.5%	30%
Direct labour	75,000 x 100	81,000 x 100
Sales	200,000	220,000
Margin	37.5%	36.8%

Direct labour expressed as a percentage of sales actually fell, which in itself would boost the gross profit margin. However, it can be seen that this has been more than offset by an increase in materials consumed as a percentage of sales. An increase in materials costs then, relative to sales, has been the cause of the decline in the gross profit margin from 19X4 to 19X5.

During 19X6 the margin pulled back to 34%, reversing the trend. How was this achieved? A similar exercise to the above will enable the reader to demonstrate that comparing 19X6 with 19X5, direct labour costs increased as a percentage of sales. However, this was more than compensated for by a reduction in materials consumed as a percentage of sales.

Turning to Clothing Imports Ltd, a reducing trend can be seen, which is cause for concern. If this trend were to continue, and the gross profit margin fell by a further 1% in 19X7, on the same level of sales a gross profit as follows would be achieved:

Sales £1,300,000 x 6% = £78,000 gross profit.

Assuming similar fixed costs, i.e., administration and distribution costs of £78,000, the company would only break even. After interest charges a loss would be incurred.

It may be that the directors of Clothing Imports Ltd deliberately reduced gross margins to boost sales. Enquiries of the directors will need to be made to ascertain the reason behind the falling trend in gross margins.

Operating Profit Margin

This is defined as $\dfrac{\text{Operating profit (PBIT)}}{\text{Sales}}$ x 100

This ratio reveals the net operating margin before finance charges and tax.

	19X4 £	19X5 £	19X6 £
Light Engineering Ltd			
Operating profit	11,000 x 100	12,500 x 100	11,500 x 100
Sales	200,000	220,000	210,000
Net margin	5.5%	5.7%	5.5%
Clothing Imports Ltd			
Operating profit	33,000 x 100	34,500 x 100	13,000 x 100
Sales	900,000	1,050,000	1,300,000
Net margin	3.6%	3.3%	1.0%

Interpretation

This ratio represents the premium gained by a business for its output over its production costs. Profit before interest and tax is used to isolate interest and tax charges from other costs of production. In interpreting this net margin it is important to observe any trend. The absolute value of the ratio will vary considerably from industry to industry, with low margins allied to high volume and vice versa. Variations in net margins from one year to another will be determined by variations in the gross profit and the overhead expenses. Having isolated the gross profit margin in the previous section, it is variations in the proportional expenses of overheads in relation to sales that will be revealed by an analysis of this ratio.

Looking at Light Engineering Ltd, it can be seen that the net operating margin is fairly steady.

Now turning to Clothing Imports Ltd, it can be seen that the net operating margin has fallen significantly during 19X6. This company has also sustained a steadily reducing gross profit margin. It is worthwhile ascertaining whether the two margins are reducing at the same rate. This is simply identified by the ratio:

$$\frac{\text{Net Operating margin}}{\text{Gross profit margin}} \times 100$$

19X4	19X5	19X6

$\dfrac{3.6}{10} \times 100 = 36\%$ $\dfrac{3.3}{8.95} \times 100 = 36.87\%$ $\dfrac{1.0}{7.0} \times 100 = 14.28\%$

The two margins are not moving in line. We shall concentrate on the greatest variation, i.e., 19X5 to 19X6, where net margin as a percentage of gross profit margin fell substantially. This must mean that there was a proportionate increase in overhead costs from 19X5 to 19X6. This can be ascertained by the following ratio:

$$\frac{\text{Overheads}}{\text{Sales}} \times 100$$

19X5	19X6

$\dfrac{59,500}{1,050,000} \times 100 = 5.66\%$ $\dfrac{78,000}{1,300,000} \times 100 = 6.0\%$

As well as a decline in gross margins, the fall in net profit margin in 19X6 was exacerbated by increased overhead costs. Overall, the decline in gross profit margins, coupled with the decline in net profit margins for Clothing Imports Ltd, is cause for concern.

2.7 Source and Application of Funds Statement

Business failure usually occurs because of a cash crisis. It is important to appreciate that a cash crisis can occur even though a business is turning in profits. Such cash crises may be preceded by a series of funds flow deficits revealed in the source and application of funds statement.

Look again at the source and application of funds statements (restated on the following page) shown for the two companies in question:

- Net Funds Generated (Absorbed) – To what extent have the companies covered their tax payments and purchase of fixed assets from their own funds generated by operations?

- Working Capital Change – If positive, can this be maintained? Increasing sales usually results in a need to increase working capital. Is working capital change 'swallowing up' all net funds generated by operations – as in 19X5 for both Light Engineering Ltd and Clothing Imports Ltd? Alternatively, is an increasing working capital requirement exacerbating an already deficit net funds generated position, as in 19X5 for Clothing Imports Ltd?

- Cash Funds Deficit – How long will the business be able to continue to fund this from increased bank borrowing? Sooner or later a business may reach the limit of its creditworthiness.

Source and Application of Funds Statements*

	Light Engineering Ltd		Clothing Imports Ltd	
	£	£	£	£
Source of funds:				
Profit before tax	7,000	5,000	26,000	2,000
Depreciation	8,200	10,000	2,000	2,000
Funds generated by operations (A)	15,200	15,000	28,000	4,000
Application of funds:				
Purchase of fixed assets	5,700	17,200 (Sale) (1,000)		7,000
Tax paid	2,000	2,200	8,000	5,000
(B)	7,700	19,400	7,000	12,000
Net funds generated (absorbed)				
(A-B) (C)	7,500	(4,400)	21,000	(8,000)
Working capital change*(D)	(10,000)	5,500	(35,000)	(27,000)
Funds available for repayment of				
Bank & H.P. liabilities (C-D)	(2,500)	1,100	(14,000)	(35,000)
Increase(decrease) in long-term debt	(6,500)	1,900	(1,000)	2,000
Increase(decrease) in net short-term				
debt	9,000	(3,000)	15,000	33,000
	2,500	(1,100)	14,000	35,000
*Working capital change:				
Increase(decrease) in creditors	6,000	(3,500)	40,000	100,000
Less:				
Increase(decrease) in debtors	7,000	(5,000)	20,000	60,000
Less:				
Increase/decrease in Stock	9,000	(4,000)	55,000	67,000
	(10,000)	5,500	(35,000)	(27,000)

*   Author's Note – Cash flow analysis and the new cash flow statement (Financial Reporting Standard 1) are explained in more detail in a future chapter.

2.8   Summary on Ratios

What the ratios revealed and the interpretation of the trends seen forms a guide to the financial health of the business being analysed. In assessing a business in this way it is important to appreciate that we are looking at historical information, but this assessment will enable the bank to have a firm basis upon which to consider future borrowing requirements. However, before the assessment can be complete, the bank will need to review the future corporate plan and forward projections of a business. What did we glean from our ratio analysis?

Light Engineering Ltd

This company is maintaining its profitability on a static sales turnover. Its gearing position is improving, in part from retained profits, but also from increasing hidden balance sheet property reserves. Liquidity and control ratios do not reveal anything untoward. The company's working capital position is not under any duress.

Overall, you may not be too concerned with present bank exposure. However, the company's future plans will need to be discussed. Will they be able to generate sufficient sales in 19X7 to maintain their position? Their 'bottom line' retained profits have been modest. There is little leeway if sales levels cannot be maintained. On the 'flat' sales turnover performance it is fortunate that they have been able to hold overhead costs at £60,000. A 10% rise in overheads on the same turnover would eliminate profits! Clearly much will depend on forecasts.

Clothing Imports Ltd

This company looks much more interesting! It has expanded its sales rapidly but only generated profit before tax of £2,000. The increased sales turnover has been accomplished only by reducing profit margins, and overall profitability has shown a marked decline. The effect of the above has been to escalate capital gearing levels, particularly the wider measure of total liabilities/net worth. Gearing is high and so the bank's margin of safety rests very heavily on the security cover. Interest cover has declined. Liquidity has declined – with the company having to extend its credit taken to finance its increased sales levels. Working capital requirements are under some strain. The company will not be able to expand sales at the same rates as in these three years without increasing its bank borrowing and/or credit taken.

Overall, the directors' strategy for 19X6 need questioning, together with their forward plans and budgets for 19X7. Do they realize the cash flow implications of another year of growth similar to that seen in 19X6?

We shall discuss the preparation and interpretation of projections in the next chapter.

Summary

As you finish this chapter you should be able to:

● Assess lending propositions from small or relatively unsophisticated business customers;

● Understand the fundamentals of ratio analysis;

● Manage the lending risk in business start up situations.

3

THE VALUE AND USE OF PROJECTIONS

By the end of this chapter you should be able to:

●   Understand the value and use of projections in lending situations;

●   Be able to construct and differentiate between a profit budget and cash flow forecast;

●   Undertake sensitivity analysis in a lending situation.

In Chapter 2 we suggested that when lending to businesses we should always have three thoughts in mind.

●   Has the business traded successfully in the past?

●   How is the business trading at the present time?

●   Will the business trade successfully in the future, and what will be the business's borrowing requirement?

We addressed the first question by looking at two businesses, Light Engineering Ltd and Clothing Imports Ltd, and considering their financial accounts. Ratios were calculated and trends analysed.

However it may be several months since the audit of the business's books was undertaken, during which time the business will have continued to trade. Prudent businessmen will prepare management accounts on a regular basis and should be in a position to advise the banker of the business's current state of health. Such a discussion will usually take place as the businessman seeks to arrange his bank borrowing requirements for the future.

The banker then needs to know whether the business is likely to be profitable over the coming months, what the borrowing requirement will be and the basis upon which it has been calculated. The lending Banker is keenly interested not only in the profitability of the business, but also its liquidity, as cash flow is the lifeblood of any business.

These questions can be addressed by analysing projections for the future, usually by way of a profit budget and a cash flow forecast. Occasionally the banker will also have the benefit of a projected balance sheet. These documents are often included in a business plan but could be prepared specially for our discussions regarding potential borrowings.

In terms of the business – what benefit can be obtained by preparing these budgets?

- To assist with decision making.
- To ensure that Management thinks ahead.
- To make sure that finance is available at the right time and in the right amount.
- To set a yardstick against which results can be compared for action as necessary.

Perhaps the major benefits are that projections make management think constructively and transfer their ideas from brain to paper. These documents also help to convince outsiders (including banks) of the feasibility of plans and proposals for the future.

When a business has its books audited the financial statements are prepared in a manner that meets the requirements of statutory and professional bodies. Management information prepared by the businessman for forecasting purposes can be in any relative and meaningful form:

Financial Accounting and Management Accounting Compared

Period involved:	Financial Accounting Historic	Management Accounting Recent Past/Future
Layout:	Profit & loss Balance sheet & source/Use of funds/Cash flow statements	Any type of monetary figures
Prepared for	Outsiders Shareholders Inland Revenue Registrar of Companies Creditors	Bankers Management Insiders
Rules made by:	Outsiders Professional bodies Legal requirements	Management can choose any format it likes.
Main emphasis:	True and fair view Detailed disclosure	Useful Timely Detailed Accurate
Area covered :	The business in its entirety	Any necessary division, department or product group

Preparation of Budgets and Cash Flow Forecasts:

To prepare a profit budget and cash flow forecast the business person will need to consider both his short term and longer term objectives and then take decisions as how these will affect his views on the future volumes of:

Sales

Production costs

Overhead expenses

Capital expenditure costs.

The businessman will need to make realistic assumptions in the following areas:

Budgets that are realistically achievable

Quantities and volumes

Economic conditions

Affect of inflation on costs and sources of income

Changes in labour, materials and expense costs

Limiting factors

Seasonality

Levels of productivity achievable

Management policy on stock levels

Starters, leavers and training

Shift work, overtime and sub-contracting

Depreciation, finance charges and notional rent on company-owned property

V.A.T./Local taxes (Care re Budgets/Cash flows)

Payment timings

Assumptions

Final budget for realism, having noted assumptions made

Before putting pen to paper it will be necessary to decide what is to be included in the Forecasts and what is to be left out.

A **Profit Budget** may be compared to the profit and loss report in the financial statements, but with the added proviso that we are looking into the future.

A profit budget may be summarized as:

Profit Budget
Include:

All sales invoiced	[Net
Materials used	of
Costs incurred	VAT]
Interest accruing	
Depreciation	

Exclude:

> Capital expenditure
>
> Repayments
>
> VAT settlements
>
> Items relating to other periods

As with the calculation of profitability in the audited financial statements, value added tax is excluded from the calculations. We need to include all sales invoiced, the materials used and the other costs incurred in the period to be covered. We must also allow for the bank and loan interest paid, and include a charge for depreciation.

All businesses have to assume that their capital assets will eventually have to be replaced. Accordingly each year they must write off a proportion of the value of these assets. The shorter the assumed life of an asset the more prudent is the business's accounting. As we shall see no cash actually changes hands and the amount included, as the depreciation charge, will not appear in the cash flow forecast.

Capital expenditure items, loan repayments and the settlement of VAT are clearly cash flow items with funds flowing out of the business, and are also excluded from the profit budget.

Before considering the preparation of a cash flow forecast we need to have regard for the timing differences that will be involved. If our business sells goods on two months credit terms, a sale made this month will be included in this month's sales records, but we shall not receive the proceeds of the sale into our bank account for a further two months. It will be necessary to allow for this timing difference when we convert our forecast of profitability into a cash flow forecast.

A cash flow forecast may be summarized as:

Cash Flow Forecast
Include:

> Sales receipts only   (Inclusive
>
> Amounts paid   of
>
> Cost paid   VAT)
>
> Interest payments made
>
> Capital expenditure
>
> Repayments, loans, H.P.

Exclude:

> Depreciation
>
> All unpaid items

A cash flow forecast will include the interest paid together with the capital element of any loan. Sales receipts and amounts paid away will allow for the timing difference and include value added tax where appropriate.

As indicated depreciation is excluded from a cash flow forecast.

Case Study 1 – Handmade Tables Ltd

Having considered the way in which we would want to present the information let us now look at a case study situation, Handmade Tables Ltd.

Handmade Tables Ltd – An example of building up the budgets

Introduction and Background

The date is February 1998.

This firm of handmade table manufacturers has been established for only three years, but during that time has made its presence felt in what is a fairly limited and specialized market. The operation has just moved from cramped garage-type accommodation to a modern 4,000 square-foot warehouse on an industrial estate, so that it could cope adequately with an increased order book. Capital expenditure in the new premises has totalled £15,000 so far, most of which has been financed by hire purchase (short-term industrial finance).

The business produces a range of nine handmade tables, three in each type of wood, i.e. oak, teak and mahogany.

The tables have a long lifespan, depending on the use to which they are put. With the growth in turnover, the principal director has found himself under increasing pressure in the day-to-day running of the company.

You have just succeeded in convincing the director of the merits of budgeting and cash flow forecasting, which should enable him to plan and control the future operation of the business in a more positive manner. He appears hesitant about how he should proceed and you have volunteered to offer general advice on the preparation of forecasts for the next six months.

Information Available

There is a seasonal pattern to sales, with a marked increase in March and April following the annual Furniture Exhibition held in London in February each year, and increased sales during the summer months.

The following sales information has been supplied by the director:

1. The average selling price of each type of table is:

   A) Oak   £100

B) Teak   £160

C) Mahogany   £140

2. Sales of the oak tables run at 35 per normal month. The teak version sells the same number in a normal month, while in a normal month 70 are sold of the mahogany model.

In the two months following the February exhibition a sales increase of 50% is seen on a normal month, while May, June and July show a 30% increase on a normal month. January and February are normal months. Due to the holiday shutdown, August can be regarded as normal.

3. Half of total production is exported.

4. U.K. sales are on a cash on delivery basis, while the average time of settlement for exports comes out at two months.

5. Close control is maintained over materials used, which form 40% of the selling price. Levels are held as low as possible and lead times are not a problem.

The receipt of purchase invoices coincides with the month in which the materials are used, and purchases are paid for two months after delivery.

6. The anticipated changes in the levels of stock during the six months are as

follows:

Stock at 28 February 1998 = £15,000.

March	+£1,010
April	+£1,010
May	- £ 528
June	+£ 472
July	- £2,020
August	- £2,944

Stock at the 31 August 1998 = £12,000

Purchases during January and February 1998 were £12,000 and £13,000 respectively.

Assume that the Stock *Purchases* figure is the materials used in the month figure, adjusted for stock levels held at the month end.

7. The company employs 10 men on the production line (5 of whom are self-employed). They are paid £80 per week each gross.

The company's National Insurance contributions for employees are 13.5% of wages.

A wage review is due on 1 August, when a 15% increase will be payable.

May and July will be 'five-week months'. PAYE is paid up to date and is always paid during the same month as the wages.

8.   Turning to the company's overhead costs, the following apply:

a)   Rent of £7,000 per annum is payable quarterly in January, April, etc., and no rent review is due during 1998/99.

b)   Rates in 1998 amounted to £1,200. Although the local authority has made no prediction for 1999, the indications are that the overall increase for 1998/99 fiscal year (i.e. commencing 5.4 1998) will be 20%. They are payable half-yearly, in May and November.

c)   The company is now employing a secretary/bookkeeper at £40 per week plus National Insurance contributions. She will also receive the August increase of 15%.

d)   Telephone usage fluctuates little during the year, the annual bill being £640, with payments made in March, June, September and December.

e)   Hire purchase (short-term industrial finance) commitments are paid by a monthly standing order for £542 (capital and interest). Annual H.P. interest charges total £2,700.

f)   Bank charges are passed quarterly and based on the following figures:

Loan of £1,650 taken up at the end of February. Monthly capital repayments are £84, first payment made in March. The annual interest is £248.

Bank Commission Charges – £500 per annum.

g)   Light and power are not appreciable affected by seasonal influences, as a constant level of heat is required to enable the materials used in manufacture to set properly.

Payments are made in February, May, August and October, and total £4,000 for the year.

h)   The fixed assets of £18,000, at cost, are being depreciated on a straight-line method over five years.

i)   Directors' salaries are £6,600 per annum inclusive of National Insurance contributions.

j)   Ignore Corporation Tax for the purpose of this exercise.

k)   It can be assumed that the remaining overhead costs detailed below are spread evenly throughout the period:

Insurance	£800 per annum
Motor expenses and travelling	£3,000 per annum
Repairs and renewals	£500 per annum

Printing and stationery	£200 per annum
Advertising	£2,000 per annum
Accountancy	£300 per annum
Sundries	£2,000 per annum

The accountant's bill is usually paid in two equal parts in October and November each year.

l) Opening bank balance to be £2,500 overdrawn.

m) Ignore inflation.

Additional Notes

VAT on tables is at 15%, *but* **export orders are exempt.**

All purchases of materials bear VAT at 15%.

VAT recoverable on other outgoings has been ignored for the purpose of this exercise.

The VAT period covers the quarters ending March, June etc. with payments to be made by the 20th of the following month.

Material Purchases:

A profit budget includes materials consumed. (*i. e. used in month*) for profit_purposes, but the VAT calculation will be based on the *purchases* in the month. A cash flow forecast includes purchases + VAT (where appropriate) with a timing allowance for terms of trade.

Let us now consider the preparation of:

1. An operating budget for a six-month period commencing on 1 March 1998.

   (This will incorporate an overheads budget for the period stating in the space provided the assumptions under which various items have been included.)

2. A cash flow forecast for the same period.

Sales Budget

First we need to prepare a sales budget from the information available. In due course we shall need to have regard for the VAT implications and the timing differences, as regards the inflows included in the cash flow forecast, but initially we should consider the assumptions upon which the sales forecast has been based.

These may include:

Questioning Sales Assumptions

● Is the company dependent on one product or customer?

- Does the sales forecast allow for discounts given?

- What assumptions have been made re growth of new markets?

- Are there any technological developments in the pipeline, which might affect sales?

- What length of credit taken by debtors has been assumed in calculating inflows?

- Are there any exchange rate risks?

- Has allowance for seasonality of sales been made?

- Are sales dependent on delivery of new plant and machinery?

- Has an allowance for bad debts been made when forecasting receipts from sales?

Once satisfied that these areas have been considered we can proceed to prepare a sales budget. We know from our discussions that sales increase by 50% in the two months following the furniture show and that May, June and July have sales 30% above a normal month. We can now prepare a sales forecast for the six-month period incorporating this information.

This shows:

HandmadeTables Ltd – Sales Budget for a six-month period to 31 August 1998

Sales	Price	Volume per month	March	April	May	June	July	August	Totals
Oak	£100	35	3,500	3,500	3,500	3,500	3,500	3,500	
Teak	£160	35	5,600	5,600	5,600	5,600	5,600	5,600	
Mahogany	£140	70	9,800	9,800	9,800	9,800	9,800	9,800	
Sub-total			18,900	18,900	18,900	18,900	18,900	18,900	113,400
+50%			9,450	9,450					18,900
+30%					5,670	5,670	5,670		17,010
Totals			28,350	28,350	24,570	24,570	24,570	18,900	149,310

£s

The monthly sales figures can be carried forward into the budget document.

Material Content in Sales

When assessing the materials content in sales we again need to question the assumptions that have been used in arriving at the figures. Such questions may include:

Materials:
- How are costs of materials assessed?

- What materials are needed and when?

- Are raw materials readily available?

- What are deliveries like?

- What minimum and maximum stock levels have been set?

- Has due allowance for discounts on bulk orders been made?

- Is the company pursuing a stocking or de-stocking policy?

- Is the company dependent on sub-contractors?

- What period of credit allowed has been assumed?

- Materials are imported – has the exchange risk been covered?

We are told that materials consumed comprise 40% of the selling price. We can therefore calculate the materials figure for inclusion in the budget:

£s	Net of VAT						
	March	April	May	June	July	August	Totals
Sales	28,350	28,350	24,570	24,570	24,570	18,900	149,310
Materials Consumed	11,340	11,340	9,828	9,828	9,828	7,560	59,724

Wages

Before calculating the anticipated level of wages for the budget period we must consider the wider aspects of the business's wages policy including any likely increases to the wages total.

We must take into consideration:

- Whether the business has allowed for known or anticipated wage increases during the budget period?

- Has due allowance for starters, leavers and training been made?

- What assumptions regarding availability of skilled labour have been made?

- Have all labour costs been included. i.e. employer's share of National Health contributions, pensions, bonuses, etc.?

- Has the cost of overtime/shift work been incorporated in the plan?

  There are several ways of entering wages in the budget, any of which are acceptable.

  They are set down here in descending order of preference:

  a) Total wages for 6 months = 15.22% of sales.

Each month should therefore bear an equivalent percentage of that month's sales as wages costs.

e.g.	March	April	May	June	July	August	Total
£	4,313	4313	3738	3738	3738	2876	£22,716

This method directly relates the wages cost to sales income.

Care In the cash flow forecast the total would have to be reapportioned as in (c) below.

b) Total wages for 6 months = £22,716 therefore each month should bear:

$$\underline{£22,716} = £3,786$$

This method treats wages as a fixed cost running on at a constant level despite fluctuations in the sales pattern

Care In the cash flow forecast the total would have to be reapportioned as in (c) below.

c) 4-week 'months' – 10 men @ £80 x 4 weeks = £3,200

+ National Insurance for 5 men @ 13.5% = £ 216

Total £3,416

5-week 'months' – 10 men @ £80 x 5 weeks = £4,000

+ National Insurance for 5 men @ 13.5% = £ 270

Total £4,270

This method more relates more closely to cash flow than to the operating budget. If sales income were split down into weekly figures it would be more relevant.

So we shall use method (a) and transfer the monthly totals into our Budget form.

In this example the workforce is paid weekly on a Thursday, and five of them are self-employed. Directors salaries are not included in the direct wages.

Overhead Costs

In this case study many of the assumptions are given but the relative calculations are:

Area	Amount	In Cash Flow
Admin Salaries:		
22 Weeks @ £40 per week	= £880	
4 Weeks @ £46 per week	= £184	
	£1,064	
x 13.5% National Insurance	£ 144	
Total Admin Salaries	£1,208	Payable monthly.

Area	Amount	In Cash Flow (cont.)
Rent: Agreed Rental £7,000 p.a. Oct.	£3,500	Payable Quarterly, Jan/April/July/
No Rent Review due.		
Rates: 1 Month @ £1,200 p.a. (i.e. 1/12) =	£ 100	
5 Months @ £1,200 p.a. + 20% =	£ 600	
Total	£ 700	Payable Half Yearly May/November.
Telephone: £640 p.a.	£ 320	Payable March and quarterly.
Insurances: Premiums of £800 p.a.	£ 400	Spread evenly throughout the period.
Light and Heat: Total £4,000 p.a.	£2,000	Payable March and quarterly.
Motor and Travelling Expenses: Estimated at £3,000 p.a.	£1,500	Spread evenly throughout the period.
Repairs and Renewals: Estimated at £500 p.a.	£ 250	Spread evenly throughout the period.
Printing/Stationery: Estimated at £200 p.a.	£ 100	Spread evenly throughout the period.
Advertising: Estimated at £2,000 p.a.	£1,000	Spread evenly throughout the period.
Accountancy: Estimated at £300	£150	Spread evenly throughout the period. Paid in two equal parts in October and November each year.
Sundries: Estimated at £2,000 p.a.	£1,000	Spread evenly throughout the period.
H.P. Interest: Annual H.P Interest Charge £2,700 p.a.	£1,350	Monthly Payments. Remember that in the cash flow we have to include the capital element of the debt as well as the interest.
Bank Charges: The annual loan interest is £248 p.a.		Loan taken up in March

Area	Amount	In Cash Flow (cont.)
The bank commission charge is £500 p.a.	£ 374	Interest and commission both paid quarterly. In the cash flow forecast we shall need to repay the capital of the loan as well.
Depreciation: Fixed assets at a cost of £18,000 To be depreciated on a straight-line basis over 5 years. £18,000 ÷ 5 = £3,600 p.a.	£1,800	A charge against profitability but not a cash flow item.

Directors' Salaries:

£6,600 p.a. to include National Insurance.

Finally check that all expenses have been included.

The total figure from the overheads budget is divided equally over the six-month period, this avoids false hopes in good months when little overheads are paid.

We can summarize our calculations in the following manner, taking 1/6 of the total as the monthly figure for inclusion in our budget:

Overheads budget for the six-month period ending on 31 August 1998

Area	Amount	Assumptions
Admin Salaries	1,208	£40 p.w. + 13.5% NI
Rent	3,500	Agreement
Rates and Water	700	+20% from April
Telephone	320	Usage
Insurance	400	Premiums
Light and Heat	2,000	Assessed
Motor and Travelling	1,500	Estimated
Repairs/Renewals	250	Nominal
Printing/Stationery	100	Assessed
Advertising	1,000	Directors' budget
Accountancy	150	As last year
Sundries	1,000	Estimated
H.P. Interest	1,350	Current contracts
Bank Charges	374	Interest and commission
Depreciation	1,800	Assessed
Directors' Salaries	3,300	6 x £550
Total	**18,952**	**i.e. £3,159 per month**

We are now in a position to finalize our operating budget.

It would be usual to present the information in the following manner:

Operating Budget for a six-month period to 31 August 1998

£s				**Totals**			
Sales	28,350	28,350	24,570	24,570	24,570	18,900	149,310
Less:							
Cost of Sales							
Materials Consumed	11,340	11,340	9,828	9,828	9,828	7,560	59,724
Direct Wages +N.I.	4,313	4,313	3,738	3,738	3,738	2,876	22,716
Total Cost of Sales	15,653	15,653	13,566	13,566	13,566	10,436	82,440
Gross Profit	12,697	12,697	11,004	11,004	11,004	8,464	66,870
Less:							
Overheads (from Overheads Budget)	3,158	3,158	3,159	3,159	3,159	3,159	18,952
Net Profit/ (Loss) (Pre-tax)	9,539	9,539	7,845	7,845	7,845	5,305	47,918

We are forecasting that the business will make a profit of £47,918 over the six-month period to 31 August 1998.

Before leaving the operating budget we should check the following areas:

Profit Budgets Check List
- Are sales realistic?
- Check the projected gross margin against past performance.
- Ensure that all overheads are included.
- Check realism of depreciation.
- Ensure that figures exclude VAT.

- Ensure that finance charges are included.
- Check arithmetic.
- Apply common sense to figures. Do they make sense?

Value Added Tax

Now that we have completed the operating budget we are in a position to consider the VAT implications of our sales and purchases.

As previously indicated VAT has been ignored on the overhead costs although in practice many of the costs would attract VAT.

We are told that VAT on tables sales is calculated at 15%, *but that export orders are exempt.*

Half the sales thus bear VAT at 15%.

All purchases of materials bear VAT at 15%.

We are told that receipt of purchase invoices coincides with the month in which the materials are used and that purchases are paid for two months after delivery.

We need to allow for the stock changes to arrive at the purchases figure for VAT purposes.

The purchases in January and February are shown to be £12,000 and £13,000 respectively.

The **Purchases** for the remainder of the period are calculated as follows:

£s

Month	March	April	May	June	July	August
Materials Consumed (40% of sales)	11,340	11,340	9,828	9,828	9,828	7,560
Stock Change	+1,010	+1,010	-528	+472	-2.020	-2,944
Purchases	12,350	12,350	9,300	10,300	7,808	4,616

15% VAT is then calculated on the purchases figures, for VAT calculations, and added to the purchases figure for outflows in the cash flow forecast.

Value Added Tax - 1998 in £s

Month	Jan	Feb	Mar	April	May	June	July	August
Total Sales	18,900	18,900	28,350	28,350	24,570	24,570	24,570	18,900
½ Sales on 2 months' credit (No VAT)	9,450	9,450	14,175	14,175	12,285	12,285	12,285	9,450
½ Sales in cash VAT	9,450	9,450	14,175	14,175	12,285	12,285	12,285	9,450
VAT on Sales	1,418	1,418	2,126	2,126	1,843	1,843	1,843	1,418
Total Purchases	12,000	13,000	12,350	12,350	9,300	10,300	7,808	4,616
VAT on Purchases	1,800	1,950	1,853	1,853	1,395	1,545	1,171	692
Net Amount	(382)	(532)	273	273	448	298	672	726
Total Payable				(641)				
Total Receivable							1,019	

Having completed our template we can see that we have VAT liabilities as follows for the first three months of the year: January £382 payable February, £532 payable March £273 due to the business. The net payment due to Customs and Excise will be £641 payable by the 20th of the following month. As we complete the second quarter's VAT calculation we see:

> April £273 due to the business
>
> May £448 due to the business
>
> June £298 due to the business

In July the business will receive a cheque from Customs and Excise for the total sum due of £1,019. We shall need to include the net payment and net receipt in our cash flow forecast.

We are now in a position to turn the operating budget into a cash flow forecast. We clearly need to have regard for the timing differences involved in the inflows and outflows of cash.

We are aware that one half of the sales are for cash plus VAT and that payment is received in the month that the sale is effected.

The other half of the sales is the export orders and although free from VAT the business does not receive the inflow of cash until the period of credit given of two months is observed.

We must begin by preparing a summary of the likely inflows from the information that we have.

Sales – Inflows for the six months ending 31 August 1998 in £s								
Sales	**Jan**	**Feb**	**March**	**April**	**May**	**June**	**July**	**August**
In Month	18,900	18,900	28,350	28,350	24,570	24,570	24,570	18,900
½ Sales on 2 Months Credit (No VAT)			9,450	9,450	14,175	14,175	12,285	12,285
½ Sales in Cash plus VAT			14,175	14,175	12,285	12,285	12,285	9,450
			2,126	2,126	1,843	1,843	1,843	1,418
Inflows in Month			25,751	25,751	28,303	28,303	26,413	23,153

With two months' credit terms involved, one half of January's sales become March's inflows; similarly one half of February's sales are the inflows in April.

Thus:

Cash sales for March £14,175, plus VAT @ 15% = £16,301.

Debtor monies in March relate to January sales of £9,450.

We can then continue to complete the analysis for the remaining months on a similar basis.

The cash sales in each month, being one half of the sales totals plus VAT are also included.

The totals calculated are ready for inclusion in the cash flow forecast.

Payments to Creditors

We are told that payments to creditors are made two months after purchase.

Therefor purchases made in January will be paid for in March. Having already calculated the purchases totals we can complete a template, setting down when the payments will be made.

Creditors' Payments Analysis   £s

Month	January	February	March	April	May	June	July	August
Materials Consumed (40% of Sales)			11,340	11,340	9,828	9,828	9,828	7,560
Stock Change			+1.010	+1,010	-528	+472	-2,020	-2,944
Total Purchases	12,000*	13,000*	12,350	12,350	9,300	10,300	7,808	4,616
Add VAT	1,800*	1,950	1,853	1,853	1,395	1,545	1,171	693
Total to be paid away	13,800	14,950	14,203	14,203	10,695	11,845	8,979	5,309
Amount Paid on 2 months' credit			13,800	14,950	14,203	14,203	10,695	11,845

*   Purchases figures given in case study.

We are now able to complete the cash flow forecast as regards both inflows from sales and outflow payments in respect of purchases.

We can also transfer into the cash flow forecast the overheads costs, allowing for the timings of payments as scheduled.

Cash Flow Forecast for six months ending 31 August 1990 in £s

Receipts	March	April	May	June	July	August
Cash Sales	16,301	16,301	14,128	14,128	14,128	10,868
Debtors (2 months)	9,450	9,450	14,175	14,175	12,285	12,285
VAT Refund	-	641	-	-	-	-
Sub-Total	25,751	26,392	28,303	28,303	26,413	23,153
Payments						
Creditors (2 Months)	13,800	14,950	14,203	14,203	10,695	11,845
Wages + N.I.	3,416	3,416	4,270	3,416	4,270	3,928
Rent, Rates and Water	-	1,750	720	-	1,750	-
Heat, Light and Telephone	160	-	1,000	160	-	1,000
Admin Salaries	182	182	227	182	227	208
HP	542	542	542	542	542	542
Bank Loan	84	84	84	84	84	84
Bank Charges	145	-	-	190	-	-
General Overheads	708	708	708	708	709	709
Directors' Salaries	550	550	550	550	550	550
VAT Payable	-	-	-	-	1,019	-
Sub-Total	19,587	22,182	22,304	20,035	19,846	18,866
Net Cash Flow/(Outflow)	6,164	4,210	5,999	8,268	6,567	4,287
Opening Balance	2,500 Dr.	3,664 Cr.	7,874 Cr.	13,873 Cr.	22,141Cr	28,708 Cr.
Closing Balance	3,664 Cr.	7,874 Cr.	13,873 Cr.	22,141 Cr.	28,708 Cr.	32,995 Cr.

As we can see there is no borrowing requirement identified, indeed good credit balances are likely to be generated. This will very much depend on the accuracy of the forecasts.

Let us examine a Cash Flow Forecast Check List:

A Cash Flow Forecasts Check List

Check that the opening balance is correct.

Check the mathematics.

Check that closing monthly balances are correctly carried forward to new month.

Ascertain terms of trade to ensure that timing differences are included correctly.

Check that debtors actually do observe the agreed credit period.

Ensure that all overheads are included.

Ensure that bank interest and commission are included.

Ensure that depreciation is NOT included.

Ensure that discounts are correctly included.

Have tax and dividend payments been included?

Ensure that all inflows and outgoings include VAT, if appropriate.

Focus on the large figures that will make a significant difference to the project.

Check that all capital expenditure has been included.

And finally:

Cash Flow Forecasts

- To be meaningful a cash flow forecast will need to be based upon agreed budgets, with allowance made for timing delays where applicable.

- They need to show that sufficient funds are available at the right time for effective trading.

- They should ensure that the capital expenditure programme is being financed in the most appropriate fashion.

- A cash flow forecast allows for the timing of receipts and payment

- It will normally show net monthly positions and not peak requirements.

- All figures are inclusive of VAT where applicable, and the net VAT settlement will be shown as a receipt or payment as appropriate.

- Depreciation is excluded (since no cash movement).

- Capital expenditure and irregular payments such as Corporation Tax should be included, as should the capital elements of hire purchase finance and loan repayments (including interest).

- The opening balance is normally that shown in the business's books, and not the bank's books.

Sensitivity Analysis

Earlier in this chapter we stated that the projections will assist with:

- Planning
- Delegation
- Control
- Motivation

A further use is to undertake sensitivity analysis, i.e. flexing the forecasts to take account of differing business scenarios. When a customer requests you to consider his financial projections for the future it is important to look critically at the figures and ask yourself what the customer's situation might be, and for that matter the bank's situation, if the forecasts were not met, or volumes were considerably lower or higher than the levels proposed.

To allow us to look at the implications of actual trading performance differing from forecast we need to apply sensitivity analysis to the proposals, and flex the forecasts.

In simple terms we must ask ourselves a series of 'what if... 'questions.

For example:

What would happen to the business if the sales forecast were not met?

What would be the position if sales exceeded forecast?

What would the borrowing requirement be if the terms of trade were different from those proposed?

What would be the effect on profitability if the overhead costs were in excess of forecast?

Let us examine a case study situation, Boffin Ltd, and apply sensitivity analysis to the customer's request for an overdraft facility of £20,000 to cover working capital requirements.

Case Study 2 – Boffin Ltd

Boffin Ltd

A new company has been formed with an initial capital of £25,000. Part of this will be used to purchase machinery (£18,000 plus VAT) and stock (£3,000 plus VAT) in the first month.

VAT rate is 15%.

The directors have found a factory and although they consider the rent to be somewhat high, no premium has been charged. They estimate that fixtures and fittings will cost £2,400 plus VAT and will be bought in the first month.

The directors have prepared a budget (see attached) and have satisfied you that their forecast figures are realistic. Their own income will be paid as wages. You know them personally and consider them to be honest and hard working.

They ask you to support them with a 12-month working capital overdraft facility of £20,000, partially to cover the immediate purchase of additional stock (£7,000 plus VAT) to bring their stock level up to £10,000, which is the amount that they intend to hold in reserve.

They offer personal guarantees supported by second charges on their homes (total values £120,000 – mortgages outstanding £70,000). Their wives are going to work as a secretary and a book-keeper in the business.

To allow you to consider their request they have prepared a profit budget and a cash flow forecast for the next 12 months. These papers show the following situation:

Profit Budget in £s

	1	2	3	4	5	6	7	8	9	10	11	12	Total
Sales	10,000	10,000	10,000	12,000	12,000	14,000	14,000	16,000	16,000	18,000	18,000	18,000	168,000
Less:													
Materials Used	5,500	5,500	5,500	6,600	6,600	7,700	7,700	8,800	8,800	9,900	9,900	9,900	92,400
Wages +NI	2,600	2,600	2,600	2,600	2,600	2,600	2,600	2,600	2,600	2,600	2,600	2,600	31,200
	(8,100)	(8,100)	(8,100)	(9,200)	(9,200)	(10,300)	(10,300)	(11,400)	(11,400)	(12,500)	(12,500)	(12,500)	(123,600)
Gross Profit	1,900	1,900	1,900	2,800	2,800	3,700	3,700	4,600	4,600	5,500	5,500	5,500	44,400
Gross Profit %													26.4%
Overheads													
Salaries and N.I.	600	600	600	600	600	600	600	600	600	600	600	600	7,200
Rent and Rates	750	750	750	750	750	750	750	750	750	750	750	750	9,000
Depreciation:													
Machinery	150	150	150	150	150	150	150	150	150	150	150	150	1,800
Fixtures and Fittings	40	40	40	40	40	40	40	40	40	40	40	40	480
Finance Costs	250	250	250	250	250	250	250	250	250	250	250	250	3,000
Other Overheads No VAT	160	160	160	200	200	200	200	200	200	240	240	240	2,400
Other Overheads With VAT	240	240	240	300	300	300	300	300	300	360	360	360	3,600
Total overheads													27480
Net Profit													16,920

Boffin Ltd – Cash Flow Forecast in £s

	1	2	3	4	5	6	7	8	9	10	11	12	Total
Receipts from Debtors Including VAT	-	-	11,500	11,500	11,500	13,800	13,800	16,100	16,100	18,400	18,400	20,700	151,800
Capital Injection	25,000												25,000
VAT Settlement				2,643									**2,643**
	25,000		**11,500**	**14,143**	**11,500**	**13,800**	**13,800**	**16,100**	**16,100**	**18,400**	**18,400**	**20,700**	**179,443**
Payments:													
Machinery, Fixtures and Fittings	**23,460**												**23,460**
Material Creditors (Inc VAT): Reserve Stock				11,500									11,500
Monthly Purchases Materials				6,325	6,325	6,325	7,590	7,590	8,855	8,855	10,120	10,120	72,105
Wages	1,800	1,800	1,800	2,250	1,800	1,800	2,250	1,800	2,250	1,800	2,250	1,800	23,400
Salaries	450	450	450	450	450	450	450	450	450	450	450	450	5,400
PAYE/N.I.		750	750	750	900	750	750	900	750	900	750	900	8,850
Rent	**1,800**			**1,800**			**1,800**			**1,800**			**7,200**
Rates	900												1,800
Finance	-	-											
Costs			750			750			750			750	3,000
Other													
Overheads:													
No VAT	160	160	160	200	200	200	200	200	200	240	240	240	2,400
With VAT	276	276	276	345	345	345	345	345	345	414	414	414	4,140
VAT Settlement	2,430	2,970	5,400										
Sub-Total	**28,846**	**3,436**	**4,186**	**23,620**	**10,020**	**10,620**	**16,715**	**11,285**	**13,600**	**17,429**	**14,224**	**14,674**	**168,655**
Net Cash Flow	**(3,846)**	**(3,436)**	**7,314**	**(9,477)**	**1,480**	**3,180**	**(2,915)**	**4,815**	**2,500**	**971**	**4,176**	**6,026**	**10,788**
Opening Balance	Nil	(3,846)	(7,282)	32	(9,445)	(7,965)	(4,785)	(7,700)	(2,885)	(385)	586	4,762	
Closing Balance	(3,846)	(7,282)	32	(9,445)	(7,965)	(4,785)	(7,700)	(2,885)	(385)	586	4,762	10,788	

Boffin Ltd – VAT Calculation in £s

		1	2	3	4	5	6	7	8	9	10	11	12
(Outputs)													
Sales		10,000	10,000	10,000	12,000	12,000	14,000	14,000	16,000	16,000	18,000	18,000	18,000
VAT	(A)	1,500	1,500	1,500	1,800	1,800	2,100	2,100	2,400	2,400	2,700	2,700	2,700
(Inputs)													
Materials		5,500	5,500	5,500	6,600	6,600	7,700	7,700	8,800	8,800	9,900	9,900	9,900
Machinery		18,000											
Fixtures and Fittings		2,400											
Stock		3,000											
Additional Stock		7,000											
Other Overheads With VAT		240	240	240	300	300	300	300	300	300	360	360	360
Total Inputs		36,140	5,740	5,740	6,900	6,900	8,000	8,000	9,100	9,100			
VAT	(B)	5,421	861	861	1,035	1,035	1,200	1,200	1,365	1,365			
Net Difference (A)-(B)		(3,921)*	639*	639*	765**	765**	900**	900..	1,035..	1,035..			
Pay or Receive					(2,643)*			2,430***			2,970..		

The directors confirm that their calculations show that there will be useful credit balances available at the end of the first year of trading. Indeed, they suggest to you that the requested overdraft facility will be only lightly used.

You are not convinced that this will be the case and arrange a meeting with the directors with a view to obtaining a better 'feel' for the business, and to have a look at the operation.

You have made a list of questions to ask the directors including:

How many product lines?

What would be the effect of changes in the product mix?

Do all products yield the same contribution?

What is the market?

What market research has been undertaken?

What contact has been made with potential customers?

Are there any firm orders?

Will the business be dependent on any one customer or product?

What technological developments may be in the pipeline?

What are the normal terms of trade?

Will any goods be exported?

Are there any seasonal factors?

Who are the competitors?

Is the plant/labour force ready to start production?

What is the production time? Budgets suggest significant sales in the first month.

What allowance has been made for bad debts?

Is there to be a discount policy?

If forecasts are to be realistic constraints to resources must be recognized. These may include the following:

Funds

Space

Demand

Labour skills

Management ability

Machine capacity

Materials availability

Only by recognizing such constraints at an early stage, and appreciating the future results of proposed present actions, can a company hope to avoid major unforeseen pitfalls.

After close questioning, the directors tell you that their forecasts are based on the following assumptions.

Assumptions

1. Credit given on sales is expected to be 2 months, (i.e. inflows from sales in month 1 will be received in month 3).

2. Credit taken on materials purchases is expected to be 3 months (i.e. purchases in month 1 will be paid for in month 4).

3. Materials will be used in the month in which they are bought.

4. Fixtures, fittings and machinery have to be paid for in month 1.

5. Rent is payable quarterly from month 1 (£7,200 per year).

6. Rates are payable half-yearly from month 1 (£1,800 per year).

7. Wages (not salaries) are paid weekly (total £600 per week gross)

There are 5 weeks in months 4, 7, 9 and 11.

8. All other cost are payable in the same month as incurred.

9. Finance costs budgeted at £750 per quarter are payable in months 3, 6, 9 and 12.

10. Depreciation on machinery is calculated at 10% per annum straight-line method.

11. Depreciation on fixtures and fittings is calculated at 20% per annum straight-line method.

12. VAT is settled: for the first quarter in month 4.

                      for the second quarter in month 7.

                      for the third quarter in month 10.

13. Both wages and salaries in the budget are gross figures including PAYE and Employers N.I. It is assumed that total deductions will amount to 25% of the gross totals each month and will be paid over to the Revenue in the month following the wages/salaries payment.

You are concerned at the suggestion that the terms of trade will be so favourable and decide to undertake some sensitivity analysis of the directors' proposals. You decide to flex the cash flow forecast by amending the terms of trade to:

Credit given: 3 months (i.e. inflows from sales in month 1 will be received in month 4).

Credit taken: 2 months (i.e. purchases in month 1 will be paid for in month 3).

Your revised cash flow forecast based on these amended terms of trade shows:

Boffin Ltd – Revised Cash Flow Forecast in £s

	1	2	3	4	5	6	7	8	9	10	11	12	Total
Receipts from Debtors													
Including VAT	–	–	–	11,500	11,500	11,500	13,800	13,800	16,100	16,100	18,400	18,400	131,100
Capital Injection	25,000												25,000
VAT Settlement				2,643									2,643
	25,000	–	–	14,143	11,500	11,500	13,800	13,800	16,100	16,100	18,400	18,400	158,743
Purchase Machy, Fixts. and Fittings	23,460												23,460
Reserve Stock			11,500										11,500
Monthly Purchases													
Materials	–	–	6,325	6,325	6,325	7,590	7,590	8,855	8,855	10,120	10,120	11,385	83,490
Wages	1,800	1,800	1,800	2,250	1,800	1,800	2,250	1,800	2,250	1,800	2,250	1,800	23,400
Salaries	450	450	450	450	450	450	450	450	450	450	450	450	5,400
PAYE/N.I.	–	750	750	750	900	750	750	900	750	900	750	900	8,850
Rent	1,800	–	–	1,800	–	–	1,800	–	–	1,800	–	–	7,200
Rates	900						900						1,800
Finance Costs	–	–	750	–	–	750	–	–	750	–	–	750	3,000
Other Overheads:													
No VAT	160	160	160	200	200	200	200	200	200	240	240	240	2,400
With VAT	276	276	276	345	345	345	345	345	345	414	414	414	4,140
VAT Settlement							2,430			2,970			5,400
Sub-Total	28,846	3,436	22,011	12,120	10,020	11,885	16,715	12,550	13,600	18,694	14,224	15,939	180,040
Net Cash Flow	(3,846)	(3,436)	(22,011)	2,023	1,480	(385)	(2,915)	1,250	2,500	(2,594)	4,176	2,461	
Opening Balance	Nil	(3,846)	(7,282)	(29,293)	(27,270)	(25,790)	(26,175)	(29,090)	(27,840)	(25,340)	(27,934)	(23,758)	
Closing Balance	(3,846)	(7,282)	(29,293)	(27,270)	(25,790)	(26,175)	(29,090)	(27,840)	(25,340)	(27,934)	(23,758)	(21,297)	

If the terms of trade are as amended then the requested overdraft facility of £20,000 is not going to be sufficient. Indeed, within three months the company is likely to be considerably in excess of the arrangement, with a likely borrowing requirement of almost £30,000, with substantial excesses seen over the remainder of the year – a different scenario from the one suggested by the directors.

How likely is it that sales will total £10,000 in month one?

What would be the effect on profitability if sales for the year were 10% below forecast?

What if they were 20% below forecast?

The sales projection in the profit budget is £168,000. The gross profit is £44,400, giving a gross profit percentage of 26.4%. The overhead costs are forecast to total £27,480.

A reduction is sales would have the following effects on company trading performance:

Area Sales %	Directors' Forecast 100% £	Forecast 1 -10% £	Forecast 2 -20% £
Sales Turnover	168,000	151,200	134,400
Gross Profit	44,400	39,916	35,481
Gross Profit %	26.4%	26.4%	26.4%
Overhead Costs	27,480	27,480	27,480
Projected Profit	16,920	12,436	8,001
Variance from Budget	-	-25%+	-50%+

As can be seen a 10% reduction in sales would reduce projected profit by over 25%. A reduction of 20% in sales would reduce the projected profit by over 50%.

If the decrease in sales were coupled to a 20% increase in overhead costs over budgeted figures, the profit for the year would virtually disappear.

Breakeven Analysis

How much turnover does the business have to achieve to avoid making a loss on trading?

This fundamental question can be answered by calculating the breakeven turnover point for the business. That is the point at which the total costs are exactly equal to sales turnover. This is often expressed as:

At Breakeven: FIXED COSTS + VARIABLE COSTS = SALES

Terminology:

FIXED COST: A cost that tends to be unaffected by variations in the volume of output.

VARIABLE COST: A cost that tends to vary in direct proportion to variations in volume of output.

SEMI-VARIABLE: A cost that is partly fixed and partly variable.

CONTRIBUTION: The difference between sales and variable costs.

In practice, deciding which costs are fixed and which are variable presents little problem because materials consumed are clearly variable and most significant overhead costs are fixed. Labour costs, however, may be fixed or variable. In the case of Boffin Ltd the costs are variable.

The most common breakeven calculation is that to establish breakeven turnover and may be defined as:

$$\text{Breakeven sales} = \frac{\text{Fixed costs x sales}}{\text{Contribution}}$$

- Contribution equates to the gross profit of a business.

- Fixed costs equate to the overhead costs of a business.

An alternative method of calculation is:

$$\text{Breakeven sales} = \frac{\text{Fixed costs}}{\text{Gross profit \%}}$$

Let us calculate breakeven levels of turnover of the directors' profit budget.

$$\frac{£27,480 \times £168,000}{£44,400}$$

Therefore breakeven turnover = £103,978

If the sales forecast proves to be accurate, and the projected gross profit margin is achieved, the breakeven point will be passed in the ninth month of the trading year. Any profits will thus be earned in the latter part of the year.

Before accepting budget figures we need to ensure that we have considered all the areas of the budget and cash flow forecasts. These will include:

Budgets:
Sales:
What are the trends?

Are sales increasing or decreasing in line with reasonable expectations?

Are sales rising in line with inflation or is genuine progress being made?

What is the sales mix?

Are the expectations of anticipated sales reasonably achievable?

What would be the effect of sales lower than forecast?

What would be the effect of sales higher than forecast?

Cost of Sales:

This shows cost of stock actually used in sales. It can include other elements of production, i.e. manufacturing wages.

Changes in materials and wages costs will effect gross profit.

> Are the materials costs realistic?

> What would be the effect of a 10% increase in materials?

Gross Profit:

This can be effected by:

> Increases or decreases in the cost of materials.

> Higher or lower selling prices.

> Pilferage

> Stock valuation

> Increases in wages costs where included in cost of sales.

What are the trends?

Is the gross profit percentage realistic and achievable?

What would be the effect on profitability if the gross profit percentage obtained was 10% lower?

Overhead Costs:

Have all relative overhead costs been included?

> Consider individual amounts.

> Examine those that will make a significant difference.

> Consider individual items as a percentage of sales.

Have likely increases in overhead costs been allowed for?

Interest:

Relate the charge to amount of borrowed funds.

> Is the degree of cover by profit acceptable?

Profit:

Is projected profit achievable?

How does it compare with past performance?

Cash Flow Forecast

Are the terms of trade realistic?

Are they being observed?

What would be the effect on cash requirements of changes in the terms of trade?

Are the timings of the payments of overhead expenses realistic?

Is the opening cash book balance correct?

Has VAT been allowed for if appropriate?

Have items been transferred correctly from the Budget?

Ensure that depreciation is excluded from the calculations.

Is any borrowing requirement projected in line with the interest charge included?

Conclusion

The potential accuracy of forecasts is dependent upon the validity of the many assumptions and estimates that underlie the proposals.

An appraisal should identify significant items in the forecasts that will make a substantial difference to trading performance outcomes and seek to assess whether the assumptions are soundly based.

The management of a business should be committed to achieving budgeted figures and use them for coordinating and controlling activities.

Particular attention should be given to those factors that are least easy to predict and are likely to have a substantial impact on profits.

4

LARGER BUSINESS LENDING

Objectives

At the end of this chapter you should be able to:

- Understand the impact of management on a business and carry out business risk analysis using SWOT and an industry analysis framework;

- Understand the new cash flow statement, FRS1;

- Have an appreciation of some stock market indicators;

- Understand the differing approaches to corporate valuation;

- Recall the main methods for capital project appraisals;

- Review typical lending covenants.

4.1   Business Risk Analysis

The Chief Examiner has recently stated in *ifs News* that:

> ' ... candidates fairly readily interpret accounting ratios and financial information such as gearing, interest cover etc., to see that a corporate has a capital structure, which contains high financial risk. Where they then fall down is that they are not able to put this high financial risk into a wider context and so are often unable to decide whether high financial risk can be tolerated in the overall circumstances of the company. Corporates face not only financial risk, but what might be described as 'business risk', i.e. threats and opportunities confronting a firm in its external environment.
>
> The analysis of business risk is about looking at a company's place in its market, its strategy for addressing its market position and its ability to manage its resources to defend/exploit its position.'

For those readers' studying for examination purposes, we therefore need an understanding of this topic. However, the analysis of business risk is difficult, because it calls for subjective judgements on qualitative issues. Basically, it is a critical review of the non-financial factors, because opposed to the financial analysis we have undertaken in the previous unit.

One of the most important aspects of any business, indeed perhaps the most important aspect, is the quality of the business's management.

The Management of a Business

How should we define Management? Perhaps the simplest definition would be 'deciding what is to be done and who is to do it'. A broad definition of management in terms of its purpose *is the efficient use of resources to achieve objectives.*

Frequently a good craftsman, chemist, engineer or salesman sets up his own business because he is good at what he does. Up to this point he has probably received little training in management skills. One of the most difficult tasks facing a bank lender is the judgement of management capability.

The quality of the management is arguably the single most important asset that any business has. We are all aware that poor management can seriously damage a traditionally good business whereas good management can restore a failing business to good health.

At the outset a lender can only reflect on what he sees, hears and reads. He must ask himself a number of questions regarding the management as regards its individual functional performances, how the management blends as a team, with a view to meeting the business's objectives.

Management Skills

A few years ago a common description of the man management function was 'command'. In recent years this has been seen to have overtones of authoritarianism, and other titles such as 'leadership' and 'motivation' are thought to be more appropriate.

In a well-balanced management team in addition to the managing director or senior partner there will be specialists in selling and purchasing, production, finance, marketing and operational control. In smaller businesses these functions may well be undertaken by a small group of individuals, or indeed, one person.

Let us consider a check list of management skills:

The Management as Individuals

● What are their professional qualifications and training?

● What is their experience and integrity?

● How good are their operational skills?

● What is their reputation in their trade or industry?

● What are their ages and how good is their health?

● How good is their ability to plan a course of action?

- How good is their commitment to the task of managing the business?
- How good are their financial skills?
- Do we know their strengths and weaknesses?
- Has management succession been considered?
- What are their personal assets and liabilities?

And more specifically:

Check List – Individual Assessment
- What impression do they make by impact of personality?

Mental Calibre
- Are they quick to grasp essentials?
- Can they penetrate to underlying facets?
- Are their reactions to problems pertinent and prompt?
- Are they open-minded to new ideas and other peoples' thoughts?
- Do they show maturity of judgement?

Initiative
- Do they show good self-confidence?
- Are there signs of overconfidence?
- Are their decisions translated into quick effective action?
- Do they provide a source of new ideas?

Cooperation
- Are they respected by colleagues? – and subordinates?
- Does they work in easily with others?
- Do they make themselves easily understood?
- Are they contributing to the development of subordinates?
- Are their personal objectives compatible with those of the business?

Responsibility
- Do they have stable personalities?
- Do they have a good sense of responsibility?
- What evidence is there of determination to 'flog through' in bad times?

- Do others rely on their judgement?

- Are they people of integrity?

- Would they provide the bank with valid up-to-date information on a deteriorating financial situation?

- Do they consider carefully the implications of providing personal security?

Track Record
- Have they succeeded in life so far?

- Are there any failures that can be attributed to them?

- Have their previous employment records been stable?

- Have they commercial awareness?

- How good is their planning?

- What is the reputation of the management team in the marketplace?

- Do they work as a team?

The Management as a Team

How good is their track record?

What is the team structure?

Are all necessary functions covered?

Is the team well balanced or is there a dominant figure?

Management Structure and Succession

Mark Homan, formerly Chairman of accountants Price Waterhouse World Firm Insolvency Group, has some interesting observations on management:

Bad management is the most common cause of business failure and a proper appreciation of the capabilities of a company's management is therefore essential in any company-monitoring exercise.

There are several common causes that the lending banker can usefully look out for.

In a family business the management of the business is frequently handed down from one generation to the next irrespective of whether management skills have been successfully inbred.

Equally dangerous is the situation where a company's management is concentrated in the hands of a single executive. The dominant chief executive can be dangerous in many respects, not least when he dies. It is a common failing in such cases to find no management succession. Regrettably, there is also more likelihood of financial impropriety where there is a dominant chief executive.

A further situation, which can give rise to problems, is where the size or nature of a business is undergoing rapid changes. An entrepreneur may be well suited to running a small, expanding business, but there comes a time when there is a requirement for other skills within the management team such as delegation and team building. Such skills are not always inherent in the initial pioneer of the business.

This is often a factor behind a business that shows early success but cannot sustain it.

It can also give rise to a loss of control of the business – particularly dangerous when early success gives rise to overconfidence and thence overexpansion.

There are other indications of management weakness that the lending banker should look out for in monitoring his customers.

A high turnover rate among key employees may indicate that management are unable to motivate staff with a real sense of purpose; while extravagant spending on travel, entertainment and office accommodation may be an indication of irresponsible management.

A reluctance to inject capital into the business may indicate a management team lacking in confidence in the business and may lead to a lack of commitment to it, and perhaps most important, a failure to take advantage of financial information (for example, by attending to variances) may indicate insufficient attention to planning and control which are so essential to good management.

In practice in many businesses the manager needs to be an 'all-rounder' capable of co-ordinating policy and planning, organization and control of the business. A manager must, of course, have the technical competence necessary to achieve the results required, but he must also have the understanding and skill needed in his unique position of having to get work done by others, that is, to lead others.

Some managers are constrained by their function and special skills to adopt a particular style of management. This may be particularly so where the manager is highly qualified, e.g. as an accountant or lawyer. In practice the manager needs to have regard for team needs and individual needs in addition to task needs.

Dr. John Adair developed a model, which illustrates how people and the work that they do interact.

Figure 4.1: People/Work Interaction

After: John Adair

Ignore the needs of the individual, and the effectiveness of both task and team is reduced.

The circles overlap. If the task circle is blacked out so too are large segments of the team and individual circles. Thus lack of attention to the task causes disruption in the team and dissatisfaction to the individual. Conversely, achievement of objectives is essential if team and individual morale is to be high.

Black out the team needs circle from the model and the other two are affected. Unless the leader actively sees that the needs of the team as a group are satisfied, his chances of achieving the required results, in the long term, are jeopardized.

SWOT Analysis

A useful company analysis framework that is very popular is to undertake a SWOT analysis.

SWOT complements and extends the CAMPARI mnemonic by looking at a business in a wider context. It stands for:

Strengths

Weaknesses

Opportunities

Threats

Strengths/Weaknesses

When looking at the strengths and weaknesses of a business, a lender will concentrate on an internal view of the performance of the business. There is a range of factors internal to any business, which will affect performance. The following illustrate the sort of topics that can be reviewed, although this list is not exhaustive:

Management	What is the level of management skills?
	What is the level of expertise and experience?
Capital	What is the liquidity, profitability and asset structure of the business?
Accounting Records	How well-informed is management about the financial position?
	How good is the information produced?
	What book-keeping systems are in operation?
Marketing	How many customers are there/What is the market share?
	Who are the main competitors?
Product	How new is the product, what is its life cycle?
	What are the volumes sold and what is the value?
Premises	What is the condition of the premises?
	How suitable are they for present/future needs?
	What is their location?
Plant and Machinery	What is the current condition of the machinery?
	What is the replacement policy?
Labour	What is the quality of labour?
	How good are labour relations?
Stock	What are the proportions of raw materials, work in progress and finished goods? Is there any obsolete stock?

Opportunities/Threats

When looking at the opportunities and threats that face a business, a lender will concentrate on the range of factors external to the business which can influence performance. These can be factors over which the business has no control. However, an understanding of the extent to which these factors can affect a business can be vital in assessing accurately the quality of the business and the ultimate credit risk. The following illustrates the issues that can be covered, but again this list is not exhaustive:

Competitiveness	What is the level of competition?
Economic Changes	What will be the impact of economic changes? Most firms are affected by pressures from business cycles, exchange rates, interest rates and inflation.

Social Changes	What will be the impact of changes in demographics, lifestyle etc.? Changes in the birth rate, the number of children per family and the average age of the population may affect a business's market. Trends in social and cultural patterns can have unpredictable effects on business, e.g., food producers reacting to a trend towards health-consciousness.
Political Changes	What will be the impact of changes in government legislation?
Technological Changes	What new technological developments will affect the business? Some businesses may be faced with obsolescence of major assets as better processes are developed.
Ecology	Ecological 'friendliness' had become one of the most visible influences on business activity in recent years, e.g. firms that discharge high levels of effluent face greater fines than before and consumers are more biased towards eco-friendly products.
Labour Markets	Demographic changes and workforce skills can affect the availability of suitable labour.

The use of SWOT is a good structure or non-financial analysis framework not only to help pinpoint the pros and cons of a particular lending situation, but also to help us to focus on some of the external factors, which are very important in larger business lending. These factors can significantly affect your view of the lending risk.

Case Study 3 – Using CAMPARI and SWOT Techniques

The following case study illustrates the use of SWOT analysis. It concerns an established and successful business which runs into difficulties, presenting the relationship banker with a series of decisions to make.

Introduction

In June 1995, HR Trailers Ltd (HRT) has asked the bank for an overdraft facility of £300,000. Your task is to review the information about HRT provided below and then, using business risk assessment techniques, assess the viability of the company to assist in making a decision about HRT's request.

Information Available about HR Trailers Ltd (HRT) as at June 1995
General information
HRT sells high-specification agricultural machinery to the agricultural industry. Although these trailers look like any other, they are more advanced and have a much greater capacity.

HRT has the exclusive rights to sell and distribute the specialist 'Visions' trailer which is manufactured by SORA Trailers (Far East) Inc. The 'Visions' trailer is a minor product among SORA's trailer product range but the market niche it fits does require specialist knowledge and commitment to service. The main requirements of HRT's customers are for a high-powered trailer with a high capacity.

HRT's machines are priced between £6,000 and £10,000 each, ignoring any customization requests. Terms are net 30 days for the basic machines to major establishments and commercial firms. Substantial deposits are taken on those orders for customized machines. The delivery period for a customized machine is about 6 weeks, which includes the time taken to configure the trailer to the customer's requirements, while standard machines, if in stock, are dispatched within 48 hours after satisfactory credit enquiries. Customers are told, on placing their customized order and paying their deposit, that delivery will be in 6 to 8 weeks. If the delivery is later than this, customers can invoke certain conditions on the sale contract. They can start to claim discounts on their final invoice and, in some circumstances, cancel their order and receive their deposit back.

The company operates from a distribution unit, with offices above, in Sunderland. Storage capacity is fully utilized at these premises and will not support further expansion. The technical support and customization department is particularly cramped for space. There is an extensive range of new and second-hand specialist equipment in the factory, which is slowly being incorporated into a formal production line.

Management

The management team is young and consists of five people. The company was formed in 1990 by Fred Young and Sally White who are joint managing directors and the major shareholders. The company's bankers have been B Bank from its very beginning and there has never been a problem with the conduct of the account. Fred Young and Sally White have been responsible for all aspects of the company's growth and for building up the present management team. They are supported by three senior people responsible for sales, technical support and distribution. Previously, they both held senior positions at SORA UK Ltd. Fred Young worked for SORA UK Ltd for seven years rising to board level. He left because he saw no possibility of a meaningful equity participation. The company employs 19 people in total.

Fred Young identified in the very beginning the niche market for specialized machines and left SORA UK Ltd, which is a shareholder in HRT, with its blessing and an agreement to be its sole distributor in the UK to this specialized market. Despite the close association between the two companies and SORA UK's investment in HRT (see overleaf), SORA UK Ltd has adopted a distinctly hands-off approach to the way in which HRT is operated. It is happy to see HRT push itself aggressively to the forefront of the market, making a name for itself and SORA's products.

Sally White is qualified in business studies and worked at SORA UK Ltd for eight years as a marketing executive. Her role at SORA UK Ltd included advising on new products, market research and responsibility for a promotional budget of £2 million. Fred is the communicator and driver of the business with ambition and energy to build the company. Sally is equally ambitious but she acts as a foil to Fred, bringing a practical and steadying influence to the company.

Market
The company's customers range across a broad spectrum. The order book is currently healthy with orders at capacity for the next four months. Throughout this niche market, HRT has earned an excellent reputation by recommending and providing the right machine for each specific use. It offers a complete range of models and 'customizations' based on the 'Visions' trailer. With HRT's advantages of a skilled and knowledgeable sales force and full customization service, HRT is approaching the quality of service and product sophistication normally associated with main suppliers.

Competitive position
The company feels it has an added advantage over its competitors by providing a customization service. This integration of distribution and customer service, from a local base within the UK, gives it added flexibility in fulfilling customers' orders. The company believes that its strong link with a major trailer manufacturer provides an effective barrier to new entrants to the market. The company aims to ensure that levels of stock of the basic machines are customer led.

Employment
Many of the workforce in the factory are school leavers trained from scratch by a core of HRT's skilled workers. The high turnover of workers in the factory has now reduced and stabilized. Labour relations appear to be good.

Expanding the business
Early in 1995, HRT used its own resources to buy out the shareholders in Scottish Trailers, its principal competitor. Following this acquisition, HRT has become the market leader in the UK and the pressure on work space is increasing. The company expects sales to grow by over 100% across the board, as a result of the purchase of Scottish Trailers, and has approached SORA UK Ltd concerning an equity investment in HRT.

After discussions SORA UK Ltd earmarked a £1.4 million financial package to support continued expansion and growth of the company, on the understanding that HRT aims to seek a full stock market listing within the next 2 to 3 years. The SORA financial package is made up as follows:

	£
Share premium	308,400
Preference shares	691,60
Total cash injected into HRT	1,000,000
(*Subordinated loan not yet drawn)	400,000
Total investment by SORA UK Ltd	1,400,000

*   The subordinated loan has been made available for a maximum period of five years of trading. It is earmarked for specific purposes relating to the expansion of the business.

The SORA UK Ltd investment is subject to various terms and conditions linked to a stock market flotation. The terms set out a timetable for the issue of shares and look for one-third of the shares to be issued within 12 months. In addition, sales are expected to achieve an annual growth rate of 7% above that resulting from the acquisition of Scottish Trailers. The shareholders, as at Jan 1995, are Fred Young (43%), Sally White (43%), and SORA UK Ltd (14%).

Share options in the future may be made available to other senior members of the management team. The directors hope that the company will achieve a stock market floatation within the next 12 months. Extensive work has been carried out by a major firm of accountants and these accountants are now retained by SORA UK Ltd to carry out 'due diligence work'. Up until June 1995, the company has operated with strong credit balances. However, even taking into account the new money invested by SORA UK Ltd, HRT has experienced a drain on its resources. This has partly been caused by buying out Scottish Trailers and partly by the increased working capital requirements resulting from the booming sales.

Financial position
As at 31 March 1995, the company has retained profits of £686,000, net assets of £836,000 and credit balances with the bank of £729,000. The financial report confirmed the first three months' cash flow forecast figures.

HRT has approached the bank for an overdraft facility of £300,000 to fund its increased working capital requirement resulting from continuing sales growth and the research and development expenditure on its new trailer system. The company expresses its key trading advantages as:

● Its technical knowledge and back-up.

● The close relationship with its main supplier, SORA Trailers (Far East) Inc.

● The support and financial commitment of SORA UK Ltd to the company through its minority share holding and investment.

● The company culture fostered by the management team.

The company appreciates that the general economic climate is on the edge of recession but believes for the following reasons that it has a very strong competitive edge. In order to reduce costs, many firms are prepared to invest in more advanced machines to cut down on manpower costs. The format of the business is well suited to the existing market conditions and is cushioned from the worst effects of the economic downturn because of its acknowledged position of service in this niche market. There is a potential to increase prices as a result of HRT's domination of this market. The integrated customization and selling operation provides low costs and flexibility.

The management team possesses a balance of skills and is highly motivated. The company has an enthusiastic and highly knowledgeable workforce.

Financial information
The following financial information has been presented at the same time as the overdraft request. HRT's financial year ends 31 March.

Summarized Profit and Loss Account for 1993, 1994 and 1995

	12 Months to 31.3.93 £000s	12 Months to 31.3.94 £000s	12 Months to 31.3.95 £000s	Forecast to 31.3.96 £000s
Sales	259	1,945	4,659	9,164
Gross Profit	148	1,127	2,988	5,699
Profit before Tax	69	202	810	1,165
Retained Profit	65	140	686	463
Net Assets	68	458	836	2,299

This is the first balance sheet showing the inclusion of Scottish Trailers.

Consolidated Balance Sheet as at 31 March 1995

	£000s	£000s
Fixed Assets	806	
Current Assets		
Stocks	1,265	
Debtors and Prepayments	834	
Bank	729	
	2,828	
Current Liabilities		
Trade Creditors	1,529	
Other Creditors	634	
Corporation Tax	281	
Hire Purchase	51	
VAT	150	
	(2,645)	
Net Current Assets		183
Creditors > 1Year		
Hire Purchase	(153)	(153)
Net Assets		836
Share Capital		150
Retained Profits		686
		836

Forecast Profit and Loss Account for Twelve Months to 31 March 1996

	£000s
Sales	9,164
Material Costs	(3,465)
Gross Profit	5,699
Labour	(1,013)
Consultancy Fees	(673)
Advertising	(661)
Other Overheads	(2,187)
Profit before Tax	1,165
Taxation	(408)
Dividend	(116)
Profit Carried down	463

Forecast Balance Sheet as at 31 March 1996

	£000s	£000s
Fixed Assets		1,793
Current Assets		
Stocks	1,745	
Debtors and Prepayments	1,825	
Bank	23	
		3,593
Current Liabilities		
Trade Creditors	1,750	
Other Creditors	435	
Corporation Tax	395	
Hire Purchase	50	
VAT	217	
		(2,847)
Net Current Assets		
Creditors> 1 Year		
Hire Purchase	(204)	(204)
Deferred Tax	(36)	(36)
Net Assets		**2,299**
Share Capital		1,150
Retained Profits		1,149
		2,299

Cash Flow Forecast for the Twelve Months Ending 31 March 1996					
Month Ending	Payments	Receipts	Net Cash Flow	Opening Bank Balance	Closing Bank Balance
	£000s	£000s	£000s	£000s	£000s
April '95	1,024	802	(222)	729	507
May	1,335	1,070	(265)	507	242
June	1,244	1,150	(94)	242	148
July	1,634	1,644	10	148	158
August	1,270	1,121	(149)	158	9
September	737	949	212	9	221
October	1,173	881	(292)	221	(71)
November	1,128	1,048	(80)	(71)	(151)
December	1,052	1,194	142	(151)	(9)
January '96	1,038	1,180	142	(9)	133
February	1,004	956	(48)	133	85
March	808	746	(62)	85	23
	13,447	12,741	(706)		

Campari and Swot Analysis

Outlined below, on the basis of the CAMPARI and SWOT, is the information available for an assessment of HRT's proposal for an overdraft facility. The analysis suggested here is not designed to be exhaustive, but to cover the main issues that should be raised. You may well have additional points which you would want to raise yourself.

Assessment using Campari

● **Character**

Information gained – The management is young and consists of five people, some of whom have worked together before at SORA UK Ltd. They appear to form a good, enthusiastic and motivated team whose skills complement each other well. The company has always been loyal to the bank and has conducted its account satisfactorily. The workforce is young but has been trained by the company and appears now to be operating well. The company appears to be aggressively sales led but may well be weak in terms of financial control.

Information required – There is very little information on the personal backgrounds of any of the management team. More information is required about their personal commitments, domestic circumstances and assets. There is some information about their business backgrounds but again this area could be explored further. From the information available, it is difficult to gain a feel for the business or the major people involved.

- **Ability**

  Information gained – The management team seem to be well qualified and experienced in their own spheres of operation. Although young, it appears to be a competent, as well as very ambitious, team. The company has captured a niche market not only by aggressive salesmanship but also by providing the right product at the right price. It has built up a solid reputation. Fred Young, in particular, seems to have had the ability to see the opportunity and to seize it. As a result of these factors, the growth of the company has been impressive. However, financial management and planning appear to be weak.

  Information required – The management team has been able to cope well so far but how well will it react when problems occur? The ability of the management to cope with more difficult circumstances needs to be explored. There does not appear to be any very coherent plan for growth apart from acquisition. The following should be examined:

  – What was the basis of the decision to purchase Scottish Trailers?

  – What was the profitability of Scottish Trailers?

  – Was Scottish Trailers borrowing and if so was this taken into account?

  – To what extent was the viability of Scottish Trailers examined?

  – What will be the impact on customer service to both existing HRT and new Scottish Trailers customers?

  – How well organized is the business to cope with such growth?

  Lack of planning seems to be indicated by the fact that the purchase of Scottish Trailers has driven the business towards an overdraft situation which is only now being addressed. Further to this, the business was already short of space before the takeover; the situation can only be worse now. How will this affect the performance of the company?

- **Margin**

  Information gained – The company has not been in the position of borrowing funds before so no margin has been set to date.

  Information required – In considering what margin to apply and other fees, it will be important to examine the extent of any other borrowings. It will also be important to explore what the duration of the overdraft is expected to be, the availability of security, the nature of the advance and its usage.

- **Purpose**

  Information gained – The overdraft is for working capital purposes in order to fund rapidly expanding sales and to fund research and development. This sales growth is mainly as a result of the purchase of Scottish Trailers. However, this has itself caused a considerable drain on resources and precipitated the requirement for an overdraft facility.

Information required – There is no very clearly defined purpose for the overdraft. To some extent it seems retrospective in terms of replacing funds drained out to purchase Scottish Trailers. If the overdraft is truly to be used to fund working capital requirements as a result of increased sales, evidence of market research to indicate the real potential for such growth over and above that which would be expected as a result of the take-over of Scottish Trailers, should be examined. What is the state of the order book? What is the debtor position – are sales being converted into cash quickly enough? The situation appears to demand a visit to the company to look into these questions in some depth.

- **Amount**

Information gained – The request is for a £300,000 overdraft facility. Gearing is satisfactory in relation to the overdraft.

Information required – There is very little information about how the figure is assessed except that the cash flow forecast indicates a maximum cash shortfall of £151,000. If this is a realistic figure, there appears to be plenty of room for contingencies. It is important to find out and test the assumptions behind the amount requested and to conduct variance analysis to explore 'what if' questions. There is no indication as to whether finance charges have been included. What other factors affecting costs have been taken into account? For example, with the absorption of Scottish Trailers and continued rapid growth, what is expected to happen to wage costs? What provision has been made for corporation tax? What plans have been made to alleviate the lack of space? It is vital to find out about all these assumptions and to test them thoroughly.

- **Repayment**

Information gained – Repayment is ultimately to come from net cash flow surpluses as a result of sales growth.

Information required – If funds are to be provided, is an overdraft the most appropriate means of doing so? If repayment is to come from net cash flow surpluses, we need to question in detail the assumptions of the cash flow forecast. For example: How efficiently are funds collected? How have terms of trade changed following the purchase of Scottish Trailers?

- **Insurance**

Information gained – The request for funds appears to have been made without the overt offer of any security. However, from the balance sheet, there is adequate cover under fixed and current assets.

Information required – Before contemplating offering the facility, the issue of security will have to be looked at very carefully to establish exactly what is available from the business and in the form of personal assets. It may be important to get the directors to make a personal financial commitment to the business to heighten their sense of responsibility and we would want to take a debenture.

4.2   Non-Financial Analysis

Lending bankers are used to analysing financial information and it is very easy to overlook the equally important aspect of the non-financial aspects of a business. One of the principal aides to non-financial analysis is SWOT analysis.

SWOT stands for:

> Strengths
>
> Weaknesses
>
> Opportunities
>
> Threats

A **Strengths and Weaknesses analysis** may be used to look at a range of factors that will affect the *Internal* areas of a business.

The following illustrate the sort of topics that should be covered:

- **Money**   What is the liquidity and profitability of the business?
- **Management** What is the level of management skills?

  What is the level of expertise, experience, drive and energy?

- **Labour**   What is the quality of labour?

  How good are labour relations?

- **Machines**   What is the current state of plant and machinery?

  What is the replacement policy?

- **Premises**   What is the condition of the premises?

  How suitable are they for present and future needs?

- **Stock**   What are the proportions of raw materials, work in progress and finished goods?

- **Product**   What is the life cycle of the product?

  How new is the product?

  How well tested is it?

  What are the volumes sold?

  What is the value?

- **Marketing**   What is the market share?

                       How many customers are there?

                       Who are the main competitors?

- **Book-keeping**   What is the state of the market? Is it growing or declining?

                       How well is management informed about the financial position?

                       How good is the information produced?

                       What book-keeping systems are in operation?

4.3   Opportunities/Threats

When looking at the opportunities/threats that face a business, a lender will concentrate on the broad environmental factors which affect the business. These are the range of factors *external* to the business which can impact on its success.

These are factors over which the business often has no control. However, an understanding of the extent to which they can impinge on a business can be vital in assessing accurately the quality of the business. Some of these factors will operate on the national or even international scale, while others will operate at the local level. In either case, you should try to be well informed about these factors so that you can qualify any information you obtain.

The following illustrates the issues that can be covered:

- **Competitiveness**   How intense is the competition?

- **Social changes**   What will be the impact of change in government? e.g. Benefits

- **Political changes**   What will be the impact of changes in government? e.g. Taxation

- **Taxation changes**   To what extent are products vulnerable to new or changing taxes?

- **Changes to the state of the economy**   What will be the impact of inflation – e.g. Interest rates?

- **Technology changes**   What new technological developments will affect the business?

- **Legislative changes**   How likely are potential legislative changes to affect the business?

The use of SWOT enables a lender to assess the overall state of a business and the direction in which it is heading. It also enables a judgement to be made about aspects of the environment in which the business operates and which can have a positive or negative effect on the performance of the business.

Let us now apply the use of SWOT to a Case Study that we have already met, H. R. Trailers Ltd.

Assessment Using Swot – Internal Attributes

- **Money**

  Strengths: Strong cash flow at the present time. Strong level of retained profits providing a good base of financial support.

  Weaknesses: The rate of growth is a drain on resources. Dependence on SORA UK Ltd and the unknown strength of SORA UK Ltd. Is the proposed flotation a sign of weakness? Why was cash paid for Scottish Trailers?

- **Management**

  Strengths: Young, enthusiastic, involved, well qualified and well matched.

  Weaknesses: Unknown and doubtful financial skills. Untried in adversity. Possibly overenthusiastic and show lack of caution. Doubtful understanding of the dangers of rapid growth. Small team with ill-defined responsibilities. There is insufficient information about the involvement of SORA UK Ltd.

- **Labour**

  Strengths: A small but trained workforce now committed to the company.

  Weaknesses: In the past, a high turnover. Low initial level of skill.

- **Plant**

  Strengths: New and second-hand equipment in use.

  Weaknesses: No apparent planned replacement policy.

- **Premises**

  Strengths: One site.

  Weaknesses: Following the purchase of Scottish Trailers, space is cramped and there is no room for expansion.

- **Stock**

  Strengths: Aims to be customer led. Delivery of standard machines in 48 hours.

  Weaknesses: Lack of storage space. Possibility of retention clauses. Is the company overstocked? Stock makes up a large proportion of working assets. How is stock valued?

- **Products**

  Strengths: Good reputation. Good quality service. Customization. Wide customer range. Strong demand.

  Weaknesses: Reliant on one supplier and one basic product line.

- **Marketing**
  Strengths: Market leader and strong marketing orientation.

  Weaknesses: Reliance on SORA UK Ltd. Lack of effective competition to keep company sharp.

- **Financial Systems**
  Strengths: No evidence.

  Weaknesses: Financial control appears to run second place to sales push. Financial systems are not sophisticated enough. There is a need for an experienced finance director.

Assessment Using Swot – External Attributes

- **Competition**
  Opportunities: Very little competition and backed by strong supplier.

  Threats: Attractive market for new competitor, especially from outside the UK.

- **Technology**
  Opportunities: Well-qualified team able to adapt technology to customer requirements.

  Threats: Vulnerable to new technology which can rapidly change the market. These are the most significant areas with regard to a SWOT analysis.

The following non-financial analysis checklist may aid you as a prompt:

The profitability of a company in an industry and the extent to which managers can dictate trading terms (i.e. speed of the business cycle) to suppliers and customers will depend on the competitive structure of the industry in which the company is placed. **Professor Michael Porter's 'five forces' model** provides a standard format for understanding a company's business position based on the view that customers, suppliers and industry competitors represent a competitive threat to the company.

Figure 4.2: Determinants of Strength of the Five Competitive Forces

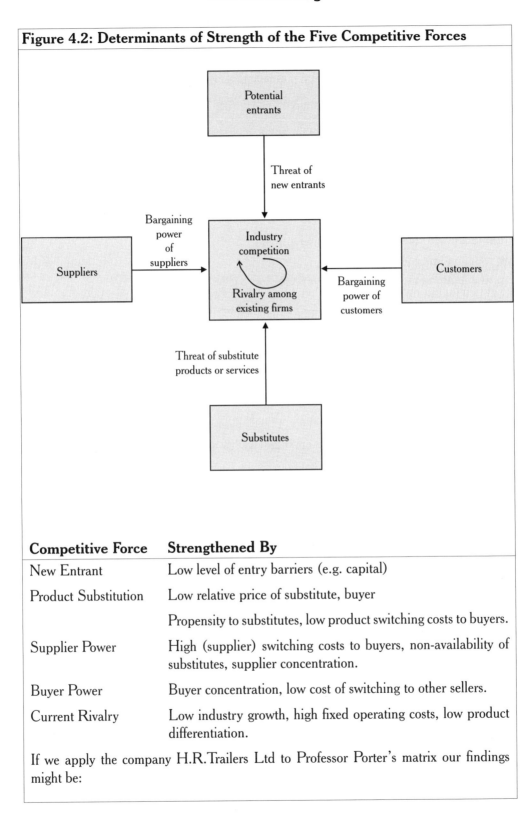

Competitive Force	Strengthened By
New Entrant	Low level of entry barriers (e.g. capital)
Product Substitution	Low relative price of substitute, buyer
	Propensity to substitutes, low product switching costs to buyers.
Supplier Power	High (supplier) switching costs to buyers, non-availability of substitutes, supplier concentration.
Buyer Power	Buyer concentration, low cost of switching to other sellers.
Current Rivalry	Low industry growth, high fixed operating costs, low product differentiation.

If we apply the company H.R. Trailers Ltd to Professor Porter's matrix our findings might be:

Threat of new Potential Entrants	Quite low in view of the expertise required and the capital involved.
Bargaining power of Suppliers	Probably quite low in respect of parts and equipment.
Bargaining power of Customers	Medium. There will be a limited alternative choice.
Threat of Substitutes	Specialized products that appear to be well liked by the marketplace.
Industry Competition	Quite low at the outset.

4.4 Boston Consulting Group - Business Portfolio Matrix

Figure 4.3: Business Portfolio Matrix

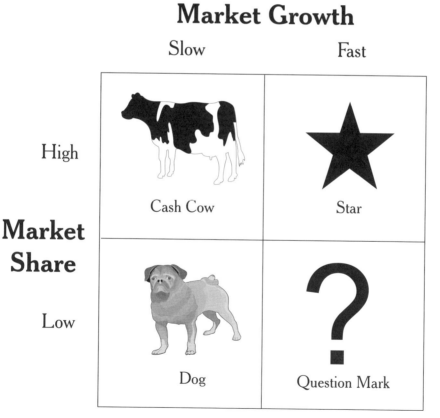

The four types of business have differing profiles in respect of:

- Profitability
- Investment Need
- Free cash flows (the cash flow from operations after it has met its Investment need).

A Dog
Market Growth Low/Market Share Low

- Low Profits (possibly loss-making)
- Low Free Cash Flow
- Low Investment (possibly disinvestment)
- Product Market in Decline

A Question Mark
Young Business/Good Growth Prospects
Low Market Share/Fierce Competition

- A High Investment Business
- Potentially High Profits
- Low (or Negative) Free Cash Flow

A Cash Cow
Mature Business/Low Growth Possibilities/High Market Share

- A Profitable business
- A Low Investment Business
- High Free Cash Flow

A Star
High Growth/High Market Share Business

- Highly Profitable
- A High Investment Business
- Low Free Cash Flow

A Risk Check List
Assessment of Macro Risks
1. Government Policies

Fiscal policies affecting purchasing power and corporate location.

Investment incentives.

Impact on labour relations.

International cooperation.

2. Inflation

Effect on total economy and international competitiveness.

3. Foreign Exchange

Volatility and effect on imports and exports.

4. Environmental Issues

Effects on product marketability and 'non-productive' manufacturing costs.

5. Country Risk

Foreign exchange convertibility, embargoes.

Assessment of Industry Risk

6. Rate of Growth

Rapid?

Mature industry.

Cyclical/fashion sensitive.

Boom time for competition?

Decline causing margin pressures?

7. Balance of Power

Between buyer and supplier.

Are there alternatives to existing buyers/suppliers?

8. Barriers to Entry

Monopoly?

Proprietary technology.

9. Government Policy

Protectionism

Statutory requirements.

10. Substitute Products

Competition?

Assessment of Company Risk

11. Asset Conversion Cycle

Under control?

Terms of trade: buyers/suppliers.

Stock and debtor control.

12. Labour Resources

Adequate?

Training facilities?

Labour problems?

13. Premises

Tenure, age, condition, suitability?

14. Plant & Machinery

Condition, age, utilization, owned or leased?

Assessment of Company Risk

15. Products and Markets

Market share?

Does the company make products and then try to find a market, or produce for a known market?

16. Costing and Pricing

What are the strategies?

Are products price sensitive?

Do they have high fixed costs?

Assessment of Management

17. Composition of Board

Balanced?

Average age close to retirement?

Succession?

Turnover?

18. Track Record

Innovative?

Keen to diversify when necessary?

Brave enough to restructure/close down unprofitable and obsolete areas when necessary?

19. Contacts

What contacts do corporate managers have in the company?

All financial?

Wider spread needed?

20. Management Information

Systems in place?

Ability to prepare budgets and cash flow forecasts?

21. Corporate Objectives

Clear?

Focused on profit/productivity/market share?

22. Motivation of Staff

Good communications?

Career planning?

Share options?

Performance-related pay?

Conclusion to the Case

A positive reaction to this request, as it stands at the moment, would not be wise. In general terms, the business has been growing too fast and there is a question mark over its ability to control the explosion of sales. It is also not entirely clear from where profits are being generated.

Encouraging the company to chase after even more growth could be disastrous. The company appears to be under pressure from SORA UK Ltd to pursue a stock market quotation, which is further encouraging a push for ever-increasing sales growth. The business faces a number of problems, including the drain on its funds as a result of the Scottish Trailers takeover and its space problems, for which there seems to be no immediate solution, without incurring considerable extra costs.

Before a more favourable reaction could be forthcoming, a number of specific issues will have to be clarified:

● There is a need to see fully-documented assumptions behind the cash flow and budget forecasts.

- Why is the overdraft required, so soon after the cash injection from SORA UK Ltd?

- The whole area of financial control and forecasting is very weak in a company with projected sales turnover in excess of £11 million.

- How can the company cope properly without a finance director?

- When Scottish Trailers was purchased, what funds were used? Why was there no consideration of borrowing requirements at this time? Why was cash paid?

- There is a considerable likelihood that the company is overtrading. It is currently profitable, but more and more funds are being tied up in the working capital requirement.

- The total reliance on SORA UK Ltd as the sole supplier is unhealthy. More information is required on SORA's trading position and standing in the marketplace.

- The stock position requires very careful scrutiny, because it represents a large proportion of the working assets.

The company is crying out for a proper plan of future development. No substantial investment should be contemplated without this. If the request is to be pursued further, a meeting with the management at the company's premises is vital.

4.5   Cash Flow Analysis

In the previous chapter, we looked at the source and application of funds. Many lenders and business people have struggled with this document to try and pinpoint exactly where the cash is coming from and how it is being used. Ernst & Young (accountants) made this statement about the new cash flow statement, FRS1:

> *The cashflow statement is potentially the single most useful/important statement for bankers. Financial Reporting Standard (FRS1) supersedes Statement of Standard Accounting Practice (SSAP) No. 10 and requires reporting entities to prepare a cashflow statement as part of their annual accounts, rather than a source and application of funds statement. The requirements laid out in FRS1 became effective for accounting periods ending or after 23rd March 1992. It was the first Financial Reporting Standard to be released by the Accounting Standards Board (ASB) after it took over from the Accounting Standards Committee on 1st August 1990. The purpose of the cashflow statement under FRS1 is to provide users of accounts, whether they be banks, creditors, shareholders or potential investors, with information as to the liquidity, viability and financial adaptability of reporting entries in a way that the source and application of funds statements seem unable.*

The cash flow statement of FRS1 has the following advantages over the source and application of funds statement of SSAP10.

- Cash flow is a concept that is easier to understand than working capital flow.

- If transactions do not affect cash, they do not appear in the statement.

- The standard format should make them more comparable with those of other companies.

The importance of the cash flow statement to bankers is that it shows:

- Whether the business has generated cash.

- Where it has come from.

- What the customer has done with the money.

However, there will be certain exceptions (e.g. small companies), but nevertheless it is a very good step forward for all business analysts.

Extract from *Financial Times* 22 February 1991:

Cashflow becomes the Determining Factor

by David Whaller and Maggie Urry

With UK corporate finances coming under pressure in the recession, attention is focusing on companies' ability to generate cash. It is, after all, cash which pays the dividends. And since companies are essentially rated by the stock market on the basis of their future dividend paying potential, cash flow is a vital measure of corporate financial health.

The stock market has not in the past put much emphasis on judging companies by their cash generating ability. Analysts have traditionally assessed a company's performance in terms of a handful of simple yardsticks, with most emphasis put on the price/earnings per share ratio. But these measures have become less reliable in recent years, as companies have become more creative in their accounting practices.

The collapse of a number of quoted companies, which from the balance sheets appeared healthy, has added to concern. As the cash squeeze on companies has tightened, many have looked to ways to conserve cash, such as cutting back on investment or squeezing their suppliers in turn. 'There have been too many surprises,' reflects one analyst. 'Throughout the 1980s companies tested the accounting rules to the limit. You just cannot afford to take a set of accounts on trust.'

This makes a company's cash flow a more important investment yardstick. As UBS Phillips & Drew conclude in a report on the UK corporate sector's favoured accounting tricks, 'whereas manufacturing profits is relatively easy, cash flow is the most difficult parameter to adjust in a company's accounts.' They add 'we believe that there should be less emphasis placed on the reported progression of earnings per share and more attention paid to balance sheet potential and most importantly of all, cash'.

The problem is, as analysts at Laing & Cruishank, the brokers, point out, 'the conventional description of cashflow is an optimistic measure.' It is simply retained profits plus depreciation. However this figure can be boosted by non-trading items, such as the profit on the sale of assets, or by capitalising interest, making the interest charge in the profit and loss account lower than the actual cash going out to a company's banks. Further the treatment of associates' profits means that a company's pre-tax profits are boosted by an amount larger than the dividend which is received from associates.

L&C has developed a system of comparing a company's traditional cashflow with their profit records, and applied it to the leading quoted companies. This throws up some interesting examples. Companies which are spending heavily on expansion may appear to have fast growing pre-tax profits. But they can be draining away cash as they spend more than they earn.

Unfortunately, these attempts to look at cashflow are far more complex than the simple price/earnings ratio. However, within a couple of months the job of assessing cashflows should become easier when the Accounting Standards Board, the arbiter of UK accounting rules, publishes a new standard FRS1 requiring companies to publish cashflow statements, instead of statements showing the source and application of funds, which show movements in the working capital rather than just cash.

The new standard has yet to be finalised, but it is likely that companies will have to show cash coming from operating, investing and financing activities. This may allow analysts to develop a new measure for rating shares based on trading cashflow.

A thorough understanding of the strengths and weaknesses of this analytical technique is therefore essential for anyone responsible for or involved in the process of taking credit decisions, which are dependent on the risk profile of a given business. (In the UK reflected in FRS1. In countries that have adopted international accounting standards, this will be prepared in accordance with International Accounting Standard (IAS) No. 7 – Cashflow Statements.)

In order to complete the analysis of the cash flow of a business, it is first necessary to develop a thorough understanding of the various components which make up the flow of cash through the business.

4.6   The Cash Flow Cycle

Cash is needed to continually finance the asset conversion cycle, to enable payments to the bank, to pay dividends to the shareholders, to pay taxes due, to purchase further fixed assets and to undertake research and development etc.

Understanding the Elements of the Cash Flow Cycle

It follows that the first key to the control of cash flow is to minimize the amount invested in the capital cycle.

Creditors – Creditors are unusual in that during the period of credit taken they represent an interest-free loan to the company, the benefit of which arises directly as a consequence of trading. Thus it is in the interests of most businesses to maximize the free credit period available from creditors. This does not necessarily mean extending the period before payment beyond the agreed terms with creditors, because this will have an impact on the business in three ways. It will affect its credit rating adversely, it could result in suppliers increasing prices to compensate for the funding cost of the delayed payment and finally creditors may withdraw from supplying while taking action to place the business into bankruptcy.

Debtors – Here the first thing to consider is the speed of collection. Is it reasonable? Can it be improved? In the UK a reasonable collection is anything from 45-75 days depending on the typical industry payment terms and quality of customer covenant. Numerous methods can be used to chase debt including dedicated credit controllers, extensive use of the telephone and so on.

Stocks – Stock is cut into three constituent parts: raw materials, work-in-progress and finished goods. Raw materials represent the basic material inputs to any manufacturing process. The main thing to consider initially is whether the purchasing is under control – who can purchase and what can they purchase. Work-in-progress and finished goods need to be reviewed and the key control here is regular stocktaking. Provisions are commonly made in accounts for slow-moving, obsolete and damaged stocks. In cash flow terms, all of these represent mistakes or lack of foresight on the part of management.

Labour Costs – Usually the second biggest input into the manufacturing process after raw materials. Consequently, the sums involved can be substantial.

Establishment Expenses – These represent the costs of occupation of property. A variety of strategies are available ranging from the reduction in the space occupied within a building, so offering the option of renting off or selling the surplus space, to the elimination for as long as is necessary of all non-essential costs such as gardening, office cleaning, decoration and non-essential maintenance.

Production Expenses – Production costs require constant review if a business is to remain absolutely competitive at all times. Measuring the output of labour is particularly important. The introduction of labour productivity measurement alone can result in significant increases in productivity as can the monitoring of all reasons for any non-productive time arising each working week. A thorough review of all the components of production costs may expose areas where an item or service might be more cheaply sourced outside the business.

Overheads – This is the remaining component of expenditure in all businesses. There is usually considerable scope to cut overheads in most businesses that are experiencing a shortfall of cash for the first time.

Selling Expenses – It is important to ensure that the costs of marketing and selling the business's output are fairly matched to the areas of margin generation.

Administration Expenses – In times of difficulties with liquidity and cash flow the administrative areas of the company come under increasing pressure to perform better with less and less resource. Capital expenditure and discretionary expenses are cut and there is an increased need for cash flow management, information and control. Liquidity problems usually arise due to lack of management foresight; consequently, in such companies there are often no budgets or forecasts. These therefore require preparation as the problems develop, in addition to the cash flow information mentioned earlier, so further stretching what is likely by this point to be an insufficient resource within the administration function.

Fixed Assets/Research and Development – This is the other major area of cash investment. The usual response to problems with cash flow is to put an embargo on all planned capital expenditure and future research and development. Selling off non-essential machinery can often yield a useful cash contribution. The premises itself occupied by the business can also provide a useful cash gain, if necessary, by downsizing or relocation of the existing business or sale and leaseback arrangements. If surplus space can be split off, it may be possible to rent it out.

4.7 FRS 1 Cash Flow Statements

Cash flow analysis allows us to draw some preliminary conclusions about the performance of a company and its investment patterns. By learning to manipulate and restate the cash flows disclosed, we can also examine the debt capacity and cash-generation patterns of the company. As it is almost impossible for a corporate to 'creatively account' these data, the conclusions gained from such analysis can be considered to be more reliable than profit-based measures of performance. The skilled analyst will then look for further confirming evidence of the preliminary conclusions drawn from the cash flow analysis.

The following table is an example taken from FRS1 and represents a single company's cash flow. Explanation of the main sections is given below.

XYZ LIMITED – Cash Flow Statement for the Year Ended 31 March 1992	£000	£000
Net cash inflow from operating activities		
(see note below)		6889
Return on investments and servicing of finance		
Interest received	3011	
Interest paid	–12	
Dividends paid	–2417	
Net cash inflow from returns on investment and servicing of finance		582
Taxation		
Corporation tax paid (including advance corporation tax)	–2922	
Tax paid		–2922

XYZ LIMITED – Cash Flow Statement (cont.)

Investing activities

Payments to acquire intangible fixed assets	–71	
Payments to acquire tangible fixed assets	–1496	
Receipts from sales of tangible fixed assets	42	
	£000	£000
Net cash outflow from investing activities		–1525
Net cash inflow before financing		3024
Financing		
Issue of ordinary share capital	211	
Repurchase of debenture loans	–149	
Expenses paid in connection with share issues	–5	
Net cash inflow from financing		57
Increase in cash and cash equivalents		3081

Note to the cash flow statement
Reconciliation of operating profit to net cash inflow from operating activities:

	£000
Operating profit	6022
Depreciation charges	893
Loss on sale of tangible fixed assets	6
Increase in stocks	–194
Increase in debtors	–72
Increase in creditors	234
	6889

Net cash inflow from operating activities

What does this value represent? Looking at the note to the cash flow statement we see there are six constituent values disclosed. The identification starts with operating profit, the next two items are depreciation and the (profit)/loss on sale of fixed assets which are added back. The objective is to identify the cash generated from operations. This is normally achieved by adding back to operating profit all non-cash items in the profit and loss account before the operating profit value is struck. Additional items in this class include loss and trade provisions, unrealized gains and losses on foreign exchange and provisions in respect of acquisitions and reorganizations.

The next three items, the increase or decrease in stocks, debtors and creditors, give us the movement in the investment in net working assets. Most businesses are constantly increasing their investment in stock and debtors to allow for the effects of inflation and growth in turnover of the business. This is usually partly offset by the increase in creditors each year, which arises for the same reasons.

Returns on investments and servicing of finance

The cash flow statement of XYZ Limited shows we have interest received and the interest and dividends paid. Interest received is the cash earned from surplus cash; we would also find any dividends received from investments in this section. Because these are earnings from investments where the business owns less than 50% of the shares and therefore does not enjoy control, it makes sense where these items are material to separate this cash flow item for analysis purposes. This is because the future flow of dividends from investments may be less certain than the business's own core-operating cash flow.

Indeed we also need to separate interest and dividends paid in order properly to evaluate the performance of the business because these payments are driven by quite different factors:

● The payment of interest is contractual and may vary significantly depending on the inflation and interest rate outlook for the business concerned and the amount of interest which is at fixed rather than variable rate.

● The timing and amount of dividends paid by the business, in contrast, is at the discretion of the directors.

Taxation

This item is the amount paid in the financial period. In the U.K. this represents the tax due in respect of profits earned in the previous accounting period. In other countries the grace period for payment of taxes due varies from monthly on account to nine months after the year end, as it is in the U.K.

Note that there is no reference to deferred tax in the cash flow statement. This is because any charge or release for deferred tax in the profit and loss account tax charge is a movement in the deferred tax provision and is therefore a non-cash item. Non-cash items have no effect on the cash flow statement.

Investing activities

This is the section where we find the value of capital expenditure made during the period under examination. The term 'capital expenditure' is often abbreviated to 'capex'. Where it is netted off against any proceeds of disposal it is often known as 'net capex'. Do not confuse the profit or loss on the sale of fixed assets (which actually represents an adjustment to the depreciation charge) with the proceeds of sale of fixed assets (which represents the cash received on the sale of fixed assets). A cash flow statement shows any proceeds of sale as a cash inflow in this section.

Net cash inflow before financing

This is a key figure. The first four items above represent the cash generation and cash absorbed in reinvestment in the fixed and working assets of the business, paying taxes and compensating providers of finance. The cash flow generated (or cash flow absorbed) is what remains after carrying out these essential activities.

The net cash inflow before financing is therefore the cash surplus achieved from carrying out the activities of the business less payments made to providers of finance. In the example above the value is positive and healthily so. However a review of a variety of cash flow statements will show you that this is not always the case.

Financing

This final section shows how the cash surplus has been used (and, if it is cash absorbed, how it has been financed). The sum of the movements on equity, debt and cash when totalled should equal the net cash inflow/(outflow) before financing.

Presentations of the financing section vary. In this case the cash has been shown separately as the final figure. Sometimes all the movements are shown, with a total that equals the net cash inflow before financing.

4.8   Additional Ratio Analysis – Stock Market Indicators

Although some of this section may be beyond the purposes of the examination, the rationale will help when we consider the topic of how to value a business.

Let us consider the various measures commonly in use and certain other measures which are not yet commonly in use that might assist us in this task. There is, of course, far more information available in respect of quoted companies, and the share price provides further valuable information about the market and investor perceptions of the value of the business.

Returns Ratios

$$\text{Operating profit to sales turnover \%} = \frac{\text{Operating profit}}{\text{Period turnover}} \times 100$$

$$\text{Return on operating assets \%} = \frac{\text{Operating profit}}{\text{Operating assets}} \times 100$$

$$\text{Return on equity \%} = \frac{\text{Profit after tax}}{\text{Total equity}} \times 100$$

Operating Profit to Sales
This ratio can easily be compared with those of other companies in the same sector and indeed compared with data derived from quoted companies. This gives us some indication as to the efficiency and quality of management, businesses displaying below sector normal performance being less efficient than the market leaders.

However, problems arise in the assessment of this ratio in unquoted companies for two reasons. Firstly the profit and loss account can contain many items that would not be present if the company were not a private company. These could include, in respect of the owner, additional rewards taken as pension fund contributions, salary, bonuses or fringe benefits. The business may also employ semi-productive employees who are related to the business owner. Secondly, owners of private companies can tend to be averse to paying taxes and run their businesses so as to minimize reported profits, by increasing overheads to absorb any significant profits. The accounting reporting bias is therefore a key consideration before relying on such a ratio as a true reflection of a private company's performance. It is common for the analyst to restate the profit and loss account, adjusting for any such items in order to gain a more useful impression of the returns achieved in a business. Thirdly, this ratio works best where the activities of the company are relatively homogeneous. Where a number of unrelated activities are being carried on in one business it may be better to examine a breakdown by sector or division.

Return on Operating Assets
This ratio is a powerful indicator of performance. It shows us the returns generated from the operating assets, before the costs of funding them. In addition to comparing this ratio to sector norms we can directly compare it with the likely return on cash deposits, the rationale being that if a business cannot generate a return on operating assets in excess of the return available on cash deposits it might as well liquidate the assets and put the money on deposit! This test acts as a good quick first approximation for performance levels if we do not have access to other comparative data such as private or quoted companies in the same business sector. Again, the problems of applying this ratio to unquoted companies revolve around the extent to which the accounts are biased towards tax minimization.

Return on Equity
An extremely useful indicator in quoted companies, but for a private company return on equity is not particularly meaningful. This is because of the denominator 'total equity' which is represented by share capital and reserves in a private company. This can be a very arbitrary value, being affected by the extent to which surplus cash is paid out as dividends or other rewards. Alternatively, the share capital may be small with the majority of the financing being loan capital from the owner as interest-free debt.

Therefore, to conclude, the problem with the return on equity ratio in a private company is that the value disclosed in the accounts as equity may not represent the true equity of the business. Assessing the performance of quoted companies can be an easier task as the quality and amount of information available upon which to base a judgement is more extensive.

Earnings per Share

The most commonly used measure of earnings for a quoted company is earnings per share (or EPS). The ratio is defined as follows:

Earnings per
Share (EPS) =
$$\frac{\text{Profit after tax, pref share dividends in pence per share}}{\text{Weighted average number of equity shares in issue in the period}}$$

The absolute value of EPS in pence tells us very little unless we compare it with the current share price. This ratio is called the price/earnings ratio (or P/E ratio):

Price/Earnings Ratio =
$$\frac{\text{The quoted market price of the share}}{\text{Earnings per share}}$$

This ratio describes the relationship between the earnings attributable to each ordinary share and the price at which those shares are currently traded. The following table illustrates P/E ratios across a sample of sectors and companies:

P/E ratios taken from the FTSE Actuaries Share Service in the *Financial Times* (June 2001).

Category	Industry/Service	Number of Companies	P/E Ratio
Financials	Banks	12	14.17
Resources	Mining	5	12.66
	Oil and Gas	11	14.42
General Industrial	Aerospace and Defence	9	21.00
	Engineering and Machinery	22	11.63
Consumer Goods	Beverages	7	18.30
	Pharmaceuticals	23	36.91
	Health	16	29.83
Cyclical Services	Leisure, Entertainment and Hotels	38	16.41
	Media and Photography	48	46.74
Utilities	Electricity	8	19.95
	Gas Distribution	2	19.04
	Water	6	13.11
Information Tech	Hardware	19	23.97
	Software & Computer Services	73	52.41

4.9 Additional Ratio Analysis – Computer-Based Spreadsheet

A good way of monitoring both ratios and cash flows is to utilize a computer-based financial analysis program. There are many such systems available. The example which follows has been produced on a system which is user-friendly to operate and produces results which are easy to understand. The company analysed in the spreadsheets is a plc. Five years' figures are quoted for comparative ratio analysis purposes. The computer also generates cash flows so it is easy to quantify the cash movements on an annualized basis.

Readers are also directed to the cash flow summaries, which are generated in a similar format to our previous FRS1 studies. These show resultant negative cash flows before financing in all the four years illustrated, together with the financing structure to cover these negative cash flow positions.

Ratios can also be applied to the cash flows. It is now common for bankers in lending documentation to refer to the cash flow interest cover ratio, usually meaning the relationship between the operating cash flow and the cash interest paid expressed as a multiple. Other ratio relationships can also be compared such as the debt principal due to cash flow available after interest service and total debt to operating cash flow. This is often the real limitation on debt capacity for many companies rather than the amount of asset security available. If a business takes on more debt than it can service relying on the existence of adequate security to get the debt in the first place, it is almost inevitable at some stage that those assets pledged will have to be disposed of in order to satisfy the debt repayment.

In the Thorntons example, readers can note both cash flow interest cover and debt payout ratios are generated by the computer and shown as additional financial ratios on the previous page to the cash flow summaries.

Also the following additional ratios are illustrated:

Ratio	Calculation Method
Efficiency Times	Sales/Total Assets
Capital Structure	Total Assets/Net Worth
Total Stock (Days in Hand)	Divide by cost of goods sold x 365
Raw Materials	
Work-in-Progress	
Finished Goods	
WI/Sales	Working Capital Requirement/Sales x 100

THORNTONS PLC: Assets

DATE: 30/06	1990	1991	1992	1993	1994
Current Assets					
Cash	12,716	13,385	16,411	7,038	11,738
ST Investments	146	126	111	111	55
Other Debtors	3,313	3,062	3,005	3,384	2,701
Trade Debtors	1,617	2,014	2,079	1,762	1,276
Stocks:					
- Raw Materials	3,056	3,657	4,070	4,580	3,483
- Work in Progress	1,067	1,171	1,010	1,167	1,175
- Finished Goods	3,834	4,799	5,925	4,926	3,823
Prepayments	1,685	2,007	2,158	2,809	2,941
Tax Recoverable	44	5	1		
Development Props	2,257	2,346			
Sundry CA					
Total Current Assets	29,735	32,618	34,770	25,777	27,192
Fixed Assets					
Premises	33,160	31,883	32,219	33,928	32,505
Plant and Equipment	39,326	44,312	50,564	58,960	56,953
Fixtures and Fittings					
Vehicles					
Accum. Depreciation	(23,526)	(26,680)	(30,543)	(36,486)	(38,436)
Net Fixed Assets	48,960	49,515	52,240	56,402	51,022
Investments					
In Affiliates					
In Other Companies					
Other					
Total Investments	0	0	0	0	0
Other Assets					
Deferred Charges					
Tax Recoverable	461	506	509	446	554
Sundry Other Assets	6	0	216	130	79
Finance Lease					
Receivables					
Sundry Other Assets					
Intangible Trademarks	15	11	9	9	6
Total Other Assets	482	517	734	585	639
Total Long-Term Assets	49,442	50,032	52,974	56,987	51,661
Total Assets	79,177	82,650	87,744	82,764	78,853

THORNTONS PLC: Liabilities/Net Worth

	1990	1991	1992	1993	1994
Current Liabilities					
Short-Term Debt	1,829	1,062	411	2,622	4,373
CPLTD	2,944	5,709	4,791	10,625	400
Dividends Payable	1,384	1,518	1,528	1,537	2,218
Trade Creditors	3,506	3,458	4,789	4,801	2,855
Misc. Taxes Payable	3,363	3,644	4,758	2,806	2,156
Other Creditors	470	386	204	413	52
Sundry CL					
Accruals	7,583	6,202	5,932	5,544	6,814
Corporation Tax	7,061	4,356	3,517	3,261	5,160
Total Current Liab.	28,140	26,305	25,930	31,609	24,028
Long-Term Liabilities					
Domestic Loans	10,074	10,619	13,115	1,876	5,842
Foreign Loans					
Total Loans	10,074	10,619	13,115	1,876	5,842
Deferred Tax	1,230	822	446	151	–
Other Provisions	634	312	234	7,352	1,712
Long-Term Tax	0	0			
Sundry LT Liability					
Minority Interests	(26)	0			
Total LT Liabilities	11,912	11,753	3,795	9,379	7,554
Total Liabilities	40,052	38,058	39,725	40,988	31,582
Net Worth					
Ordinary Shares	6,290	6,326	6,366	6,369	6,428
Preferred Shares					
Share Premium	7,808	8,220	8,680	8,718	9,334
Other Reserves					
Revaluation Reserve	3,148	2,280	1,875	1,864	2,039
Retained Earnings	21,879	27,766	31,098	24,825	29,470
Total Net Worth	39,125	4,592	48,019	41,776	47,271
Total Liabilities and Net Worth	79,177	2,650	87,744	82,764	78,853
Operating Lease Commitments	–	4,432	4,823	6,800	7,171
Contingent Liabilities					

THORNTONS PLC: Profit and Loss Account

	1990	1991	1992	1993	1994
Sales	77,289	80,996	85,265	92,476	96,572
Net Sales	77,289	80,996	85,265	92,476	96,572
Cost of Goods Sold	(43,378)	(48,619)	(51,373)	(55,352)	42,516)
Gross Profit	28,911	32,377	33,387	36,624	54,056
Depreciation	(4,045)	(4,233)	(4,724)	(5,700)	(5,551)
SG&A	(9,518)	(11,083)	(11,877)	(13,683)	(29,793)
Other Costs	(5,872)	(6,167)	(7,059)	(7,887)	(6,136)
Operating Profit	9,476	10,894	9,727	9,354	12,576
Exceptional Items	-	-	(824)	(13,175)	-
Miscellaneous Expense					
Interest Expense	(1,273)	(1,636)	(2,000)	(1,718)	(856)
Interest Income	1,662	1,395	1,435	740	387
Sundry Other Income	663	514	716	-	-
Profit from Prop. Sales	783	713	148	-	-
Profit before Tax	11,311	11,880	9,202	(4,799)	12,107
Current Tax	(3,212)	(4,144)	(3,276)	(3,097)	(4,653)
Deferred Tax	(218)	192	348	295	357
Profit after Tax	7,881	7,923	6,274	(7,60l)	7,811
Extraordinary Items	950	350	-	-	-
Profit after Extraord.	8,331	3,278	6,274	(7,60l)	7,811
Minority Interests	10	-	-	-	-
Net Income before Div.	8,841	8,278	6,274	(7,601)	7,811
Dividends	(2,076)	(2,273)	(2,324)	(2,333)	3,151)
Net Income	6,765	6,005	3,950	(9,934)	4,660

THORNTONS PLC: Ratio Summary

	1990	1991	1992	1993	1994
Return on Equity	22.6%	18.6%	13.1%	−18.2%	16.5%
Profitability	11.4%	10.2%	7.4%	− 8.2%	8.1%
Efficiency times	1.0	1.0	1.0	1.1	1.2
Capital Structure times	2.0	1.9	1.8	2.0	1.7
Profitability Ratios					
Sales	77,289	80,996	85,265	92,476	96,572
%Change in Sales	N/A	4.8%	5.3%	8.5%	4.4%
COGS/Sales	62.6%	60.0%	60.8%	60.4%	44.0%
Gross Profit/Sales	37.4%	40.0%	39.2%	39.6%	56.0%
Operating Profit/Sales	12.3%	13.5%	11.4%	10.1%	13.0%
PBT/Sales	14.6%	14.7%	10.8%	−5.2%	12.5%
PAT/Sales	10.2%	9.8%	7.4%	−8.2%	8.1%
Taxation/PBT	28.4%	34.9%	35.6%	−64.5%	38.4%
Divs/NI before Divs	23.5%	27.5%	37.0%	−30.7%	40.3%
Efficiency Ratios					
Debtors Days on Hand	15.6	13.8	12.9	13.4	10.2
Total Stocks DOH	60.0	72.3	77.4	69.7	72.8
- RM DOH	23.1	27.5	28.6	29.9	29.9
- WIP DOH	8.1	8.8	7.1	7.6	10.1
- FG DOH	28.9	36.0	41.7	32.2	32.8
Creditors Days on Hand	26.5	26.0	33.7	31.4	24.5
Accruals DOH	57.2	46.6	41.7	36.2	58.5
WI/Sales	2.4%	6.2%	6.4%	7.1%	4.6%
Financial Ratios					
Interest Cover	7.4	6.7	4.9	5.4	14.7
Tangible Net Worth	39,110	44,581	48,010	41,767	47,265
Working Capital	1,595	6,313	8,840	(5,832)	3,164
Current Ratio	1.1	1.2	1.3	0.8	1.1
Liquid Assets	17,792	18,587	21,606	12,295	15,770
Quick Ratio	0.7	0.8	0.9	0.5	0.8
Gearing	0.4	0.4	0.4	0.4	0.2
Leverage	1.0	0.9	0.8	1.0	0.7
Cash Flow Interest Cover	N/A	7.9	8.1	0.8	23.7
Total Debt Payout	N/A	1.3	1.1	11.4	0.5

THORNTONS PLC: Consolidated Cash Flow Statement

	1991	1992	1993	1994
Net Cash Inflow from Operating Activities				
Operating Profit	10,894	9,727	9,354	12,576
Add: Depreciation	4,233	4,724	5,700	5,551
Change in Stocks	(1,670)	1,378)	332	2,192
Change in Trade Creditors	(48)	1,331	12	(1,946)
Change in Trade Debtors	(397)	(65)	317	486
Change in other Debtors	251	57	(379)	683
Tax Recoverable	(7)	50	1	0
Development Props.	(89)	2,346	0	0
Sundry CA	0	0	0	0
Other Creditors	(114)	(152)	209	(361)
Sundry CL	0	0	0	0
Accruals	(1,381)	(270)	(388)	1,270
Prepayments	(322)	(151)	(651)	(132)
Exceptional Items	0	(824)	(13,175)	0
Miscellaneous Expense	0	0	0	0
	0	0	0	0
Sundry Other Income	514	716	0	0
Profit from Prop. Sales	713	148	0	0
Extraordinary Items	350	0	0	0
Net Cash Inflow	12,927	16,259	1,332	20,319
Returns on Investments and Servicing of Finance				
Interest Expense	(1,636)	(2,000)	(1,718)	(856)
CP Ltd	(2,944)	(5,709)	(4,791)	(10,625)
Dividends Paid	(2,139)	(2,314)	(2,324)	(2,470)
Interest Income	1,395	1,435	740	387
Net Cash Inflow/Outflow	(5,324)	(8,588)	(8,093)	(13,564)
Taxation				
Taxes Paid	(6,849)	(4,115)	(3,353)	(2,754)
Misc. Taxes Payable	281	1,114	(1,952)	(650)
Deferred Tax	(216)	(28)	0	206
Tax Paid	(6,784)	(3,029)	(5,305)	(3,198)

THORNTONS PLC: Consolidated Cash Flow Statement (cont.)

	1991	1992	1993	1994
Investing Activities				
Net Capital Expenditure	(5,656)	(7,854)	(9,873)	4
Inv. in Affiliates	0	0	0	0
Inv. in Other Companies	0	0	0	0
Other Investments	0	0	0	0
	0	0	0	0
	0	0	0	0
Deferred Charges	0	0	0	0
Tax Recoverable	(45)	(3)	63	(108)
Sundry Other Assets	6	(216)	86	51
Finance Lease Receivables	0	0	0	0
Sundry Other Assets	0	0	0	0

THORNTONS PLC: Consolidated Cash Flow Statement

	1991	1992	1993	1994
Net Cash Inflow from Operating Activities				
Other Sources and Uses(cont.)				
Other Provisions	(322)	(78)	7,118	(5,640)
Long-Term Tax	0	0	0	0
Sundry Long-Term Liab.	0	0	0	0
Minority Interests	26	0	0	0
Other Reserves	0	0	0	0
Retained Earnings	(118)	(618)	3,661	(15)
Net Cash Flow from Investments	6,105) (8,767)	1,055	(5,705)	
Net Cash Flow before Financing	(5,286)	(4,125)	(11,011)	(2,148)
Financing				
Short-Term Debt	(767)	(651)	2,211	1,751
Long-Term Debt	6,254	7,287	(614)	4,366
Capital	448	500	41	675
Net Cash Flow from Financing	5,935	7,136	1,638	6,792
Net Movement in Cash	649	3,011	(9,373)	4,644
Actual Movement in Liquid Funds	649	3,011	(9,373)	4,644

4.10   Corporate Valuation

Occasionally questions will arise within the examination that call for comment on value. Valuing businesses is a complex topic, but it is important that you have an understanding of the alternative approaches to valuation. Currently, there are six main approaches to valuation in general use in different contexts:

● Earnings-Based Approach

● Discounting Cash flows

● Dividend Discounting

● Market-to-Book Ratios

● Ratio-Based Measures

● Asset-Based Valuations.

We shall concentrate on the two most likely methods that you will encounter – the earnings-based approach and the asset-based valuation method.

Earnings-Based Approaches to Valuation

A method of valuing the total equity of a business is by applying a multiplying factor to sustainable earnings. This mirrors the relationship between share price and sustainable earnings per share (EPS) in respect of a quoted company, usually known, as we read earlier, as the price/earnings (P/E) ratio. This can be known as P/E-based valuations.

The value of a particular equity share (or stock) of the whole business is represented by a value which is a given multiple of the earnings per share or the value of the sustainable earnings relevant to the equity shareholders. The value of the multiple, known as the P/E ratio, is determined by an examination of published price and earnings data in respect of similar businesses in the stock market. The size of the multiple is broadly equivalent to the relative consistency of the earnings stream and the anticipated growth rate in earnings.

Prior to the development of cash flow valuation methods this was the principal method of pricing new issues and arriving at an estimate of value in large acquisition and disposal situations. While remaining extremely valuable, particularly for assessing the reasonableness of pricing by comparison with other similar quoted businesses, this method has been criticized because it is based on profits rather than cash flow, vulnerable to variations in accounting practice between companies and lacks the formal rigour of a cash flow valuation.

The annual accounts of all quoted companies normally show the value of the earnings per share generated each year and usually also disclose the trend of EPS change over the previous few years. The UK Financial Reporting Standard 3 (FRS 3) defines earnings per share as follows:

'The profit in pence attributable to each equity share, based on the profit (or in the *case of a group the consolidated profit) of the period after tax, minority interests and extraordinary items and after deducting preference dividends and other appropriations in respect of preference shares, divided by the number of equity shares in issue and ranking for dividend in respect of the period.'*

The International Auditing Standard (IAS) exposure draft E52 – Earnings per Share – follows essentially the same approach, defining the earnings figure to be used for the calculation of basic earnings per share as follows:

'For the purpose of calculating basic earnings per share, the net profit or loss for the period attributable to ordinary shares should be the net profit or loss for the period after deducting all claims against it other than those of the ordinary shareholders.'

Using published or forecasted earnings or EPS data as a starting point this is adjusted by the valuer for any distorting or one-off items to arrive at a sustainable earnings or EPS value, which is then forecasted forward to give a feel for the likely growth rate and future share price performance.

A P/E multiple is then selected by comparison with published price data for other similar companies and applied to the stream of earnings or EPS data to arrive at a valuation or anticipated share price.

Sustainable earnings are the earnings generated from the bona fide long-term activities of the company. Unusual, one-off or speculative gains should be ignored because such income is not predictable or regularly recurring. Speculative gains are such items as currency gains, gains from property or other asset disposals, sales of businesses or windfalls arising from insurance recoveries or successful legal action.

Significant formulae

$$EPS = \frac{\text{Relevant earnings}}{\text{Av. no of ordinary shares in issue}}$$

$$P/E \text{ ratio} = \frac{\text{Current share price}}{EPS} \quad \text{or} \quad \frac{\text{Value of the business}}{\text{Relevant earnings}}$$

Thus this becomes: Value of the business = Relevant earnings x P/E ratio

Criticisms of the earnings-based valuation method

- In assuming that the value of a business is encapsulated in the relationship between the market price of a business's shares and its anticipated earnings, the method assumes an indefinite life for the business. Thus it is really suitable only for businesses of reasonable size and critical mass whose future is likely to be indefinite in the absence of unforeseen circumstances. We are assuming that the business will continue to produce a hopefully increasing flow of earnings into the future. If the business is vulnerable in any way to any specific risk other than the general risks faced by all similar companies in the sector, care should be taken before assuming similar P/Es can be applied.

Earnings will often provide the starting point for valuation in smaller businesses. However their relative vulnerability and less certain profit flows will result in the selection of a lower P/E multiple to reflect the increased business risk and risk of failure they face.

- No two businesses are the same. The multiples used are usually derived from observing the market price and P/E multiples achieved by other similar businesses which are listed on a recognized stock exchange. Care must be taken to weight each one appropriately for the actual differences in size, profitability, geographical spread, product offering, growth rate and capital structure. They are not directly comparable. When performing a real valuation exercise this involves carrying out a detailed ratio comparison exercise on the different businesses in the sample chosen in order to identify significant differences and attempt to rank the businesses in some sort of order. Also, it is usual to use data only from a market in the same domicile as the target company.

- Differences in accounting policies. EPS and total earnings figures need to be adjusted for differences in accounting policies among different companies in the same sector. Usually accounting policies in particular industries tend to similarity, so any anomalies this exercise reveals should be carefully considered. Also, in the 1980s, it was normal practice to take a profit figure for the calculation of EPS based on profits before extraordinary items. The argument in favour of this approach is that these were exceptional one-off costs or revenues and should therefore be ignored. Increasingly, however, companies attempted to have all unusual costs so allocated that extraordinary items started to appear regularly in accounts. This is why the definition of earnings per share for disclosure is now after extraordinary items. Financial analysts have come to realize that reporting cash flows is a more factual disclosure of the results of a business. The identification of profits or earnings is much more judgmental, involving areas such as depreciation, stock valuation and provisioning, which require the application of subjective estimates.

- P/Es can be high for two reasons. Firstly, because the company and the sector it is in are highly rated and the company is perceived to have exceptional growth prospects. Secondly, the company might have achieved unusually low profits in the previous year so that the P/E ratio looks flattering. Care should be taken to examine the published accounts of the other companies chosen to ensure there are no special or unusual circumstances that might warrant adjustment of their results.

- The effects of taxation may need to be considered, particularly in asset-rich companies with large potential capital gains liabilities. The tax charge in all companies consists of two things. Firstly, the amount of corporation tax payable on the profits for the current year. Secondly, the value transferred to or from the deferred tax reserve. Where full provision is not being made for potential liabilities it may be necessary to adjust the figures.

Also advanced corporation tax (ACT) is levied whenever a dividend is paid, and is recoverable against a corporate's liability to corporation tax generally on its earnings, which is known as 'mainstream' corporation tax. For multinationals, where the majority of their income arises abroad, there can be insufficient mainstream corporation tax for them to offset their ACT each year. They are obliged to carry forward and eventually write off the surplus ACT if there is no possibility of final offset and therefore recovery. This has the effect of increasing the real level of taxation paid by such businesses.

However, having given all these limitations, the earnings model is a quick way of arriving at a tentative valuation for a company. A first estimate of the value of a business can be arrived at in minutes using this methodology. Before the arrival of cash flow methodologies, earnings-based valuations were the prime method of valuation, used by corporate financiers to value equity since stock markets came into existence. In essence is it a commonsense approach. What do similar businesses trade for in the marketplace? Adjust our view of value for any different features of our particular product and that is the price. The fact remains, however, that the model is over-simplistic. Paragraph 52 of the FRS 3 – Reporting Financial Performance – states:

It is not possible to distil the performance of a complex organisation into a single measure. Undue significance, therefore, should not be placed on any one such measure which may purport to achieve this aim. To assess the performance of a reporting entity during a period all components of its activities must be considered.

The comments above are directed mainly towards performance assessment. However they are equally relevant to valuation. Here is the prime weakness of this valuation approach. Reported earnings are only one facet of value. In a sense they are a lagging indicator of value. A company could have been investing for many years in people and training, all investments which would depress reported historic profits when compared with their competitors, the pay-off coming in enhanced results and growth in the future. The earnings-based model does not recognize such future issues.

Asset-Based Valuation Method

This is a method of valuing constituent parts of a business by applying a market-derived value to each of the assets forming the business. It is also known as a break-up valuation, worst-case valuation or receivership or liquidation value.

Asset valuation is relevant to two different situations:

- If a business is generally considered to have no goodwill associated with it, usually because it is not generating any profits or positive cash flow, the idea that it can be considered to generate a steady stream of earnings breaks down. At this point the value of the business drops to its worst-case value. This is the break-up value of the underlying assets in the control of the business. These are valued individually, added up and offset against any liabilities that might be assumed by the purchaser to arrive at the total value of the business.

- Certain sectors, such as property and leasing, are essentially asset-management businesses. Valuation of such businesses is dominated by the asset value of the portfolio managed. This method of valuation is probably used more often in the real world than any other. In a dynamic economy thousands of businesses ranging from newsagents to multinationals are changing hands each year. Asset-based valuation represents the worst-case scenario in all valuation situations and therefore should always be considered carefully from the risk management point of view. If things should go wrong the only recoverable value from the situation may be the underlying residual asset value. While business is usually about managing assets successfully to unlock their profit-earning potential, the assets themselves are tradable and have an intrinsic worth of their own. Generally asset-valuation approaches are usually appropriate to situations where the business is worth more in terms of its net asset value (the market value of the assets less liabilities) than as a profit or cash-flow generating entity.

This situation usually arises in the following scenarios:

● The business is trading poorly and generating losses.

● The business while generating some cash is not generating sufficient cash to service all its liabilities.

● The business has ceased to trade, or is in receivership or liquidation.

● The business controls assets that are more valuable than the trade itself.

● The business is an asset-management business trading in marketable assets such as property or quoted securities.

● The business controls intangible assets such as brands, distribution agreements, patents, intellectual property or know how.

The value of an asset at any moment in time is its fair market value. This is defined as the price the asset would fetch in the market if traded at arm's length between a willing buyer and seller. The fair market value is determined by a number of subsidiary issues, any one of which might be dominant (and hence the key determinant of value at a given moment in time):

● The supply and demand position in the open market for that asset. If there is considerable demand for that asset in the second-hand market prices will be robust. If there is oversupply of the assets in the second-hand market prices will be depressed. In extreme conditions there may be no willing buyers at all!

● The extent to which the asset is still current with technology in its market. In other words the extent of technological obsolescence. This is as relevant to buildings as it is to machinery.

● The condition of the asset.

● The replacement cost and availability. (This is effectively a comparison with the cost effectiveness of acquiring an equivalent new asset.)

- The earnings potential of the asset and its remaining useful life as an income-generating asset.

- The location of the asset.

In situations where the business is an asset-management business such as a property or leasing company the value of the portfolio of assets is normally determined by professional valuers. They report in writing listing and describing the assets concerned together with their assumptions and finally their opinion as to value.

It is also necessary to introduce the issue of liabilities in the context of asset valuation, because it is certainly relevant.

When a manager purchases a group of assets (essentially a business), usually from a receiver or liquidator, it is because those assets are collected together in one location and usually in a condition such that they can be quickly be made productive. Contrast this with the problems of acquiring such assets piecemeal, where many additional costs would be incurred in creating the same entity and making it quickly productive. Indeed in many cases it would take years to reach the level of integration and volumes that the business to be purchased may have already achieved.

Thus the buyer has some incentive to also assume existing liabilities which will crystallize in the future if this is necessary in order to effect the purchase, providing they are offset directly against the asset value. The assumption of liabilities may also reduce the amount of cash required to acquire control of the assets. The most common liability to acquire is the contingent liability to employees relating to their redundancy entitlement in the event of their being made redundant in the future, this being based on their length of service prior to the receivership. Receivers will often offer assets and imply to bidders that bids assuming this liability are likely to be preferred.

A buyer may also choose to assume all trade liabilities (on a direct offset basis) in order to protect and preserve the ongoing nature of the business, rather than allowing the receiver to damage the company's existing market position by crystallizing them into bad debts.

Criticism of this Method

- Assets usually turn out to be worth less than you pay for them, whereas liabilities always increase in value over time.

- It is not what you do know when you acquire such a business that matters, it is what you do not know that subsequently causes grief!

From the above, the following conclusions can be drawn:

- Asset valuation is an important skill in most business situations. Having a feel for the worth of assets assists in the recognition of new opportunities to create value added in a business.

- The purchase of the operating assets of a business in difficulty is a situation involving big opportunities and downsides. Effective risk-management skills are key to achieving a clean entry to the assets. Quality-management skills are also at a premium in the critical restart period.

4.11   Capital Project Appraisals

You will recall that the basic object of any investment is that after paying out a certain amount of cash today, a larger amount will be received back over a period of time. A lender of funds for capital investment has, therefore, to be certain that a realistic assessment of the project has been undertaken. From the accountancy text book, *Management Accounting for the Lending Banker*, written for the Chartered Institute of Bankers by M. A. Pitcher ACIB, ACIS, AMBIM, first published in 1979, there are four main methods of assessing capital investment projects:

Payback – this involves the calculation of the time it will take to recover the initial outlay.

Average Rate of Return (Return on investment) – this indicates the average annual percentage return on either the average or alternatively the total amount of the investment.

Discounted Cash Flow (Net present value return on investment) – this method involves the discounting of future cash inflows from the project. It adjusts the return to allow for the time value of money.

Yield (Internal Rate of Return) – this method uses the same principles as the net present value approach but with the objective of establishing the discount rate at which the present values of the cash inflows and outflows match.

Traditionally, project-appraisal approaches have centred on either (a) identifying the payback period of the project, or (b) identifying the accounting rate of return on the project. However, with the evolution of discounted cash flow techniques, there are more sophisticated approaches: (c) identification of the net present value (NPV) of the project cash flows, or (d) identification of the internal rate of return (IRR) for the project.

Payback Method

The payback period of a project is found by identifying the number of years it takes before the cumulative forecasted cash flows equal the initial cash outlays related to the project.

For example:

Project	Year 0	Year 1	Year 2	Year 3	Payback Period	NPV at 20%
Z	–5,000	+5,500			1 Year	– 416.67
Y	–5,000	+1,000	+4,000	+7,000	2 Years	2,662.04

Applying only payback criteria to decide between the two projects would result in the selection of Project Z, because it has a payback period of less than one year (if we assume that the cash flows accrue evenly during the year). Reviewing the cash flows associated with the two projects reveals that the returns from Project Y are expected to be substantial and increasing. Finally, the NPV of Project Y is positive, whereas Project Z is negative.

Advantages
● Simplicity. It is easy to understand and communicate to others.

● May be useful in conditions of high uncertainty, where forecasting itself is difficult or meaningless. However, it is important to consider whether a rational investor should be attempting to invest or do any business in such conditions.

Disadvantages
● It ignores the time value of money – equal weight is given to the cash flows prior to the cut off point. This can be overcome by discounting the cash flows to arrive at the discounted payback period. Although this is an improvement on the straight payback approach, it still ignores the cash flows after the payback point.

● It ignores the different levels of specific project risk.

● It ignores the cash flows after the payback point.

Accounting Rate of Return
The accounting rate of return or ARR is also know as the average return on book value. It can be calculated by dividing the average forecasted book profit of a project after depreciation and taxes, by the average book value of the investment. The resultant ratio can then be compared with the book rate of return for the parent business or against other external measures, such as average book rates of return for the sector.

Where the investment is fully depreciated with no residual value at the end of the project life, the average book value of the investment is usually half of the original investment. This is illustrated by the example below:

	Year 0	Year 1	Year 2	Year 3
Investment at cost	12,000	12,000	12,000	12,000
Accumulated depreciation	0	4,000	8,000	12,000
Net book value	12,000	8,000	4,000	0

The investment at cost is 12,000. The average net book value is 6,000 throughout the three-year period of the project.

The following three projects all have the same initial investment of 8,000 with no residual value and a life of three years.

		Year 1	Year 2	Year 3
X	Income after depreciation and taxes	1,500	500	1,000
	Equivalent cash flows	2,000	2,500	500
Y	Income after depreciation and taxes	1,000	1,000	1,000
	Equivalent cash flows	2,000	2,500	500
Z	Income after depreciation and taxes	4,000	1,000	–2,000
	Equivalent cash flows	5,000	2,500	500

All three examples have an average income after depreciation and taxes of 1,000. All, therefore, achieve an ARR of 1,000/4,000 = 25%. However, it is evident from examining the data that the examples are actually quite different.

Advantages

● Calculation is relatively straightforward using traditional profit and loss account and balance sheet accounting techniques.

Disadvantages

● The averaging of profits ignores the actual timing of the returns. Projects yielding their returns earlier are more valuable. ARR does not reflect this.

● ARR is based on profits rather than cash flows. Profits take account of non-cash items such as depreciation and provisioning. Cash flows may not correlate with profits and may be materially better. Profits are also more subjective and more easily manipulated than cash flows.

● The fixing of a benchmark return for comparison and cut off is inherently subjective. It will typically be based on the historic book returns of the existing business.

● ARR ignores the relative risk of future income projections.

Therefore, ARR, like payback, is a fundamentally flawed methodology. It ignores the time value of money and is not based on the project cash flows. Its application may lead to a business that has high rates of return from existing businesses rejecting viable projects, and those businesses with low rates of return accepting poor projects. Both of these methods have now largely been superseded by the more contemporary discounted cash flow techniques.

Discounted Cash Flow Techniques

The following process should be followed:

● Identify the relevant project cash flows.

● Summarize the cash flows to identify the (typical) annual net cash flow relating to the project.

● Discount the cash flows using an appropriate discount rate.

- Sum the discounted cash flows to identify their net present value (NPV).

- Evaluate the findings.

The following property investment project illustrates the methodology. The project involves the purchase of a building for £10,000 at the beginning of year 1. The property is immediately rented on a 4-year lease at £1,000 payable in advance and increasing by 10% after 2 years. At the end year 4, the property is expected to be worth £18,000 and will be sold for that amount.

- Identify the relevant cash flows for the evaluation – this can often be the most difficult part of a evaluation exercise because it may involve making forecast assumptions.

- Once the cash flows have been identified, they are then summarized in an annual summary format as show below. (Note that the initial investment and receipt of the first rental payment in advance are shown as Year 0 – this is a common convention meaning that each cash flow is assumed to be at the end of the year concerned.)

	Discount Rate	Year 0	Year 1	Year 2	Year 3	Year 4
Cash In:						
Rent		1,000	1,000	1,100	1,100	–
Disposal Proceeds						18,000
Cash Out:						
Acquisition Cost		–10,000				
Net Annual Cash Flow		–9,000	1,000	1,100	1,100	18,000
Discount Factor	20%	1	0.8333	0.6944	0.5787	0.4822
Discounted Cash Flows		–9,000	833.33	763.89	636.57	8680.56
Net Present Value		1,914.35				

- The summarized net cash flows then have to be discounted, using a discount rate which should reflect the opportunity cost of funds to the project. (In this project, we are assuming a discount rate of 20%.) The future cash flows are then discounted to identify the present value of each.

- The sum of the discounted cash flows are used to identify the net present value (NPV) of the project, which in this case is a positive cash flow of £1,914.35. This means that if we embark on this project, we would be immediately £1,914.35 better off assuming the actual cash flows match the forecasted cash flows and assuming that we can lend and borrow money at the assumed cost of funds. This is because this amount could be borrowed and spent on day one of the project and the subsequent cash flows from the project would repay the borrowing and the interest incurred on it at the discount rate.

This method can cope with an infinite variety of cash flows over any future timescale. Unlike the previous methods, it recognizes the impact of the time value of money and adjusts for it in the discounting process. The discount rate can vary to reflect the different levels of risk. Alternatively, the rate can be fixed at the cost of funds and the risk/uncertainty of future cash flows can be reflected in the forecast.

Yield (Internal Rate of Return)

This method uses the same principles as the net present value approach, but with the objective of establishing the discount rate at which the present values of the cash inflows and outflows match.

In our discounted cash flow techniques example (see above), the discount rate of 20% gave us a positive NPV of £1,914.35. In many cases, it is possible to identify the discount rate value that will result in a NPV of zero. This value is known as the internal rate of return (IRR). It is also known as the discounted cash flow rate of return. In our project example below, this is a discount rate of 26.7%.

	Discount Rate	Year 0	Year 1	Year 2	Year 3	Year 4
Cash In:						
Rent		1,000	1,000	1,100	1,100	
Disposal Proceeds						18,000
Cash Out:						
Acquisition Cost		−10,000				
Net Annual Cash Flow		−9,000	1,000	1,100	1,100	18,000
Discount Factor	26.7%	1	0.7892	0.6229	0.4916	0.3880
Discounted Cash Flows		−9,000	789.26	685.22	540.82	6,984.71
Net Present Value		0				

This rate can then be compared with, for example, the average rate of borrowing to undertake the project or the corporate's average cost of capital.

4.12   Facility Letters and Covenants

Short-term lending is repayable on demand or within 12 months. The trend over the last decade or so is towards longer-term lending by way of long-term loans. The longer the term of the loan, the higher the potential risk to the lender. In such cases, facility letters setting out the terms of the loan, and the circumstances under which the bank may demand repayment, are drawn up and signed by all parties.

Such facility letters often contain many covenants which place certain restrictions and duties on the customer. If the bank has any doubts about the long-term ability of the borrower, for example if he has high gearing, a poor profit record or other lines of credit elsewhere, then covenants would be required.

Typical covenants are:

● Change of Ownership – Ensures the company will not change ownership, particularly if it is part of a larger group.

● Negative Pledge – An agreement not to give security to other lenders.

● Interest Cover – Usually two times cover is the minimum. (Profits and/or cash flow covenant.)

● Gearing Restriction – A limit is placed on the gearing ratio of the business.

● Leverage Restriction – A limit is placed on the leverage ratio of the business.

● Minimum security cover.

● Maintenance of Minimum Levels of Assets covered by a debenture, e.g. overdraft to be covered by x times debtors of, say, 60 days or less, monitored monthly.

● Timetable for production to the bank of interim management accounting information for monitoring purposes.

Summary

After having studied this chapter carefully, you should be able to:

● Understand the impact of management on a business and carry out business risk analysis using SWOT and an industry analysis framework;

● Understand the new cash flow statement, FRS1;

● Have an appreciation of some stock market indicators;

● Understand the differing approaches to corporate valuation;

● Recall the main methods for capital project appraisals;

● Review typical lending covenants.

5

BUSINESS LENDING AND SECURITY

Objectives

After studying this chapter, you should be able to:

- Quantify risk exposure on business lending;
- Clarify when security should be taken;
- Consider the various forms of security available from business borrowers and the valuation discounts;
- Understand the concept of break-up analysis.

It is not intended to deal with the technicalities of charging security, which are well covered in other books. Readers are referred to other books on the recommended reading for this subject.

A lender should consider taking security where the purpose of the advance is to acquire a specific asset, e.g. a medium-term loan for the purchase of machinery, or a bridging loan for premises purchase or where the risks of repayment are assessed as such to make it essential to have a controlled repayment alternative.

If a business is unable to repay its debts, in order to assess the outcome of this event, it will be necessary to carry out a break-up analysis of the balance sheet. This will give a significantly different picture to the balance sheet as a going-concern. For example, many assets lose value as soon as trading ceases. Asset values need to be discounted by the banker to carry out this type of gone-concern approach to credit analysis. The discount factors to be applied will vary from business to business. For example, stock may be out-of-date, obsolete or include work-in-progress.

5.1   The Assessment of Risk

When assessing the risk to the bank, the full extent of the bank's exposure to the customer must be understood. In addition to overdrafts and loans, the bank may well be asked to enter into many other types of contingent liability for the customer and it will be necessary to incorporate these additional risks into the overall risk 'exposure'.

Bank Risk Percentages for Contingent Liabilities

The figures below are approximations. Precise views on the level of risk in these products vary from bank to bank.

	%
Acceptances	100
Discounts (trade bills)	30
Discounts (accommodation paper)	100
Foreign bills negotiated	30
Forward currency contracts	20
Irrevocable letters of credit	100
Engagements:	
– Guarantees	100
– Bid Bonds (tender bonds)	20
– Performance bonds	100
– Advance payment guarantees	100
– Bonds to HM Customs and Excise	20
– Indemnities re freight irregularities in shipping documents etc.	10

Guidelines

Acceptances – 100%

When the bank accepts a bill on behalf of a customer the customer then obtains possession of the underlying goods in exchange for the bill. At maturity the bank must honour the bill at face value.

Discounts (trade bills) – 30%

When a bill is discounted the bank is, in effect, buying (with recourse) the underlying debt from its customer. On breaking up a balance sheet you allow 70% for debtors and assuming you will obtain 70% value for the debt your uncovered risk is 30%. The bank may be able to secure a lien over the underlying goods if it feels the need.

Discounts (accommodation paper) – 100%

An accommodation bill is a bill drawn by your customer on himself for a funding operation not linked to any underlying trading transaction and your customer will be expected to cover the bill at or before maturity. Thus, your customer is the ultimate debtor and our risk is 100%.

Foreign bills negotiated – 30%

Treat on the same basis as discounts (trade bills).

Forward currency contracts – 20%

Loss could be sustained if the customer is unable to complete the contract. This would necessitate the bank having to buy or sell the currency at spot rate in order to complete. Your risk is dependent upon movements in the exchange rate and for practical purposes you adopt a risk factor of 20% (some banks are as low as 10%).

Irrevocable letters of credit – 100%

In establishing a credit we undertake to make payment in accordance with the terms thereof. Thus, this risk is assessed at 100%.

Guarantees – 100%

Where you have detailed knowledge of the finances of the individual or company being guaranteed (the principal debtor), e.g. recent balance sheet, the risk is capable of accurate assessment. Where you do not, this risk must be 100%. Some banks automatically weight such guarantees at 100% risk.

Bid bonds (tender bonds) – usually 20%

In effect, this is an assurance by the bank that a customer's tender for a contract is not of a frivolous nature, i.e. in the event of the contract being awarded to the tenderer, that he will not withdraw, thereby leaving the beneficiary to recommence tender procedure. The bond itself will be outstanding only until a contract is awarded, at which stage it will be cancelled (if the customer has not been awarded the contract) or replaced by a performance bond. The risk factor is therefore 100%, but because the bonds are short term and because many underlying tenders will not be accepted, some banks adopt a 20% risk factor.

Performance bond – 100%

Default under a performance bond could arise through your customer's:

● inability to fulfil the contract; or

● withdrawal from the contract.

The former case is only likely to arise from insolvency because contractors are highly unlikely to withdraw once the bond has been given.

A performance bond is essentially an insolvency bond which generates no cash flow whatsoever. It merely has the effect of placing the contractor in the position that he can go ahead with the contract which in itself may or may not generate cash flow. If and when default occurs you are still not able to quantify your risk at less than the full amount, because it is possible that the whole of the bonded amount will be required to rectify the shortcomings of the contract. Also remember that you are in the beneficiary's hands in that he holds an 'on demand' guarantee and you must pay in full when called upon to do so. Thus, the risk factor is 100%.

Advance payment guarantee – 100%

When a bank's customer is paid in advance for goods not yet delivered, the purchaser may demand in exchange a guarantee of repayment in case of non-delivery. As with a performance bond this is, in effect, an insolvency bond which is not capable of quantification at less than the full amount.

Customers' balance sheets may show these advance payments in different ways. In some cases the amount of the advance payment is shown as a liability whereas in others it can be shown as a deduction from work-in-progress.

Bonds to HM Customs and Excise – 20%

These are mainly guarantees for deferred VAT and import duty. The bonds normally specify a maximum figure per month, but Customs and Excise could wait until two months' payments are in arrears before claiming.

Indemnities re missing bills of lading, Irregularities in shipping documents etc. – 10%

It is highly improbable that any customer will ask you to assist him (through the issue of an indemnity) to procure goods that are not intended for delivery to him. Irregularities in shipping documents are invariably clerical discrepancies and your action in giving indemnities against discrepancies merely oils the wheels of commerce. It is, therefore, considered that the risk factor in these instances is notional at 10%. Indeed, some banks take the view that for an established, reputable customer there is nil risk.

Break-up Analysis (The Gone-Concern Approach)

If a business goes into insolvency, you need to be able to assess the risk of any loss on your lending by analysing the business's assets on a 'gone-concern' basis. Break-up values can be calculated from the latest audited (or interim) figures. Experience has shown that amounts recovered in asset realizations are almost always far less than expected. If there is a general recession hitting a trade or area, the market for the assets will be depressed and when a business fails, many debtors will look for reasons not to pay.

Suggested percentages for asset realization values ('gone-concern' basis):

	%	
Marketable investments	80	of current market value
Debtors	50-70	Depending on age, spread, quality
HP debtors	60	
Stock	15-40	
Work-in-progress	20	
Property – freehold	40	of balance sheet or manager's valuation with vacant possession; or
	60	of recent professional valuation
	%	
Long leasehold (30 years plus)	33	$1/3$ of manager's valuation or recent professional valuation
Private dwelling house – freehold or leasehold	66	$2/3$ of manager's valuation with vacant possession (some banks may not allow managers to value)
Plant and machinery etc.	10-20	Depending on how specialized
Vehicles	20	
Office furniture, tools etc.	10	
Payments in advance	Nil	
Ships	50	of recent professional valuation
Farming		
Cattle and livestock	60	
Harvested crops	50	
Deadstock – feed	Nil	
Tillages – preparation	50	

Note: For examination purposes, these percentages are to be adopted in the majority of cases, but they are not regarded as rigid. If it is felt necessary to include a different valuation, the reason should be stated in your answer.

5.2 Debentures

When the bank has a debenture charge, monthly figures (as well as monitoring business performance through ratio analysis, cash flow and management information) can be called for to help to monitor the bank advance. After considering the nature of the debenture charge in general, we shall look at the type of monitoring that can be used.

Bankers frequently encounter situations where a company customer has executed a debenture charge to the bank. This type of security will give the bank differing priorities over the company assets. Forms of charge vary between banks, but a debenture usually gives the bank the following security:

(a)   A legal fixed first charge on freehold and leasehold property whether registered or unregistered title, together with building fixtures, including trade fixtures and fixed plant and machinery. The definition of fixed plant means machinery fixed to the floor. This should not be confused with the accountancy definition of fixed assets, which will include moveable assets such as vehicles, which would not be covered by the debenture's fixed charge.

(b)   An equitable fixed first charge on all future freehold or leasehold property, together with building fixtures including trade fixtures and fixed plant and machinery.

(c)   An equitable fixed first charge over all book debts and other debts now and from time to time owing, and over goodwill and uncalled capital.

(d)   A first floating charge over all other assets whatsoever both present and future. The principal assets remaining to be caught under the floating charge are stock, moveable plant and machinery and motor vehicles.

(e)   A floating charge over intellectual property rights.

The receiver's powers will generally include the right to:

(a)   take possession and sell off assets;

(b)   carry on the business and borrow money on the security of the assets;

(c)   appoint managers and agents to assist with the running of the business;

(d)   carry out acts incidental to the performance of his duties.

Limitations of the Charge

Any preferential creditors, e.g. VAT, PAYE, will erode available floating-charge recoveries. However, a bank can rank in priority with other preferentials in respect of advances for wages and salaries. Under the Insolvency Act 1986, Sch. 6, para. 11, money advanced and actually paid to employees during the four months prior to winding-up will be valid subject to a maximum guideline in respect of each employee.

Furthermore it must be remembered that under s. 245 of the Insolvency Act 1986, floating charges granted within 12 months prior to the commencement of winding-up are invalid, unless it can be proved that the company was solvent at the time the charge was created.

Usually, however, Clayton's case will assist, in that the debt will often have been turned over by receipts and payments through the account, and the advance will be deemed to represent new money. In these cases the floating charge will then be valid.

Setting a Formula

In setting a formula for cover of the bank debt by current assets, the banker will need to consider both the balance sheet strength and the nature of the risk. For example, for an old-established, successful business having substantial fixed assets, a finer margin of cover may be stipulated than for a relatively new, expanding business with few fixed assets.

Furthermore, regard must be given both to the annual accounts and also to the current levels of book debts to make sure that any formula set is workable. A formula could be two-and-a-half times cover of the bank debt by stock and debtors, with cover of one-and-a-half times by book debts.

A further guide to workable formulae is to look at profit/cash budgets (if these documents have been prepared) and derive from them a monthly projected balance sheet. There are many possible variations of the formula, but whatever the margin of cover decided upon, any breach of the set formula may be used by the banker as a 'trigger' to call for interim financial accounts or call for an independent review of the company's affairs by an accountant.

Monitoring the Formula

To enable effective monitoring of the formula, it is advisable to use some kind of debenture monitoring form. A suggested layout is shown in the example below. With such a form the listing of figures for debtors, stock, creditors, etc. from the latest available annual accounts forms a useful base for comparison with current figures on a month-to-month basis. The bank balance used should be as per the company's books. Sales per annum and sales per month have been included. If businesses are carrying out any monitoring at all it is almost certain to be sales! This information will enable you to monitor current sales activity. Capital expenditures or disposals should be minuted – they will have an effect on liquidity movements. The current assets total line A should then be compared with the agreed lending cover formula to ensure compliance.

Critical Analysis of Variations

As well as monitoring the debenture cover formula of bank debt to current assets, the monitoring form is also useful in highlighting the net current asset movement position (net of totals: A – B), as the following example shows.

ABC Co Ltd

The figures shown in the example are applicable to this company.

For ABC Co Ltd:

(a) The formula was 2.5 times cover by debtors and stock – this was easily maintained each month.

(b) The net current assets position (A – B) shows an improving trend from January to May but suddenly drops back in June. (Why did this occur?) However, comparing the June end position with the opening figures shows an improvement of £47,825 (£346,795 – £298,970). Although this does not always represent a profit figure, it does show as a healthy sign – this positive movement can only be caused by profits earned or funds injected or sale of fixed assets or a combination of all three. Equally, if the movement was negative (as occurred from May to June), further enquiry would be justified.

(c) The annual sales of £2.4 million average out to £200,000 per month. Monthly sales recorded on the form look good in comparison, and it will be interesting to see the full 12-month picture.

Company Name: ABC Co Ltd Financial Year End 31 December

Agreed Formula: 2½ times debtors plus stock

	From Annual Accounts Date 31.12.X5	From Company Books					
		January	February	March	April	May	June
	£	£	£	£	£	£	£
Current Assets							
Cash	2,500	1,800	2,600	1,500	2,800	3,200	1,800
Debtors	484,500	472,653	486,152	517,250	586,220	570,185	526,590
Stock	120,000	135,500	140,200	120,700	115,800	112,100	110,500
Total (A)	607,000	609,953	628,952	639,952	704,820	685,485	638,890
Current Liabilities							
Bank	115,850	108,950	120,680	105,700	102,800	100,849	98,774
Creditors	192,180	210,525	200,520	225,600	210,723	202,576	197,821
Total (B)	308,030	319,475	321,200	331,300	313,523	303,425	296,595
Net Off (A)-(B)	298,970	290,478	307,752	308,150	391,297	382,060	346,795

Capital Expenditure - NIL

ABC Co Ltd Sales Record

	Per Annum	Per Month					
		January	February	March	April	May	June
	£	£	£	£	£	£	£
Sales	2.4m	215,280	325,650	350,320	325,000	328,520	255,650

The next example illustrates the difficulties that can be encountered with debenture monitoring figures. R Co Ltd is engaged in manufacturing and was established in 19X3. Sales have progressed and the bank account reveals the following statistics:

Year End	Average Balance	Turnover
19X3	£5,818Cr.	£1,600,000
19X4	£79,663Dr.	£2,600,000
19X5	£124,212Dr.	£3,100,000
19X6 (to date August 19X6	£50.003Dr.	£3,000,000

19X6 analysis:	
Best balance:	£77,454 Cr
Worst balance:	£185,917 Dr
Overdraft limit:	£200,000
Security:	Debenture
Formula:	2.5 times current assets

A summary of the annual accounts for 19X4 and 19X5 illustrates profitable trading and retentions:

Year ended:	December 19X5	December 19X4
Sales	£2,900,000	£2,400,000
Gross Profit %	31%	34%
Profit	£ 136,000	£ 190,000
Net Worth	£ 367,000	£ 256,000

Note that while turnover has increased, it has been at the expense of the gross margin. However, everything looks straightforward until the debenture monitoring figures held at the branch are reviewed. An extract of the net liquid position appears in the example below.

The debenture formula has been easily met (bank x 2.5: current assets), but what has happened to the liquid surplus totals (A – B)? The surplus has fallen from £927,000 in January to £844,000 in June. Further review will show that the stock figure looks 'silly'. It cannot be static for four consecutive months in a manufacturing business!

Interim management accounts were called for and they showed:

To June 19X6:

Sales	£2,600,000
Gross profit	30%
Net profit	£116,000

Certainly a much healthier position than revealed in the debenture monitoring figures. The problem was of course the stock figure – not even estimated – it was only a repeat of the previous quarter-end figure. The 'true' stock figure, when verified, was almost £200,000 more.

Company Name: R Co Ltd Financial Year End 31 December

Agreed Formula: 2½ times cover

	From annual accounts date 31.12.X5	From company books:					
		Jan	Feb	Mar	Apr	May	Jun
	£000	£000	£000	£000	£000	£000	£000
Current assets							
Debtors	811	822	928	929	1,014	1,059	1,045
Stock	673	693	693	663	663	663	663
Total (A)	1,484	1,515	1,621	1,622	1,677	1,722	1,708
Current liabilities							
Bank	107	107	109	75	126	240	165
Creditors	380	425	443	514	612	634	664
Hire-purchase	65	56	66	71	30	23	35
Total (B)	552	558	618	660	768	897	864
Net of totals (A-B)	932	927	1,003	962	909	825	844

Additional Analysis

You will have seen how important it is to understand fully the figures presented on the debenture monitoring form. For this reason it is suggested that the following additional analyses are made, by way of supplementary forms attached to the debenture monitoring form.

Debtors

This figure needs breaking down into normal trade, intercompany, and doubtful debt. Care should be taken not to include any debts that have been factored under a factoring agreement. Further, it is useful to get an indication of debtor spread and debtor control.

Debtor Analysis:

Debtor	Totals	Age (Days)				Remarks
		Current	30	60	90	
£1,000 and over						
Others						
Percentages	100%					

Debtor Analysis by Major Customer Account: Age (Days)

Name	Total Balance	Current	30	60	90	Remarks
Totals						

Stock

This figure is a difficult one for many businesses to provide. Frequently, there will be many differing stock lines and the only accurate way is to carry out a physical stockcheck. However, this difficulty can be overcome if the stock file is computerized. Usually, though, in practice you will have to accept the directors' estimate based on stock movements during the month. A quarterly physical stocktake should be encouraged to give a clear indicator of the actual stock position – useful to both the banker and the customer!

A further complication is in businesses where there is on-going product manufacture or job contracts – then it will be necessary to estimate work-in-progress.

Also stock can be invoiced from a supplier subject to reservation of title (Romalpa terms). This reservation means that goods supplied remain the property of the supplier until he is paid. Again the directors should provide details. The example below illustrates stock analysis.

Analysis of Manufacturing Stock

Month Ended: ....

Stock	£	as a %
Raw Materials		
Work in Progress		
Finished Goods		
Total Stock*		

*Reservation of Title £........

It is useful, when stock is physically taken and valued, to mark the stock figure on the debenture monitoring form accordingly.

Creditors

In addition to age analysis to see if there is pressure for payment on the business, it is also very useful to split the creditors total into normal trade and preferential. We are very interested in the preferential creditors for the reasons stated at the beginning of this section when we considered the debenture charge. We should establish if there are any set-off trading positions between creditors and debtors that might lead to counterclaims.

Creditor Analysis:

Creditor	Totals	Current	30	60	90	Remarks
			Age (Days)			
£1,000 and over						
Others						
Percentages	100%					

Creditor Analysis by Major Customer Account

Creditor	Totals	Current	30	60	90	Remarks
			Age (Days)			
Trade:						
Preferential Creditors – VAT, PAYE, NIC etc.						
Percentages	100%					

5.3　Protecting the Bank's Position

Readers are cross-referred to the chapter on Problems with Business Lending for more details on the appointment of an investigating accountant. However, for the purpose of this chapter, it is worth giving a brief introduction.

It is always difficult to advise on timing of the appointment of a receiver and manager. Sometimes the company directors will request it; but often it is a case of the company directors hoping for better times and wanting to carry on – while the bank is anxiously looking at the trading of the business and pressure on the bank account. How best can you protect the bank's position? If it is a hopeless case, then you must act decisively. Delay may cause further deterioration.

If all parties are slightly unsure of their ground, then a useful interim step is to get the company to agree to the appointment of an investigating accountant. His brief will vary but essentially it is to:

(a) comment on and analyse recent trading;

(b) draw up a current statement of affairs;

(c) comment on the future viability of the business;

(d) comment on the bank's exposure and security.

The appointee should be an accountant with proven expertise, with knowledge of the particular trade (if possible), and if receivership follows you must feel sure that he will be the man for the job.

The investigation can be quick and it may only take from three to five days to get a 'feel' for the business and make a preliminary report. The company directors should cooperate, because it must be also in their interest to know where they stand.

The following case study will illustrate the speed with which the bank's position can deteriorate.

Case Study 4 – M Group Ltd

This group was involved in cash-and-carry wines and spirits, with three warehouses and six retail shops. The business commenced in 1960 and had grown rapidly in recent years. The board of four directors included the proprietor and his wife, a sales director and a chartered accountant acting as finance director.

You have been unable to obtain recent debenture figures, due to the company transferring records to computer. There has been pressure of late on the bank account and you have had to report temporary excess positions to the control department. The company directors have told you that the bank account problem is only temporary and is mainly caused by the cost of a move of premises.

However, draft accounts have just been produced to the company year-end 31 March, and when you compare them with previous years, the following is revealed:

	Draft Accounts	Audited Accounts		
	31.3.X6	19X5	19X4	19X3
Sales	£36.1 m	£30.4m	£19m	£9.3m
Gross profit	1.2 m	£1.3 m	£909,000	£586,000
Gross profit %	3.4%	4.2%	4.8%	6.2%
Overheads	1.7m	£1.1m	£689,000	£485,000
Profit (Loss)	(£484,000)	£147,000	£220,000	£101,000

The group results indicate the rapid growth of the business in the last four years, with sales going from £9.3 million to £36.1 million, and with a fine (and deteriorating) gross margin, down from 6.2 % to 3.4 %. The draft accounts reveal both a drop in gross margin and at the same time increased overheads, to £1.7 million, resulting in a loss of £484,000.

With the move of premises and transfer to computer, no management accounts were prepared during the latter part of the year to 31.3.X6, and consequently the considerable loss came as a shock to the directors.

The directors agreed to the appointment of investigating accountants to try to pinpoint the current trading position and cash flow requirement. The accountants subsequently reported:

(a) a serious imbalance of trade between volume of sales, gross margins and overheads incurred;

(b) that the accounting records maintained were most inadequate for a business of this nature with fine gross margins and high volume of turnover.

The following figures were provided to illustrate the bank's position:

	At 31.3.X6		At 20.5.X6	
	Estimated Draft balance sheet £000	Estimated break-up balance sheet £000	Estimated balance sheet £000	Estimated break-up balance sheet £000
Assets subject to fixed charge:				
Freehold deeds	283	175	283	175
Leasehold	9	–	9	–
Goodwill	70	–	70	–
Trade debtors	1,318	1,197	1,102	956
(A)	1,680	1,372	1,464	1,131
Assets subject to floating charge:				
Fixtures and equipment	420	50	420	50
Motor vehicles	60	30	60	30
Stock	5,568	4,202	4,150	3,058
	6,048	4,282	4,630	3,138

	At 31.3.X6		At 20.5.X6	
	Estimated Draft balance sheet £000	Estimated break-up balance sheet £000	Estimated balance sheet £000	Estimated break-up balance sheet £000
Less: Preferential creditors:				
PAYE/NIC	(28)	(28)	(58)	(58)
VAT	(299)	(299)	(799)	(799)
Wages and holiday pay	(10)	(23)	(10)	(23)
Other preferential debts	(3)	(3)	(66)	(66)
	(340)	(353)	(933)	(946)
Net floating charge (B) assets	5,708	3,929	3,697	2,192
Total realizable (A+ B)	7,388	5,301	5,161	3,323
Bank	2,510	2,510	2,743	2,743
Surplus on bank's (C) charge	4,878	2,791	2,418	580
Unsecured creditors	4,459	3,759	1,999	1,399
Net assets/(liabilities)	19	(968)	419	(819)

The accountants also made the following report:

The group business has such a high turnover of stocks, with very short periods of credit given and taken, that the balance sheet can change dramatically in short periods of time. This is highlighted by the reduction of surplus on the bank's charge on a going-concern basis between 31/3 and 20/5 from £4.8 million to £2.4 million. [See also break-up basis, £2.8 million to £580,000: line (C).]

In our view the bank's position is not satisfactory ... the bank can never be sure as to what the position is. ... Losses are highly likely to be continuing.

A few weeks later a receiver was appointed.

5.4   Debenture Realizations: Break-Up Values

What you recover as a percentage of book debts, stock or fixed assets varies enormously from trade to trade and area to area. The recovery unit in your bank's regional office will be able to give you a guide based on their experiences. Full recovery on each asset is rare – that is why we set a formula for cover in the first place, which we hope will provide an overall margin at the end of the day.

Here is an interesting case study to show you what can happen.

Case Study 5 – Company X

Company X were UK distributors for domestic kitchen appliances. Sales were mainly to electrical wholesalers and kitchen specialists. The goods carried no manufacturer's guarantee, but were distributed by Company X with their own 12 months' warranty. Company X traded profitably in their early years, but later incurred substantial losses due to abortive ventures into new kitchen and bathroom products. At the same time, high warranty charges were encountered with one major product line and business overheads also increased during 19X1 and 19X2.

Year Ended December:	19W9	19X0	19X1	19X2
Sales	£2.57 m	£3.56 m	£4.23 m	£2.3 m
Gross Profit %	19%	18%	18%	17%
Overheads	£493,000	£641,000	£965,000	£783,000
Overheads/Sales %	19%	18%	23%	34%
Net profit/(loss)	–	–	(£202,000)	(£323,000)

Investigating accountants went in in September 19X3 (after the bank received the disastrous 19X2 trading figures) and reported that the bank debt should be covered on a break-up basis:

Estimated Statement of Affairs as at 30.9.X3

	Book Value £000	Break-up Value £000
Assets subject to fixed charge:		
Debtors	425	335
Less: Bank	(393)	(393)
Surplus/(Shortfall) to debenture holder		
under fixed charge	32	(58)
Assets subject to floating charge:		
Stock	497	251
Plant/Machinery/Motor Vehicles	33	15
	530	266

	Book Value £000	Break-up Value £000
Preferential creditors:		
PAYE/NI	36	
Rates	12	
VAT	130	
Employees (Holding Pay)	3	
	(181)	(181)
Surplus/(Shortfall) under floating charge	349	85
Surplus/(Shortfall) to debenture holder	32	(58)
	381	27
Unsecured Creditors	(553)	(553)
Shortfall to Unsecured Creditors	(172)	(526)

(You will see that most of the bank's cover was on book debts as a fixed charge.)

When receivership took place later in December 19X3, the bank's cover on debtors was quickly dissipated with many counterclaims from customers to set off on warranty work and retentions in case of future complaints on warranty work. Finally, by 19X6 the total recovery from book debts amounted to only £134,000 as against the initial book value of £425,000. Stock also suffered, although previously discounted by 50% to £251,000. Eventual realization was only £125,000 (50% of the discounted figure).

5.5   Debenture Security Disadvantages

Fixed Charges

(a) **Land**

Experience shows that the value of land can be overestimated. Clearly there are many factors that must be borne in mind, e.g.:

- Market conditions.
- Type and age of building, including state of repair.
- Nature of usage.
- If leasehold, length of lease.
- Access and position.

(b) **Debtors**

Realization is usually considerably lower than book value (averaging 50/70%), as debtors attempt to escape payment. Reasons may include:

- Doubtful/irrecoverable debts, particularly inter-group.
- Claims for breach of contract. This is particularly relevant for companies that are

involved in long-term contracts, i.e. the construction industry, or companies that offer after-sales service contracts. In such cases, a receiver may be appointed to enable the contracts to be completed. The bank might be prepared to advance money to the receiver to enable this to take place if this would protect and ensure that the pre-receivership debt could be recovered in full. Clearly, this course of action would need to be analysed closely.

- Counterclaims by debtors, who are also owed money.

- Claims that the goods are below the required standard.

- Attempts to avoid payment, particularly where small debts are involved. The debtors hope that a receiver/liquidator will have so many other problems, that it is not cost-effective to pursue legal remedies.

Breach of contract, counterclaims or substandard goods may result in the receiver/liquidator scaling down the debt by negotiation, or may allow the debtor to escape completely.

(c) **Fixed Plant and Machinery**
Realization values of all machinery are usually considerably lower than book value. Reasons may include:

- Old plant may be worth no more than scrap value.

- Specialized machinery may have a limited market.

Fixed charges cover only machinery that is bolted to the floor. Should the machinery be unbolted it is difficult to trace and to prove that it was bolted to the floor! For these reasons, where any item of machinery is a significant part of the bank's security, a specific charge should be taken.

Floating Charge

(a) **Preferential Creditors**
These usually take priority over the floating charge in a winding up or if a receiver is appointed.

(b) **Stock**
Realization values in most industries tend to average between 15 and 40%. Reasons may include:

- Stock proving to be out-of-date or unsaleable.

- Work-in-progress – Difficult to complete and may, in a manufacturing business, have to be scrapped.

- Raw materials – While being of some value, will need to be discounted to enable any potential purchaser to collect, etc.

A receiver may be able to trade on, and therefore turn some finished goods. This should enable these items to be sold for a figure much nearer to book value. Any such sale proceeds will still be added to floating realizations, although this would improve the bank's position if a preferential claim for payment of wages can be made. In addition, trading on may also allow completion of contracts, which might protect pre-receivership debts, and therefore obviate debtors escaping by claiming breach of contract.

Stock may be subject to reservation of title clauses in the creditor's invoices. These are commonly known as 'Romalpa clauses' (after the case which first gave rise to the test of the principle in English Law – *Aluminium Industrie Vaassen BV v Romalpa Aluminium Ltd 1976*). Such clauses will often be contained in a supplier's conditions of sale, and give the supplier the right to retain the title to goods supplied, until payment is received. Their wording dictates the extent to which the suppliers can proceed to recover goods, which effectively belong to them. A simple clause that would work might be 'Title to the goods shall not pass until payment is received in full'.

This clause will therefore significantly affect the bank's recovery from stock.

5.6 Other Forms of Security

Residential Property

First mortgages over the houses of business proprietors are often taken as security for business borrowing. Caution must be exercised with matrimonial homes, with letters of consent obtained from the interested parties. Banks will usually lend up to 80% of the house valuation. If a second mortgage is being taken, the amount of the first mortgage should be deducted from the valuation. It must also be considered that the first mortgagee can force a sale of the property if the loan is in default, and that, although legally obliged to sell for the best possible price, will have an aim of clearing the first mortgage and not any other amounts secured on the property. Therefore, if there is only a minimal amount outstanding on the first mortgage, it can be worthwhile to take over the first mortgage to have complete control of the situation.

Directors' Guarantees

See Chapter 2, Small Business Lending, for a full explanation.

Company Guarantees

The company's memorandum of association must first be checked to establish if it deals with the giving of guarantees/third-party charges. The benefit of the company giving a guarantee or third-party security should be investigated, e.g. where there is a relationship – parent/ subsidiary or landlord/tenant, or if there is a trading relationship, which is vital to one or both parties. Where the guarantee is intra-group, it must be considered whether the failure of the guaranteed party might place sufficient financial pressure on the guarantor, such that the guarantor is unable to honour its guarantee. If a parent company is guaranteeing a subsidiary, the financial ability of the group must be assessed.

Letters of comfort are not legally enforceable (Decision – *Kleinwort Benson Ltd v Malaysian Mining Corporation Berhad* 1987). Therefore, no security value should be attached to them. However, it is still frequent banking practice to take a letter of comfort as an indication of group commitment.

Summary

After having studied this chapter, you should be able to:

- Quantify the total risk exposure on business lending;

- Clarify when security should be taken;

- Consider the various forms of security available from corporate borrowers and the valuation discounts;

- Understand the concept of break-up analysis.

Case Study 6 – Sparks Ltd

Sparks Ltd have banked with your bank for over 20 years and act as wholesalers and suppliers of a range of electrical components to industrial customers. The directors, Richard Lee (aged 49) and Charles Proctor (aged 52) own 50% of the company each, and draw remuneration in the same proportions. Lee looks after sales and Proctor is responsible for finance and administration.

The company currently has overdraft facilities of £300,000 secured by a debenture.

The overdraft was renewed for 12 months a short while ago, at which time the company supplied a profit and loss forecast for the year to 30 September 1997.

Richard Lee calls to see you. He tells you that Proctor has recently suffered a mild heart attack and is seriously considering giving up work. He wants Lee to buy him out of the business and has put a value of £400,000 on his shares. Lee wishes to go ahead and buy the shares at this figure, and his initial thoughts are as follows:

1. He can raise £100,000 himself – £50,000 from savings and £50,000 by increasing the mortgage on his house (value £300,000, existing mortgage £40,000).

2. The company buys back sufficient shares to cover the remaining £300,000. He sees this being financed by:

    (a) a 10-year loan of £200,000;

    (b) utilizing the existing overdraft facility to provide the balance of £100,000.

3. A book-keeper will be employed to replace Proctor at a salary of £25,000 per annum.

Required:

Set out, with reasons, your response to this request.

SPARKS LTD: Profit and Loss Summary

Year to 30 September	1994 £	1995 £	Draft 1996 £	Forecast 1997 £
Sales	1,731,672	1,909,452	2,024,434	2,250,000
Gross profit	626,400	611,970	649,378	720,000
Directors' remuneration	136,066	171,753	172,500	180,000
Interest paid	21,180	23,830	20,714	22,500
Profit before tax	87,372	30,042	21,437	112,500
Retained profit	78,372	18,042	9,887	–

Balance Sheet

As at 30 September	1994 £	£	1995 £	£	1996 £	£
Current Assets						
Cash	7,261		7,327		7,402	
Debtors	423,216		474,668		482,925	
Stock	385,998	816,475	359,973	841,968	367,338	857,665
Current Liabilities						
Creditors	255,007		239,677		309,750	
Bank	151,109		167,030		109,311	
Hire Purchase	38,917		48,223		46,179	
Taxation	9,000	(454,033)	12,000	(466,930)	11,550	(476,790)
Net Current Assets		362,442		375,038		380,875
Fixed Assets						
Leasehold Property	13,500		12,000		10,500	
Fixtures and Fittings	24,106		23,831		17,876	
Motor Vehicles	97,212	134,818	104,433	140,264	115,938	144,314
		497,260		515,302		525,189
Financed By:						
Ordinary Shares		2,500		2,500		2,500
Profit and Loss Account		494,760		512,802		522,689
		497,260		515,302		525,189

Accounting Ratios

	1994 (Draft	1995 (Forecast)	1996)	1997
Net gearing (%)	36.8	40.4	28.2	–
Current ratio	1.80:1	1.80:1	1.80:1	–
Acid test	0.95:1	1.03:1	1.04:1	–
Credit given (days)	89	91	87	–
Credit taken (days)	84	67	82	–
Stock turnover (days)	127	101	96	–
Gross margin (%)	36.2	32.0	32.1	32.0
Net margin (%)	5.0	1.6	1.1	5.0
Interest cover (times)	5.1	2.3	2.0	6.0

Operation of Bank Account

	High £'000	Low £'000	Average £000
1994	202 Dr	5 Cr	145 Dr
1995	225 Dr	30 Dr	172 Dr
1996 to date	180 Dr	60 Cr	139 Dr

Interest margin 3% over base.

Suggested Answer

Sparks Ltd

This question was about a company wanting to buy back its shares and the effect it would have on its balance sheet etc. Share buybacks are allowed under Section 162 of the 1985 Companies Act but there must be sufficient undistributed profits to enable the buyback to take place. In this case there are.

The existing proprietors, Lee and Proctor, have built up a good business and they must have been competent managers to do so. However, Proctor will not be there in future and his talents could be missed – who will replace him? If the management become stretched, will Lee be able to devote the same amount of time as before to his marketing role, particularly as the company's projections require sales to increase by over 11%. Weakening the management team at the same time as putting the business under greater financial pressure by reducing the capital it has available is not an ideal situation.

The first issue to be considered is the price being paid. On a net asset basis, £400k looks a high price for 50% of £525k of net assets. On a P/E basis the price is too high, with the price earnings ratio being 81 times on the 1996 figures! The price can only be justified based on the 1997 forecast adjusted for a reduction in costs as a result of the lower directors' remuneration.

Looking at historical financial performance it can be seen that the current balance sheet structure is strong with low gearing. The business is liquid with both current ratio and acid test showing a healthy position, which is also reflected in the good credit given and taken figures and low overdraft usage. However, profitability has been disappointing, particularly at the net level. The last time the business made a decent net profit was two years ago when the gross margin was 36.2% rather than the 32% it is now. At the raw net profit level, it does not look as though the business could carry a lot more debt, but it has to be recognized that the directors have been able to pay themselves high remuneration and this could be regarded as 'quasi profit'.

If projections for 1997 look optimistic their achievement will require much tighter overhead control than has taken place in the past. Although the sales targets look ambitious, the company has a good track record of achieving good sales increases in the past.

Turning now to the proposition itself. Given his income and despite his age, Lee should be able to raise the extra mortgage he suggests so the main issue is whether the company can carry the extra debt burden. There is headroom within the overdraft facility to accommodate £100k but this will almost certainly create a hard core and it will be better to fund this element by way of loan. The deal will require cash outflow in terms of interest and loan repayments of circa £50k, against which can be set net directors' salary savings of £60k – last year say £85k less a book-keeper's salary of £25k. Repayment does therefore look theoretical possible.

Gearing would rise significantly:

	£
1996 Net Debt	148,088
Add New Debt	300,000
	448,088
1996 NTAs	525,189
Less buy back	300,000
	225,189

So net gearing will be nearly 200%. The new capital structure will be uncomfortable. What is needed is a detailed business plan going forward with sensitivity analysis.

As security in the new scenario only once debtor cover would be available and there would be less than two times current asset cover, so security is thin. Moreover as a wholesaler the business is at high risk of reservation of title in relation to the stock. Given the level of gearing and the thin security cover, Lee's guarantee looks necessary, supported by the equity in his house which will amount to £210k after the re-mortgage.

This is a marginal proposition which could be argued either way. Repayment looks feasible but gearing and security are uncomfortable and this tends to suggest that the price being paid by Lee is too high. He should be advised to go away and renegotiate the price. If an absolute reduction is not achievable some of the consideration could be deferred on to an 'earn out' basis.

Whatever the decision, what is required is a detailed business plan, probably produced with the assistance of outside accountants.

6

MAKING CREDIT DECISIONS

Objectives

By the time you have read this chapter you should be able to:

● Have a wider understanding of the basic principles of corporate lending.

● Have a greater understanding of what lies behind the figures used in financial appraisal.

The joint authors to this book were involved in many corporate credit decisions during their careers with Barclays Bank and were also active in Line Management training. Based on our experiences we would suggest that the key areas of decision making are as follows. These thoughts were confirmed by C. N. Rouse FCIB in his Chartered Institute of Bankers publication *Bankers' Lending Techniques* first published in 1989.

The areas covered in a corporate lending proposition are:

The key areas:

● Markets

● Resources

● Management

Followed by:

The interpretation of money numbers in financial reporting:

● the significance of net worth and gearing

● the financial assessment of risk

● the creation of assets

● inflation and money numbers

● the ability to repay

    and

● an assessment of the quality of management.

An assessment of the quality of the management of the business is of prime importance and should follow an appraisal of all the performance areas of the business so that our judgement can be as objective as possible. Management is considered more fully in Chapter 4.

The concept of balance-sheet lending has much less credibility when we see the extent to which the values of assets fall away upon the failure of a business.

The basic points that should be covered in any lending proposition are:

- The nature of the business

- Purpose

- Repayment

- Historical performance

- Security/Collateral

We need to be aware that PROFITS can only be created by SALES TURNOVER.

There is a danger that we can become too security conscious, concentrating too much on asset values, and forget what it is that makes assets valuable – their ability to generate profitable business. An evaluation of markets, products and competition represents a dynamic understanding of the opportunities for the future/chances of survival. We then need to evaluate what resources, physical and people, a company has to meet the challenge of the market place.

The money numbers of financial reporting are a way of expressing only some of the business realities. We must be able to assess the marketplace for customers' products and services.

Difficult though this is, the much greater challenge faced by a lending banker is that he has not only to understand the business as it is today, but also predict the future trading prospects. Any lending decision must involve predictions of the future.

6.1   The Lending Decision

Predicting the Future

Markets   What markets are expected to be available?

Resources   What resources will be required?

Management   How capable are they to cope with the future?

If we are in the business of predicting the future – what is the relevance of the past? Experience has found that many plans and budgets are accepted by lending bankers in support of applications that are quite irreconcilable with the past performance of the business. The past may not necessarily be a guide to the future, but there must be good reasons why the future will differ from the past.

Predicting the future and an evaluation of:

- Markets
- Resources
- Management

are the foundation blocks of the analysis.

Lending bankers spend many hours each year analysing historical accounts. All this effort is wasted unless the information obtained is interpreted to help us to predict the future. Every analysis of historical accounts should lead to questions about the future.

Historical Accounts

What trends are shown? What is the effect of extrapolating the trends into the future?

Do the forecasts show a change in:
●   Trends
●   Sales
●   Profitability
●   Cash position?

If so, question closely. Why should the future be better than the past?

Let us now look at one of the key sources of historical information – the financial accounts and other financial reports.

The Lending Banker and Profit

A business has value in proportion to the profits it will generate. This valuation is of little relevance to the bank lender because he does not participate in profits. He seeks only to get his money back plus a margin. The lender is, however, very concerned about future profits – because profitability generates cash flow and lendings are repaid from future cash flows.

If we ask ourselves what are the most critical factor that will determine whether a company survives or fails we may identify a number of answers. The most obvious areas are sales and profitability. A company with high and increasing sales can fail due to overtrading, or where sales are at below cost, and a profitable company can run out of cash – as with overtrading.

Overtrading

This occurs when a firm conducts a volume of trade far in excess of that justified by shareholders' funds so that the financing of current assets is over dependent on outside finance.

More companies fail through undertrading than through overtrading. Undertrading occurs when the assets cannot be sufficiently utilized to generate sales and cash.

Survival is determined by:

Adequate Cash Flows

Every business needs to have both profit and liquidity objectives. These two objectives have to be compatible with each other. We usually define **cash flow** as:

Net profit after tax adding back non-cash items – depreciation being the most common.

CASH FLOW is the prime source of debt repayment, of investment in fixed assets, of financing growth in working capital and of paying interest and dividends. Lending bankers know an increase in depreciation reduces reported profit. Cash flow is really profit *before* depreciation and any other non-cash charge and, therefore, changes in depreciation charged will not affect a company's cash flow.

Before looking further at the concept of cash flow, let us examine the construction of the balance sheet. Initially we may examine the:

Net Worth/Net Tangible Asset Value/Customer's Stake

and define this as:

- original capital, subsequent capital injections and retained profits

  or

- the difference between total assets and total non-shareholder liabilities.

It indicates the size of the financial stake of the shareholders in the business.

The benefit of a large equity base is:

(a) It evidences shareholder commitment.

(b) It reduces the risk to the lending banker.

Commitment

The customer must have a big enough stake in the business so that real financial loss will ensue if the business fails. This is particularly true of start-up businesses where the temptation is to walk away if greater than anticipated problems are encountered.

Risk

> '*Net worth shown in the balance sheet is important because it represents a margin or buffer which stands between creditors and disaster. It is the stake the proprietors have in the business and would all have to be lost before creditors suffer.*'
>
> from *Interpretation of Balance Sheets*   Hutchinson

Because a balance sheet is based on costs, not values, net worth ceases to have any meaning when disaster strikes. Whatever creditors are able to recover will be determined by the saleability of the assets. Net worth is determined critically by asset values.

On liquidation, a balance sheet disintegrates and becomes little more than a list of accounting liabilities and assets. Most of the latter will have liquidation values that bear no resemblance to the monetary numbers that appeared in the balance sheet.

A company with large net worth might have most of its assets as specialized machinery which no other company would want to acquire. On the other hand, a company with little net worth may have assets consisting almost entirely of good debtors and readily saleable stock. Lending bankers customarily measure net worth against borrowings to produce the gearing ratio.

Note that the ratio debt/equity or borrowings/shareholders funds are often described as the capital or financial gearing ratio.

As we saw in Chapter 2 a typical definition of **capital gearing** is:

All borrowings from the bank

All borrowings from other banks and financial institutions

Hire purchase/capitalized leases

Mortgages

Debentures

Directors' loans

Inter-group debt

The calculation excludes:

Trade, expense and sundry creditors

Tax

Dividends

Capital gearing developed initially as an investment concept: the proportion of share capital to long term debt. Since debt carries less risk than equity, the required return on debt will be lower and the introduction of debt thus serves to reduce the average cost of capital.

Having made the calculation we must then consider what ratio of capital gearing should we regard as acceptable. In some cases 1:1 may be considerably too high and, in other cases, gearing levels over 1:1 may be manageable. It will depend how volatile profits are, volatility being defined as the extent to which profits are sensitive to changes in sales turnover. This is determined by the level of:

Operational Gearing

To explain what is meant by operational gearing, we need to consider the relationship between risk and differing company cost structures.

The critical question relating to risk is to establish to what extent costs reduce as sales decline. This will indicate whether variable costs account for a large proportion of sales revenue. Operational gearing is determined by the relationship between fixed costs, variable costs and net profit, where fixed costs are incurred regardless of sales turnover and variable costs are directly proportional to sales.

Let us now consider two businesses with different cost structures. The first is an engineering company selling high-value added machine tool parts, the other is a supermarket business.

	Engineering Business	Supermarket Business
	£	£
Sales	200,000	1,200,000
Direct Costs		
Labour	50,000	
Depreciation/		
Leasing	50,000	
Materials	20,000	1,100,000
Cost of Goods Sold	120,000	1,100,000
Gross Profit	80,000	100,000
Overhead		
Expenses	60,000	80,000
Net Profit	20,000	20,000

Which company is the more sensitive to a decline in sales; e.g. if sales fell by 15%, which would show the greater fall in profit?

This question cannot be answered without knowing which costs would decrease as sales declined. We have to ask which costs are fixed and which are variable – what costs fall away with decreasing sales and which stay fixed irrespective of the level of activity.

The split between variable and fixed cost for both companies is shown below:

	Engineering Business	Supermarket Business
	£	£
Sales	200,000	1,200,000
Less: Variable Costs:		
Materials	20,000	1,100,000
Contribution	180,000	100,000
Less:		
Fixed Costs	160,000	80,000
Net Profit	20,000	20,000

Material costs in both these companies are regarded over the short term as being the only variable costs. The labour cost in the engineering business is skilled and would be laid off only if business declined considerably.

What would each company's profit be if sales fell by 15%? Only variable costs would fall by 15%.

If sales fell by 15%

	Engineering	Supermarket
Sales	170,000	1,020,000
Less:	.	
Variable Costs	17,000	935,000
Contribution	153,000	85,000
Less:		
Fixed Costs	160,000	80,000
Net Profit/(Loss)	(7,000)	5,000
Previously	20,000	20,000

It can be seen that the engineering business is profit-sensitive to sales, because it has a cost structure of high fixed costs. Very little of its costs reduce with declining sales. Variable costs are a low proportion of sales revenue.

If we calculate the breakeven level of sales using the formula of:

Fixed Costs x Sales ، Contribution = Breakeven Level of Sales turnover

we see:

£160,000 x £170,00 ÷ £153,000 = £178,000

The breakeven point is £178,000.

On sales of £170,000, £8,000 below breakeven point, a loss of £7,000 is made. The operational gearing is so severe that profit is affected dramatically with relatively small changes in sales turnover.

If we sought to finance this type of business with a high proportion of debt (high capital gearing), we would impose additional cost by virtue of the interest charges, thus making the business more vulnerable and increasing the risk to shareholders and creditors. This is why manufacturing companies, which are usually more capital intensive than service companies, are expected to have a lower levels of capital gearing.

Now let us look at the Supermarket business. The profit on £1.2m sales is £20,000, the same profit as shown by engineering business on sales of £200,000. This business is less sensitive to changes in volume because for every £1.00 of sales that are lost it loses 91.6p of costs.

Lendings to businesses of this type would often be primarily to assist in the financing of fast-moving stock. If controls are good, the demand for finance should decline as sales decline. Higher gearing levels could be acceptable. If the company's stock control system is good, interest would effectively be a variable cost because as sales declined the stock cover required in terms of days sales would result in a lower financing requirement.

Although profits in this type of business are not sensitive to volume changes, they are sensitive to changes in gross profit margin. The current gross profit margin calculated using the formula:

Gross Profit x 100 ÷ Sales = Gross Profit Margin

shows

£100,000 x 100 ÷ £1,200,000 = 8.3%

If we calculate the breakeven level of sales turnover following a fall in sales of 15% we find:

£80,000 x £1,020,000 ÷ £85,000 = £816,000

As a bank lender, we are in the high-volume low-margin business. An erosion of gross margin has a very severe impact upon our profitability. We have to remember that gearing must be related to the cost structure of a business. Can it take the risk of adding to its existing fixed costs?

When lending to a highly geared company, we need a wide margin of safety, i.e the margin between breakeven point and current or planned sales. If lending to a company with low operational gearing, we should examine:

(1)   The competitive situation, i.e. what pressure could the gross margin come under?

(2)   The company's ability to monitor the gross margin.

One of the main weakness of capital gearing as a measure of risk is that it is based on balance-sheet values at one moment in time. A more dynamic lending risk ratio is interest cover that measures the number of times pre-tax pre-interest profit covers interest charges. It provides a measure of the margin of safety before profits fail to cover interest charges.

This is a useful ratio that was covered in Chapter 4 and is widely used but, like every ratio, it does have its limitations. Low interest cover makes a company vulnerable to rising interest rates or falling profits, as well as having implications about the sufficiency of retained profits to finance other areas of the business, and debt repayment.

Measures of gearing, both capital and operational, provide an indication of the risk to a company of adding to its existing fixed costs by additional interest charges.

We can consider vulnerability by asking questions such as:

What if sales fall by 20%?

What if gross margin falls by 2 %?

This technique is known as **Sensitivity Analysis**.

A company would clearly be at risk if sales declined sharply. But, it tells us nothing about the factors that could cause such a decline or their likelihood of occurring. Therefore, a careful analysis – based on a SWOT approach – to assess the likelihood of the risks becoming real threats is required.

Some risks are merely possibilities. Others are bound at some time to occur. These latter risks are the ones associated with the cyclical nature of many businesses. The lending banker's customary three years' balance sheets are inadequate to span the business cycle.

A company's best defences against recessionary downturn are:

(a) A strong balance sheet with high equity and good liquidity;

(b) Strong margins in favourable conditions where a major reduction would still to leave company in profit;

(c) Tight control over costs and efficiency;

(d) Tight control over current assets to allow a downward adjustment if recession threatens.

Poor management information systems often hinder the successful monitoring of the changing environment. Budgetary control being a historical technique is not adequate for such control. A company must be continuously forecasting and re-forecasting during a budget period.

For some customers, the order book is a significant monitoring device. Is it increasing/decreasing? How do orders taken this week compare with orders taken last week etc.?

We should ensure that our customers consider:

(a) How far could profits (and cash flows) could fall in a downturn.

(b) To what extent and how quickly current assets could be turned into cash to ensure repayment and servicing of borrowings.

(c) How quickly capital expenditures could be reduced in order to maintain viability.

(c) How quickly fixed assets could be sold in an emergency. The important factors are the marketability of the assets and the levels of second-hand values.

Having briefly looked at cost structures, risk implications and the effect of volume changes on profit, let us now examine the cash flow of the engineering business.

		£
Sales		200,000
Direct Costs		
Labour	50,000	
Depreciation/		
Leasing	50,000	
Materials	20,000	
Cost of Goods Sold		120,000
Gross Profit		80,000
Overhead Expenses		60,000
Net Profit		20,000

If we seek to establish the cash flow of the business, the answer will depend on whether the depreciation/leasing charge is depreciation or gearing. If it is all depreciation, the sum of £50,000 may be added back to the net profit, giving a sum of £70,000. If all leasing, which is a charge against profitability, then the cash flow would be £20,000.

We always need to look at the quality of profits. A company reporting losses but with a high depreciation charge could have a positive cash flow. Depreciation is a method of releasing a cost held as an asset in the balance sheet steadily through the profit and loss account as an expense. Depreciation arises out of the 'matching' concept in accountancy, that expense should be matched against the sales revenue to which it relates.

Accountants argue that if a machine will generate production and, thus, sales revenue for 10 years, its cost should be charged against sales revenue over those 10 years and not expensed in full for the profit and loss account in the year that it is purchased.

It is sometimes thought that depreciation creates a reserve for replacement. This is a common misunderstanding. An alternative to depreciation would be to charge the cost in full when the asset is bought, rather than sharing it out over several periods. Clearly, expensing a cost to the profit and loss account cannot create a reserve. Depreciation is merely delaying recognition of a cost. The timing of the release of assets as expenses is a fundamental problem in accounting.

Current assets increase in volume and money terms, only partly financed by trade creditors (if you are not a supermarket). The financing 'gap' becomes increasingly large.

Let us now consider two other areas:

- The structure of borrowings
- The ability to repay

To address these areas we need to resolve whether the borrowing is to short term, medium term or long term. What would determine the term of lending?

1) The purpose
2) The cash flow projections

We should attempt to match the period of the facility to the time during which the asset or assets will work for the business.

What about the overdraft facility? It is usually requested:

1) To assist with working capital finance/finance current assets
2) To cover temporary cash fluctuations

Why is the overdraft considered suitable for working capital financing when, in many companies – especially those with a stable pattern of business – the working capital requirement is as fixed as the fixed capital requirement? In those circumstances, the account will show only small net cash movement swings each month.

Assuming a company had a positive cash flow, what could pre-emp[t] operations reducing the overdraft? The reasons could be:

1) Increases in current assets

2) Fixed asset purchases

3) Repayment of loans

4) Reducing creditor positions

Repayment will not come from profits or, indeed, from cash flow if these other factors absorb cash – because the bank account is the residual funding facility.

The mix of current and capital, expense and income entries passing through the account make analysis of cash flows particularly important – to understand why there is a particular trend or why swings have disappeared. The fact that the bank account is the residual balancing item becomes very useful in determining the cash requirement by using a projected balance sheet. If a profit and cash budget can be drawn up, then so can a projected balance sheet.

6.2   Test for Adequacy of Cash Flow

Based on profit and asset projections draw up a projected balance sheet. If growth is projected, calculate increased current asset positions. Allow reasonable increase in creditor support. Calculate the fixed asset increases, net of specific financing. The balancing figure in the projected balance sheet is 'the bank balance.' We can then see whether the business is a cash generator or a cash consumer.

We should remember that profit is an accounting concept – only cash repays the bank, and the cash flow generated can easily be absorbed elsewhere.

Finally, the topic we have emphasized before and many of us would consider the most vital.

6.3   Management

It is extremely difficult to judge a man or management team quickly. A good case can be made for extreme caution in this area. If we are to assess the quality of management effectively, the assessment must be made only after there have been searching enquiries into all areas of the business operations.

What preliminaries would allow an adequate assessment of management or 'the man' to be made? After:

● visits have been made to company premises

● discussions have taken place with subordinates

● we have seen how well the business is run

● we have evaluated his attitude to customers and employees

Business Lending

...ound, track record and experience

...ves and his lifestyle

...derstands all facets of he has his business

...can make an objective evaluation.

...y and particularly before committing thoughts to paper
...nto a logical sequence. The following is intended as a
...to consider. Not all the areas will be appropriate for

A.   Introduction

1.   Brief History

Brief history of the company, its reputation and experience. In the case of a group structure a family tree should be provided showing details of interrelated shareholdings. The company(ies) to whom the bank are lending must always be clearly defined.

2.   Management

a)   Age, health, experience, expertise.

b)   Assess performance/ability/integrity.

c)   Depth – balanced management team – continuity/succession.

3.   Product/Service, Market and Trading Outlook

a)   Details of the product or service.

b)   What is the present order book position?

c)   Is the order book static, increasing or decreasing?

d)   Is the company dependent on a few suppliers?

e)   Are sales dominated by any one customer?

f)   What is the life cycle of the product/service? At what stage is the customer in the product life cycle?

g)   What is the competition?

4.   Premises/Machinery/Vehicles – Major Items

a)   Age, condition and life expectancy. Suitability for purpose used?

b)   Location.

c)   Adequacy.

d)   Insurance/depreciation.

5. Labour

a)   Skilled, availability/Industrial relations record.

B.   Trading Performance

1.   Audited Accounts

a)   Comment on any significant changes in the figures or ratios.

b)   Liquidity/Cash generation. Highlight salient features.

c)   Other borrowed money/facilities.

d)   Hidden assets.

e)   Specific comment required if accounts are more than 12 months old.

2.   Trading since Last Audited Accounts

a)   What management information systems exist?

b)   Do directors monitor performance against budgets?

c)   If there are no management accounts, what do the directors say has happened and is this supported by the run of the bank account? Do they have effective control?

C.   Conduct of Account

1.   Conditions of Previous Sanction Met?

a)   Have the facilities been respected?

b)   Has the security formula set (if appropriate) been met?

c)   Are management accounts and debenture figures produced to the bank on time?

2.   Have the Facility Letter Covenants been Observed?

D.   Requirements

1.   Amount

a) Comment if appropriate, where there is a loan and overdraft required.

b) Is the amount required in line with the customer's stake?

c) Is the customer seeking headroom?

2.   Purpose

Why is the borrowing required? Be specific.

3.   Term

State the term required for each facility.

4. **Ability to Repay and Source of Repayment**

    a)   Is the business viable?

    b)   Can the borrowing be serviced and capital repayments met by cash generated from trading?

    c)   Is there a hard-core overdraft? If so, why and can this be isolated onto a loan?

    d)   Are there any other financial commitments nearing completion or commencing in the near future?

5. **Budgets and Cashflow Forecast**

    a)   Are the assumptions realistic bearing in mind the present climate?

    b)   Have the assumptions made been tested?

    c)   What is the margin of safety?

    d)   Have past forecasts been accurate?

E.   Security

a)   Draw attention to any significant changes.

b)   Ensure that security is shown in full on any schedule.

c)   Are valuations extended on properties held as security realistic? Who undertook the valuations and when?

e)   Is there a debenture formula? What is the system for the reporting to the bank of the debenture figures?

F.   Monitoring and Control

Elaborate on proposals for monitoring of information and control of account.

G.   Remuneration

a)   **Interest Rates**
Is the interest rate correct for the type of lending and the strength of the customer? Comment on reasons for any changes recommended.

b)   **Commission**
State terms. Comment if full recovery not to be obtained.

c)   **Fees**
State basis of negotiation and amounts generated.

H.   Business Development Opportunities

What other opportunities are there for introducing other services available from the bank or the group?

I   Conclusion

This section should bring together the weak and the strong points of the application, and end with a recommendation to the credit controller/credit committee.

Now let us look at a lending case study.

Case Study 7 – Western Trading Company Ltd

The Western Trading Company Ltd designs and supplies men's fashion clothing. The company banks with one of your competitors. The directors have become disenchanted with their present bankers and have called to see you to ask whether you would be prepared to take over the company's account and grant an overdraft facility of £100,000.

The company commenced trading on 1 March 1993 and the directors have provided you with audited accounts for their first year and draft figures for the following 6 months.

The company sells its clothing mainly to leading retailers with several outlets. The garments are manufactured by sub-contractors, held in stock by them, and delivered direct to the stores. All invoices are factored and the factoring company advances up to 55% of the company's outstanding debtors. It has a fixed charge on book debts but would be willing to allow the bank a second charge.

In conversation with the directors, you establish that the factoring company has refused to increase its lending percentage and that the overdraft is needed to meet future expansion needs. Its present bank has refused to grant overdrafts above £10,000.

The company does not produce management accounts or forward projections but needs the extra facility to meet an expanding order book. The directors are willing to give you a debenture (ranking behind the factoring company facility) and their personal guarantees for £100,000.

Required:

Analyse the business and give, with reasons, the response you would make to the company.

The Western Trading Company Ltd: Balance Sheet

	28 February 1994				31 August 1994 (draft)	
	£	£	£	£	£	£
Fixes Assets						
Leasehold Improvements		1,690			1,690	
Motor Vehicles		10,162			13,612	
Fixtures and Fittings		7,558	19,410		16,182	31,484
Current Assets						
Cash	57,804			418		
Debtors	222,792			438,296		
Stock	106,208	386,804		202,882	641,596	
Current Liabilities						
Factoring Advances	40,228			231,570		
Creditors	325,162			311,752		
VAT	7,564			37,226		
Directors' Loans	5,000			5,000		
Overdraft	-			9,214		
Tax	6,296	384,250		6,296	601,058	
Net Current Assets			2,554			40,538
			21,964			72,022
Financed By:						
Share Capital			5,000			5,000
Profit and Loss Account			16,964			67,022
			21,964			72,022

Profit and Loss Summary

	12 Months to 28 February 1994	6 Months to 31 August 1994 (Draft)
	£	£
Sales	763,406	1,129,178
Gross Profit	164,792	256,424
Purchases	598,614	872,754
Directors' Remuneration	25,800	17,000
Interest Paid	7,375	8,266
Profit before Tax	20,010	50,058

Accounting Ratios

	28 February 1994	31 August 1994
Net Gearing % (directors' loans treated as capital)	–	313
Current Ratio	1.01:1	1.07:1
Acid Test	0.73:1	0.73:1
Credit Given (days)	107	71
Credit Taken (days)	198	130
Stock Turnover (days)	65	42
Gross Margin %	21.6	22.7
Net Margin %	2.6	4.4
Interest Cover (times)	3.7	7.1

Suggested Solution: Western Trading Company Ltd

This business is being offered to the bank 'off the street' so caution is needed. This is particularly the case because it has been in existence only a very short time.

In the short timescale the achievement of the directors in building up sales is not inconsiderable. They must have flair and/or marketing skill. Moreover, the fact that they have obtained a factoring facility for a rag trade business – a type of business factors do not like – says something about their persuasiveness. It also reflects a reasonable degree of financial sophistication because the company would not have been able to obtain finance to the extent it has in any other way. The fashion clothing business is a high-risk industry with many failures, so the lack of a formal plan for the future and projections/management accounts is a concern.

Looking at the historic accounts, it needs to be appreciated that this is a seasonal business with spring and autumn peaks, which could affect ratio comparison, although in this instance the dates are probably at similar points for their relative seasons. The business is very liquid and the high gearing is a concern. In fact the business would probably collapse if the factoring facility was withdrawn. Moreover, the liquidity position is worsening as the business expands.

In February 1994, creditors, VAT and tax could fund stock and debtors, but by August there was a big shortfall. All the indications are that the borrowing requirement will increase steadily with further expansion, which now needs to be controlled.

It looks very much as though the factoring facility is already near full utilization.

The gross profit margin has held up well given the rapid expansion, and the improvements in net margin and interest cover suggest good overhead control. Directors' remuneration has been modest.

The security offered is unlikely to be adequate. Lending against a second charge on debtors behind a factoring company is highly unattractive. If 55% lending is safe for the factors (who are the professionals in lending against debtors) the bank should not lend any more. Effectively the bank will be lending against the stock, which would have to be heavily discounted in a receivership. We do not know what the directors' guarantees are worth but these too would not be attractive security unless backed by charged, readily realizable security.

The business overall is probably not bad but its expansion is out of control and the bank should not be in a hurry to take it over. Any further working capital need ought to be financed by the factoring company. It might be worth having our own bank's factoring company have a look at the proposition to see if it would be prepared to advance more against the debtors, and another alternative might be to reconsider the proposition with the benefit of the government's Loan Guarantee Scheme.

Case Study 8 – James the Grocer

James the Grocer wishes to expand his retail supermarket business by acquiring the premises next door. The cost of the new premises will be £75,000 and Mr James is requesting a loan of £45,000. However it is anticipated that extra costs including legal, building and shop fittings will amount to £11,000.

You are asked to consider whether the company can afford to borrow £56,000 given an interest rate of 17%.

James the Grocer Ltd: Trading and Profit and Loss Accounts

	Two Years Ago £	Last Year £	This Year £
Sales	451,053	511,248	593,489
Less:			
Cost of Goods Sold	384,243	439,162	514,553
Gross Profit	66,810	72,806	78,936
	14.8%	14.1%	13.3%
Rent	17,500	17,500	17,500
Rates and Water	3,240	3,681	4,156
Wages and National Insurance	19,857	20,528	23,825
Heating and Lighting	2,086	2,450	2,937
Postage and Telephone	791	869	917
Motor and Travelling Expenses	978	1,317	1,189
Repairs and Renewals	737	285	341
Bus Advertising	4,000	4,000	4,000
Directors' Remuneration	9,000	10,500	12,000
Sundry Trade Expenses	889	1,011	393
Accountancy and Audit Fees	500	550	600
Bank Charges	74	87	105
Depreciation - Shop Fittings	2,150	2,150	2,150
– Motor Van	1,000	1,000	1,000
	62,802	65,928	71,113
Net Profit before Tax	4,008	6,158	7,823
Less Corporation Tax	1,650	2,568	2,707
Retained Profit for the Year	2,358	3,590	5,116
Retained Profits brought forward	9,871	12,229	15,819
Retained Profits carried forward	12,229	15,819	20,935

James the Grocer Ltd: Fixed Assets	Two Years Ago		One Year Ago		Now	
	£	£	£	£	£	£
Fixed Assets						
Leasehold Premises at Cost		2,150		2,150		2,150
Goodwill		20,000		20,000		20,000
Shop Fitting at Cost	21,500		21,500		21,500	
Less:						
Depreciation	4,300	17,200	6,450	15,050	8,600	12,900
Motor Van at Cost	5,000		5,000		5,000	
Less:						
Depreciation	1,000	4,000	2,000	3,000	3,000	2,000
Current Assets						
Stock	22,150		24,817		33,724	
Debtors	11,897		14,632		18,150	
Cash and Bank	6,857		15,424		22,154	
	40,904		54,873		74,028	
Less:						
Current Liabilities						
Creditors	50,247		54,897		66,449	
Accrued Expenses	5,128		6,789		5,987	
Corporation Tax	1,650		2,568		2,707	
	57,025		64,254		75,143	
		(16,121)		(9,381)		(1,115)
		(27,229)		(30,189)		(35,935)
Representing						
Share Capital						
Authorized, Issued and Fully Paid						
15,000 shares of £1 each		15,000		15,000		15,000
Retained Profits		12,229		15,819		20,935
		27,229		30,819		35,935

James The Grocer - Suggested Solution

Some readers may recall having seen this case study featured on an *ifs* video. The project is to take the opportunity of acquiring the premises next door to expand the retail supermarket business.

At first glance, the balance sheets show an adverse liquidity position (current assets minus current liabilities). However, this can be typical of many retail supermarkets where the stock is being turned over quicker than the payment terms to suppliers.

Also, there is a healthy and accumulating cash balance. Net worth is improving through profit retentions and the business has no bank debt. Turning to trading: although values have been increasing, there is a small deterioration in the gross profit margin – possibly due to more sales at lower prices strategy. The resultant profits are low and do not seem sufficient to meet the projected loan costs (£56,000 @ 17%).

However, James has been a long-standing customer and upon enquiry he explains that business advertising of £4,000 will not re-occur and he is of course expecting extra sales from the expanded unit space. Restating the profit and adding back depreciation will generate sufficient cash flow to service the loan.

Case Study 9 – Tubular Glass Ltd

Tubular Glass Ltd has banked with your bank for over 25 years. It manufactures and sells specialist glassware products, which are used to measure liquids to a high degree of accuracy. The main customers are scientific laboratories, universities, schools etc. Over recent years, the company has suffered increased competition from plastic products which, although less accurate, are much cheaper to make and distribute. (Packaging is a major cost for the company.) Losses have been made and, although the company has stayed comfortably within its overdraft limit of £350,000, a hard core of £200,000 has developed and is increasing.

The original founder of the company, John Tumbler, is 75. He remains a director, but following his resignation as chairman in March 1995, he no longer takes an active part in its management. The current chairman and managing director is John's son, Michael Tumbler, aged 50. John is steadily transferring his shares in the company to Michael, who now owns 60% to John's 40%.

Although Michael has worked in the company all his working life, he feels that he has not been allowed by his father to fulfil his potential. He believes the company has stagnated recently and needs to change. He is introducing a new packaging system which is cheaper and will improve gross margins in the 1997 financial year. He has also been talking to the public company which owns Tubular's biggest UK competitor for glass products. It is willing to sell this business to Tubular, and Michael Tumbler believes the costs will be as follows:

	£'000
Goodwill	15
Plant and Machinery	31
Patents	8
Stock	85
Legal and Professional Costs	10
	149

In addition, he believes there will be a need for an extra £60,000 for working capital (based on debtors £72,000 and creditors £12,000).

The new business will be integrated within Tubular's existing leasehold premises, where there is surplus capacity. There will be some initial one-off costs, but Tumbler believes the following additional sales and profits should be produced over the next two years:

	Year 1 £'000	Year 2 £'000
Sales	463	400
Gross Profit	163	160
Gross Margin	35.2%	40.0%
Overheads	129	79
Profit before Tax	36	81
Profit Margin	7.8%	20.3%

These figures are in addition to those shown in the company's 1997 budget. Tumbler asks you to increase the company's overdraft facility to £550,000 to accommodate this acquisition. You already have a debenture over the company's assets and an unlimited guarantee from Michael Tumbler supported by a second charge over his house, which has equity of £75,000.

Required:

Set out, in note form, your analysis of the company and its plans. Give, with reasons, the response you would make to the request for an increased overdraft.

Suggested Solution: Tubular Glass Ltd

Managing succession in a family business can be difficult and this question looked at the problems of an underperforming family business, and a plan to do something about it. The company is a long-standing customer so the bank would want to be positive, but the business had clearly been suffering badly for a number of years without much being done about it by the management.

The son's suggestion that it is all his father's fault could be true – recent performance has improved (albeit still a loss) since he took charge. However it is stretching a point to say that he bears no responsibility for what has happened in the past, after all he is 50! It is positive that he is prepared to implement change but the effect of the implementation of the new packaging system has yet to be seen. He is now proposing to buy another business but the acquisition will, among other things, put a strain on the management and the management's current quality is at best unproven.

Questions need to be asked about the sense of making the acquisition. The current product is struggling so does it really make sense to acquire a bigger market share of a reducing market. Could not some sort of diversification be a better strategy?

Despite the company's recent decline, the balance sheet is still quite strong. Gearing is only 42% with a significant element of borrowing being term debt. The proposed acquisition would worsen the position with the capital base being reduced through the acquisition of new intangible assets and the expense involved, while the extra borrowing required would adversely hit gearing, although on a best estimate this would still be only around 71%, which would be acceptable in the short term.

At present liquidity as shown by the current ratio and the acid test is good, but there is evidence of a steady deterioration in the cash position with an increasing hard core and credit taken being extended. One positive sign is the improved stock turnover in 1996 which could be evidence of the son's improved management.

While profitability remains abysmal, the 1996 sales performance looks good in a difficult marketplace and the improved gross margin is a positive sign. However, some caution needs to be exercised over the 1996 figures which are still draft. The budget requires further sales increases which may be tough to achieve in the current marketplace. It is clear that the cost savings to be achieved from the packaging change will be crucial in achieving profitability.

In the meantime, can something be done to reduce overheads and in particular directors' remuneration which looks high now that the father is making little contribution to the business?

Looking at the acquisition a little more closely, the price looks cheap if the long-term profits can be achieved. However, questions such as why the competitors are prepared to sell so cheaply need to be asked. Some sort of accounts for the business being acquired should be seen and there should be some due diligence by, say, Tubular's auditors. The future sales projection looks conservative – implying some further loss of business – so overall the deal looks good if synergies can be achieved and profit added to the existing business.

A major strength for the company in the bank's eyes is the good security cover available. The debenture gives good cover for the existing facilities – 5 times current asset cover including 2.5 times debtor cover as at 31 March 1996. Moreover, the finished stock should be readily saleable in a business such as this.

After the acquisition current asset cover will be as follows:

Debtors	£554,000	+	£72,000	=	£ 626,000
Stock	£563,000	+	£85,000	=	£ 648,000
					£1,274,000

To cover £199,000 + £209,000 = £408,000.

The debtors should be well spread and of good quality so a 1.5 times debtor formula plus stock should be adequate. The son's guarantee and the second charge over his house will provide essentially moral support only but is evidence of commitment.

The proposition is marginal but given evidence of some improvement and the acquisition making business sense, plus the good security cover available, it should be possible to agree facilities. Consideration could be given to factoring/invoice discounting for a large portion of the requirement, but in any event a significant element of the hard core ought to be put on to a medium-term loan to ensure this is reduced over a period.

Summary

By the time you have read this chapter you should be able to:

● Have a wider understanding of the basic principles of corporate lending.

● Have a greater understanding of what lies behind the figures used in financial appraisal.

7

PROBLEMS WITH BUSINESS LENDING

Objectives

After studying this chapter, you should be able to:

● Identify early problems with business lending;

● Define what actions to take;

● Know what action to take to minimize loss on problem advances;

● Understand the role of investigating accountants.

Research has indicated that the bad-debt performance of many banks could have been improved if earlier action had been taken when danger signs first became apparent. Therefore, it is very important to monitor business performance by:

● comparing actual results against projections;

● monitoring debenture figures when appropriate;

● investigating the reasons for any excess or hard-core positions when they appear on the current account.

7.1 Identifying Warning Signs

Recognizing potential problems at an early stage can be assisted by monitoring a company's progress through security formulae and regular financial reviews. However, this may not highlight all the warning signs and security is not always taken from business customers.

Two key warning signs for a business are:

● Pressure on the account

● Irregular changes in the business

Pressure on the Account

● Increase in facilities requested

This may be an indication of poor financial planning.

- Frequent/unauthorized excess positions
  The company should have built in an overdraft headroom limit for exceptional payments, and occurrence of excesses suggest a company's cash flow requirements are altered. Where excesses do not have prior authorization, it suggests that the company does not consider that the excess would be agreed if it made a formal request.

- Cheques returned unpaid (in or out)
  Outwards – The borrower's suppliers may restrict trade credit if this is the case, with a consequent knock-on effect increasing a business's working capital needs.

  Inwards – This may suggest that the borrower is seeking poorer quality of business in order to maintain sales levels.

- Increasing average debit balance (or hard core)

- Rapid increase/decrease in account turnover
  Increase in turnover suggests overtrading, stock disposals and debtor collections.

  Decrease in turnover may occur due to loss of orders or perhaps dual banking.

- Cheques issued in round amounts
  May suggest either cross firing or the holding of payments to appease pressing creditors.

- Delays to receipt of funds
  The company may be having problems fulfilling orders or perhaps its debtors are under cash flow constraints. This may cause a knock-on effect.

Irregular Changes within the Business

- Delays in production figures/late audited accounts
  The company may be having financial management problems or the release of figures may be delayed because the company does not wish to report a deteriorating financial condition.

- Change of auditor/qualified accounts

- Material differences from forecasts to actual figures
  Forecasts can never be wholly accurate, however material divergencies would be such things as unplanned capital expenditure or a substantial reduction in sales over more than one period.

- Financial covenants/security/debenture formula – Are these being met?

- Request for release of personal guarantees/personal security

- Pressure on margins

- Changes in key personnel

- Increased used of special presentations of cheques (in or out)

- Significant increase in preferential creditors
  The non-payment of preferential creditors (e.g. VAT and PAYE). All creditors need to be met on time in accordance with the negotiated terms of trade.

Action Check List

If the above monitoring confirms that there is cause for concern, then you should take prompt action:

- Discuss matters with the customer. Very occasionally warning signs can mislead and you may find that there is no problem.

- Collect as much information as possible. Use CAMPARI and SWOT techniques to assist you in your new assessment.

- Consider what information you have – do you need to know more? Visit the business premises.

- Check the existing security – is it complete and effective? Is additional security available?

- Set objectives for the way forward. At this stage you may have to decide to accept some eventual loss. Investigate what went wrong with the original proposal.

- Obtain the borrower's understanding of, and commitment to, any plans for repayment, particularly timing and amounts. Get agreement in writing if possible.

- Take firm control of the position. If agreements are not carried out by the customer, take speedy and firm action.

- Keep your controlling office advised of the situation.

A summary of warning signs would include:

From Bank Records:
- Interview Notes
- Visit Notes
- Management Accounts
- Unauthorized Excesses
- Additional Facility Requested
- Turnover Increasing
- Turnover Decreasing
- Hard Core
- Unpaid Cheques
- Round-Amount Cheques

- Uncleareds
- Cross-Firing
- Special Collections
- Status Enquiries
- Court Judgments
- Stopped Cheques
- Cash Withdrawals
- Rumours

From Visits to Customers' Premises/Interviews:
- Elusive Directors
- No Long-Term Aims
- Failure to Meet Orders
- Reliance on One Customer
- Diversification
- Delays in Receipts from Debtors
- Requests for Release of Security
- Changes in Terms of Trade
- Two Businesses in One Set of Premises
- Dead Stock
- Creditor Pressure
- Management Changes
- Old Management – No Succession
- Management Team Unbalanced
- Change in Attitude Since Last Meeting
- State of Company Records
- Condition of Equipment/Premises

From Audited Financial Financial Statements:
- Evidence of Other Borrowings
- High Gearing
- Surplus/Net Tangible Asset Value Small

- Losses
- Late
- Still In Draft
- Two Sets
- Change of Auditor
- Qualified
- Other Bankers
- Unusually High Audit Fee
- Re-valued Assets
- Figures Do Not Compare with Management Accounts

From Management Accounts:

- Late
- Sketchy
- Non-Existent
- Security Formula Breached
- Increase in Preferential Creditors
- Targets/Budgets Not Met
- No Assumptions With Forecasts
- Losses
- Loss of Customers
- Customers Not Well Spread
- Pricing By Guesswork

7.2 Remedial Actions

When a company is in difficulty, action will generally need to be taken to improve profitability. However, businesses do not go into liquidation through a lack of profits, they do so because they run out of cash. In the short term therefore the problem company will need to make the best use of the limited cash resources that are available. In order to do this, it will have to ensure that profit margins are set at a level to generate both adequate demand and cash flow. Also that all assets in the business are fully utilized and what assets can be utilized to help improve the cash flow position. The following list gives some ideas to assist cash generation.

Stock

A full review of stock should be undertaken to:

● Concentrate on lines most readily turned into cash.

● Sell off cheaply any static or slow moving lines.

● Seek suppliers who are cheaper or who offer more credit.

● Reduce order quantities by keeping closer control.

● Shorten production runs – this may however affect profitability.

Debtors

● Improve credit vetting before allowing credit.

● Review invoicing system, with the aim of speeding it up.

● Reduce credit terms allowed, if possible (by offering discounts for early payment if necessary).

● Tighten credit control.

● For large orders, seek advance payments of cash.

● Consider factoring or invoice discounting.

Creditors

● Take full credit given and not be tempted by discounts to make early payment.

● Find alternative suppliers with longer credit terms.

● Renegotiate term loans, or other instalment finance, if possible without penalties.

Assets

● Dispose of surplus non-performing assets.

● Consider sales and leaseback.

● Lease or buy using hire purchase rather than pay cash.

Products

● Concentrate on those products that turn over quicker for cash and have the biggest impact on cash flow and profits.

● Drop those products that use up the most cash for production – i.e. are 'cash hungry'. However, consideration must be given to whether contribution to fixed costs will be lost.

● Consider the life cycle of the product.

Labour

- Reduce staffing, if possible.
- Consider sub-contract labour, where staff would be otherwise under-employed.
- Consider short-time working.

The above measures must be considered carefully with regard to redundancy costs/union problems.

Capital Expenditure

- Non-essential new projects to be suspended or postponed.
- Review existing projects.
- Update capital expenditure appraisal techniques.
- Review plans for research.
- Review any advertising costs.

Management

- Can management be trusted to take 'tough' decisions?
- Are management changes needed?
- Does existing management need advice? Would the involvement of investigating accountants help?

7.3   Avoiding Lending Loss

It should be remembered that the key point of any remedial action is to minimize the risk of loss to the bank. There are choices as to the way forward:

Continuing the Banking Relationship

If the provision of banking facilities is still considered acceptable, the following can be undertaken:

- State new terms from this new starting point.
- Restate criteria for the continuing support of your bank (possibly a new facility letter).
- Clearly state your position, with regards to monitoring and control.
- Review facility pricing to reflect the risk.

Most experienced lenders will recognize situations where they have lent more to a borrower to keep a business going. With the benefit of hindsight, it could have been wiser to accept a limited loss on a borrowing rather than lending more to a business that is in difficulties, hoping performance will improve.

Terminating the Banking Relationship

If the on-going provision of banking facilities is not considered a viable route, the following steps could be taken:

- Consider a structured recovery plan, if possible to ensure eventual repayment of the debt.

- Cancel any additional ancillary facilities.

- If currently unsecured, press to place borrowing on a fully secured basis if possible.

- Wind-down banking relationship with a view to exiting from the situation.

- Press for realization of security.

7.4   Using Investigating Accountants

It is always difficult to advise on timing of the appointment of a receiver and manager. Sometimes the company directors will request it; but often it is a case of the company directors hoping for better times and wanting to carry on – while the bank is anxiously looking at the trading of the business and pressure on the bank account.

How best can you protect the bank's position? If it is a hopeless case, then you must act decisively. Delay may cause further deterioration.

If all parties are slightly unsure of their ground, then a useful interim step is to get the company to agree to the appointment of an investigating accountant. His brief will vary, but essentially it is to:

a)   Comment on and analyse recent trading;

b)   Draw up a current statement of affairs;

c)   Comment on the future viability of the business;

c)   Comment on the bank's exposure and security.

The areas of the business to be considered will normally embrace:

- Directors/Shareholders

- Organization Structure/Chart

- Memorandum and Articles of Association

- Bankers, Borrowing Facilities and Security

- Solicitors, Outstanding Litigation, Leases, Licences, Agency/ Commission

- Agreements, Intellectual Property Rights

- Auditors, Accounting Policies, Audit Comment Letters

- Audited Accounts 3 years

- Corporation Tax Computations 3 Years
- Business Plan
- Budgets and Cash Flow Forecasts
- Management Accounts, Information Systems, Ratio Analysis
- Forward Order Book, Work in Progress
- Insurance, Salaries and Pensions
- Terms of Trade
- Credit Control, Debtors Age Analysis
- Internal Control, Security
- Creditors Age Analysis, PAYE, NIC, VAT
- Product Lines
- Product Costings, Gross Contribution, Net Contribution
- Fixed Asset Register, Capital Expenditure, Research and Development
- Trading Locations

The appointee should be an accountant with proven expertise, with knowledge of the particular trade (if possible), and if receivership follows you must feel sure that he will be the man for the job. The investigation can be quick and it may only take from three to five days to get a 'feel' for the business and make a preliminary report. The company directors should cooperate, because it must be also in their interest to know where they stand.

Investigating accountants' reports vary enormously in both volume and style. The following case study is to illustrate.

Case Study 10 – Lendal Holdings Ltd (Problem Loan)

This case study features both pig breeding and the related industry of pig-building manufacturing; both sector activities are undertaken by Lendal.

Readers are encouraged to study this and analyse carefully the accountant's recommendation at the end of the report.

December 1993

The bank's head office credit analyst peered gloomily over the latest bank statements on this account, following on from a terse telephone call from the bank manager branch X. This was not the first call and there had been many difficulties of late. After summarizing the latest figures, the bank account trends were as follows:

Lendal Holdings Ltd: Bank A/C					
	Worst	Best	Avg. Bal.	Limit	Dr T/O
1993 JAN	92,326D	47,578D	66,528D	171,000D	67,268D
FEB	94,368D	35,200D	59,119D	171,000D	50,253D
MAR	82,037D	37,940D	59,864D	171,000D	55,996D
APR	106,384D	77,484D	92,107D	171,000D	43,167D
MAY	124,576D	88,249D	109,173D	171,000D	43,612D
JUN	147,941D	126,024D	138,287D	171,000D	35,540D
JUL	178,824D	134,831D	155,332D	171,000D	75,544D
AUG	196,553D	173,210D	185,590D	171,000D	33,341D
SEP	254,647D	201,254D	222,618D	171,000D	81,607D
OCT	230,183D	186,357D	211,211D	171,000D	66,275D
NOV	260,692D	212,026D	230,033D	171,000D	62,789D
DEC	264,100D	216,027D	241,362D	171,000D	61,718D
	Dr T/O		Av Bal		
1991	384,737D		38,427D		
1992	694,727D		56,453D		
1993	680,342D		129,694D		

The analyst concluded the trends were quite alarming and responded to the Bank Manager:

'You will see from these figures that our bank's position looks very difficult and that I am far from happy with these trends and am bound to conclude that we have a cash flow crisis on our hands!

As you know the bank has paid the account up to £264,000 (Wednesday's overnight position) compared with the limit of £171,000 which actually formally expired last August!!

The company has told you that it is having temporary cash flow problems, but are sure that they are trading profitably. I have reservations because it is difficult to relate the profit claimed with the run of the bank account. Other areas which give cause for concern include:

● I am worried about their financial controls exercised.

● Their continuing hope of an up-turn in the pig industry.

● Are all debtors good?

● Creditors – what level of pressure is being exerted? Are there any writs outstanding?

I have come to the conclusion that we must get a lot closer to their cash flow position in order to decide where we go from here. I know you share a lot of my concerns about where exactly do we stand and I wondered if the way forward would be to call for a visit from an independent accountant who has extensive experience in these types of situations?'

Later, following agreement by the company, an investigating accountant was invited to visit the company – below are extracts of his report following the visit:

Lendal Holdings Ltd: Accountant's Call Report

Group Balance as at 12.1.94	£286,120 Dr
Group Limit	£171,000

As requested, I am writing to report following my visit to the company.

The areas I looked at specifically were:

1. The management accounts produced as at 31 August 1993, and projections to 28 February 1994.

2. Quality of management and controls exercised.

3. The valuation of assets in a forced-sale situation.

4. The products and associated industry.

5. Debtors.

6. Creditors. With the current high level of creditors, is pressure being exerted? Any writs in existence?

7. The American and Canadian investments.

The Product Range

The basic set-up is manufacturing from Leeds Industrial Estate; a pig breeding, weaning and follow-on demonstration unit at Cliffe; a demonstration pig fattening unit at Cleckheaton; a newly established manufacturing business in Iowa, America, and a pig breeding and weaning demonstration unit at Calgary, Canada. Lendal manufactures portable containerized pig units, which gives an environmentally-controlled producing and growing situation for pig farming. The price range varies from £5,050 to a maximum of £27,000 before VAT. The advantage of the units to the farmer is the controlled environment which produces a higher number of weaners per sow per annum to be sold, together with a better food conversion ratio. The products look good, and demand has increased over the years:

1991	Turnover	£524,263
1992	Turnover	£1,095,273

Although the pig industry at the moment is pretty depressed, there is still a reasonable order book for units, together with repeat orders for the replacement of old pig housing units. As regards management, David Ball was away in America and I did not have the opportunity to meet him, and most of my discussions were with Ron Naylor whom I think would be best described as general manager. He is technically competent, and certainly close to the technical production of the different pig units.

Audited Consolidated Balance Sheet as at 31 October 1992

To illustrate the growth of the companies, I have extracted the following figures from the consolidated balance sheet as at 31 October 1991 and 31 October 1992.

	1991	1992
Capital Employed	£95,712	£148,415
Sales Turnover	£524,263	£1,095,273
Trading Profit For Year (before taxation)	£19,330	£57,327
As a percentage of sales	3.68%	5.2%

A more recent picture can be obtained from the following management documents:

Lendal Holdings Ltd and Subsidiary Companies: Management Consolidated Balance Sheets	Actual 31/8/93 £	Projected 29/2/94 £
Sources of Capital Employed		
Authorized	10,000	10,000
Issued and Fully Paid		
1,000 Ordinary Shares of £1.00 Each	1,000	1,000
Reserves	113,824	138,004
	114,824	139,004
Minority Interests in Subsidiary Companies	1,194	1,194
Deferred Taxation	56,000	56,000
Directors' Current Accounts	14,750	14,750
	186,768	210,948
Application of Capital Employed		
Fixed Assets	435,689	447,068
Less Loans	35,160	23,156
	400,529	423,912
Current Assets		
Stock	209,265	210,115
Debtors *	272,313	312,000
Cash in Hand	9	8
	481,587	522,123
Less: Current Liabilities		
Creditors	451,825	405,087
Bank Overdraft	243,525	330,000
	695,350	735,087
Net Current Liabilities	13,763)	(212,964)
	186,768	210,948

* includes USA 99,900 and Canada 142,00

This management balance sheet as at 31 August 1993 has been prepared on the basis of a statement of affairs, and a stocktake was carried out as at the end of August. The figure of £113,824 for reserves was, therefore, a balancing figure. There are no supporting monthly profit and loss, or quarterly profit and loss accounts to support this balance sheet.

The fixed asset valuation at £435,690 is analysed as follows:

Schedule of Fixed Assets – as at 31 August 1993

Group	Total	Land	Buildings	Plant & Machinery	Fixtures & Fittings	Motor Vehicles	Leased Fittings
Written-Down Value	326,742	49,258	132,032	96,102	4,519	35,830	9,000
Sales for Period	(12,880)	-	-	-	-	(3,880)	(9,000)
Additions	154,571	2,876	89,489	31,734	-	30,471	-
	468,434	52,134	221,522	127,837	4,519	62,421	-
Depreciation	32,744	-	-	19,175	64	13,004	-
	435,689	52,134	221,522	108,662	3,955	49,417	-

A total of £121,223 has been expended mainly on buildings, plant and machinery at Cliffe, the main demonstration unit site, and Cleckheaton, the fattening unit site.

Stock

Stock as at 31 August 1993 totalled £209,265 as follows:

Stock & W.I.P. 31/8/93	£209,265

Analysis:

L/Agricultural	76,451
Engineers	72,630
Pigs	56,027
Construction	4,157
	£209,265

This includes £63,000 attributable to work in progress, and the resulting balance of £145,000, some of which is subject to Romalpa terms (reservation of title). The company could not identify the amount so affected. The debtor figure at £272,313 includes the American and Canadian developments at £75,000. Also it is my understanding that a further deduction should be made of £27,000 as a provision for bad and doubtful debts. This reduces the debtor balance to £170,000. The creditor figure at £451,825 includes the American and Canadian ventures, together with preferential creditors of around £30,000. It is not possible to identify the American and Canadian amounts.

Turning now to the projected balance sheet to 29 February 1994. This time the basis of compilation was to estimate profit and the resulting reserves balance, based on the turnover calculation and estimate of the net profit percentage. The problem here is that without a full analysis of overheads, bearing in mind the American and Canadian activities, it is impossible to conclude that the company would have achieved a net profit percentage of around 5%, which would, on a £1.3M turnover projection, give the required level of profit to increase the reserves to the figure quoted at £138,004. The remaining figures have been progressed as can be seen – the debtor figure at £312,000 includes American and Canadian total investment projected of £114,100. The balancing figures on the balance sheet are creditors at £405,087 and bank overdraft at £330,000. The increased bank facility therefore is partly required to make a reduction in the creditor balance. The details of the companies' retained earnings calculation are given:

Retained Earnings

		£
Sales		
Agric. – 21K per week x 26 weeks		546K
Engineering – 4K per week x 26 weeks		104K
		650K
	@ 5% net profit	32.5K
Less:		
Loss on pigs (80 x £4 x 26 weeks)		8.3K
	NET	24.2K

Management Information Available as at 31 December 1993 (at the time of my visit)

Debtors (Gross) - £317,947
Although this will show a lower position of £193,000 after deducting £125,000 for the total American and Canadian investments as at 31 December. From this figure should be deducted £27,000 for provisions, giving the net debtor figure of around £166,000.

Creditors (Gross) - £314,378
This does not include PAYE (estimated 2 months - £30,000) or any accruals. Ron Naylor told me that there had been two writs levied against them, while he was away recently in America, but this had now been cleared up.

Sales turnover to 31 October is estimated at total sales across the group of £1,330,149. This level of activity is up on the previous year's turnover of just over £1M. As mentioned before, no monthly or quarterly profit and loss accounts are compiled and, therefore, the only basis of profit projection would be to estimate at 5% net, giving a projected profit of £66,500, but this is, of course, only feasible if the level of overheads has been contained, and this must be questionable bearing in mind the American and Canadian ventures.

American Venture
This business was set up in America in 1993, and currently operates from a factory of

10,000 sq. ft. in Guttenberg in the State of Iowa. The factory employs 16 people, and they are currently manufacturing two pig units per week. According to Naylor there is a great demand for pig housing in America, particularly in Iowa due to the extremes in climatic conditions – the average number of weaners sold per sow per annum is only 14, whereas with the controlled housing environment in excess of 20 weaners per sow per annum are being obtained at the demonstration unit at Cliffe. Capital was introduced by Lendal UK of $177,013, and capital provided by Double L (American businessman) $105,000. At that time, a line of credit of $70,000 was negotiated with the Security State Bank of Iowa, supported by David Ball. I also understand that Ball purchased a house in Guttenberg for $85,000, on which there is a mortgage of approximately 50%. This house is also held as supporting security by the American bank.

There have been significant changes since that date in that Double L, the American, tended to be unreliable, and Lendal has bought out Double L by paying back the $105,000 for capital, plus $15,000 attributable to stock, giving a total pay out of 120,000 American dollars. This in turn led to an increased line of credit being obtained from the Security State Bank at $130,000, and Naylor told me that this is the maximum that the Security State Bank can lend to a corporate client. Capital employed, shown at $151,026 at a conversion rate of 1.42, gives a figure of £106,356.

The capital injection into America, plus the funds needed to buy out Double L, has meant that Naylor is preparing a business plan for when he intends to revisit America, mid to end of February, to make a presentation to the Iowa Development Credit Corporation and the Norwest Bank to endeavour to raise additional monies to fund the manufacturing operation. He hopes to be able to return some capital back to the UK from this additional funding – I feel this is unlikely, as no bank will be keen to lend additional funds on the basis that funds are to be returned to the UK.

A management balance sheet has been produced for the American investment as at 31 October 1993:

Lendal Holdings USA Ltd: Balance Sheet – 31 October 1993

Sources of Capital Employed

Capital provide by Lendal UK	$177,013.00
Capital provided by Double L	$105,000.00
	$282,013.00
Less setting-up costs	($130,987.00)
	$151,026.00

Application of Capital Employed

Fixed Assets

Leasehold building improvements	35,862.00	
Plant and equipment	21,811.00	
Office, fixtures, fittings and furnishings	17,044.00	$74,717.00

Current Assets

Credit on bank current account	6,236.00	
Stock (10-week purchases)	172,406.00	
Debtors (accounts receivable – 5-week sales)	85,276.00	
	$263,918.00	

Current Liabilities

Creditors (7-week purchases)	117,609.00	
Bank loan	70,000.00	
Deficit on bank current account	-	
	$187,609.00	

Net Current Assets	76,309.00
Company Net Worth	$151,026.00

Canada

Two trial units are located in Calgary, to show the potential of the sow units and early weaning units. No formation statement is yet available for the Lendal Agricultural (Canadian) Ltd position, but I understand that the formation will be as follows:

David Ball	25,000 Canadian dollars already invested by way of the production units.
Pierre Moreau	10,000 Canadian dollars
Alan Toles	10,000 Canadian dollars

On the basis of a 10,000-Canadian dollar investment each, David Ball should have

15,000 Canadian dollars to come back to the UK. At a dollar conversion rate of 1.78, this equates to £8,426. At this stage there is therefore no intention to manufacture in Canada!

Conclusion

It is my opinion that the companies' cash resources have been strained to the maximum, with the subsequent effect on the bank account balance and creditor position. To summarize, during 1993 they have further developed their head office; developed the fattening unit at Cleckheaton; developed the demonstration unit at Cliffe; entered a manufacturing situation in America, and a demonstration unit in Canada.

Asset Valuations

Estimates of valuations would be as follows:

		*Estimated Forced Sale Valuation
Factory Unit 40,000 sq. ft, approx. at £1 per sq. ft. rental over 7 years £280,000		£140,000
House, 4½ acres of land, and pig accommodation for 176 sows to 11 weeks at £1,000 per sow place £176,000		£50,000
		£190,000
Debtors as at 31/12/93	£318,000	
Less USA/Canadian	£125,000	
and provision	£27,000	
NET	£166,000	£80,000
Stock	£209,000	
Less work in progress	£64,000	
(Less Romalpa)**	£145,000	£50,000
		£320,000
Less preferential creditors estimated		£30,000
Less realization costs		£290,000

** Reservation of title by suppliers – Additionally, there is Ball's unlimited guarantee.

* NB: Fixed assets, P and M and motor vehicles discounted

Recommendations as to the way forward:

1. The audited accounts to 31 October 1993 to be produced as a matter of urgency.

2. Quarterly profit and loss figures, together with a stocktake, should be carried out at

31 January 1994, to give an indication of progress for the first three months of the current trading year.

3. There has been no monitoring of liquidity figures, and this must be set up. I would suggest an urgent meeting with Ball, here at my office to discuss the future of his business connection vis-à-vis the cash flow requirements.

4. A short-term cash flow forecast must be produced as a matter of urgency to pinpoint the way ahead, as regards cash requirements, bearing in mind the American and UK manufacturing set-ups.

5. If between the auditors, Blower & Co, and the company, they are unable to come up with the information that is required, I would recommend an independent firm of accountants go in to help to prepare the information which is desperately needed, before it is too late to come up with a rescue plan.

6. It is my opinion that the group of companies is highly geared, cash flow is under extreme pressure and expansion must be slowed down, to give the companies time to generate profits and positive cash flow which needs to be retained within the business to give it a chance to survive.

Case Study Postscript

Remedial action certainly needs to be taken quickly as readers will have seen from the report. Warning signs should have been seen much earlier – particularly from the bank account trends, which show many excess positions and the development of hard-core borrowing.

The cash flow problems were, unfortunately, extremely severe and a few weeks later the borrower went into liquidation.

Case Study 11 – Ashton Baker Marketing Ltd

Ashton Baker Marketing Ltd was established three years ago by an ex-public company marketing executive, Edward Ashton (41), and Colin Baker (42), who previously worked for a major advertising agency. The company provides marketing consultancy and research services. The two directors each own 50% of the company.

The business got off to a slower start than the directors expected and has only just started to make a profit in audited account terms. They have acquired some top-class clients and 38% of their revenue comes from work undertaken for the British subsidiary of the world's largest soft drinks company. A further 18% comes from a major European food company. At present, they are working with 15 different clients.

The company's relationship with your bank has not been an easy one. It has banked with you since it was formed. Originally, you agreed an overdraft facility of £20,000 but this was increased to £40,000 in 1994 to cover cash flow shortages. A hard core developed, and further pressure on the limit resulted in the bank later switching £20,000 onto a 5-year loan, while retaining a £40,000 overdraft limit in return for a full security package of a debenture plus guarantees of £60,000 from each director (supported by second charges over their houses, which have equities of £80,000 and £120,000). Since then, the company has honoured the new arrangement, but a further hard core has developed and there is again pressure on the limit.

The directors call to see you. They are under pressure from creditors to bring payments up to date, and the Inland Revenue in particular are insisting PAYE is kept current. They estimate that they need an extra £20,000 on the overdraft. They believe the business has turned the corner now because, although their accounts for the year to 30 September 1996 show only a small profit, performance for the second half of the year was as follows:

6 months to 30 September 1996

	£	
Sales	222,512	
Gross profit	166,875	(75%)
Net profit	29,700	(13.3%)

They expect October to be their best month ever, because their work-in-progress figure at the end of September was the highest it has ever been, at £31,000, and this should produce a profit of £6,500 when invoiced.

They give you a copy of their 1997 budget, which they believe is conservative, and ask you to lend the additional £20,000 they need.

Required:
Analyse the company's position and set out, with reasons, the response you would make to the request.

Ashton Baker Markting Limited: Profit and Loss Account

	1994	1995	1996	Budget 1997
12 months to 30 September	£	£	£	£
Sales	128,158	208,038	315,588	450,000
Less: market research costs	(23,709)	(50,061)	(88,502)	(110,250)
Gross profit	104,449	157,977	227,086	339,750
Net profit	(19,920)	(43,041)	1,304	67,500
After:				
Depreciation	6,317	9,657	17,363	17,500
Directors' remuneration	28,512	46,657	55,492	100,000
Interest paid	5,988	12,841	11,992	13,522

Balance Sheets as at 30 September

	1994 £	£	1995 £	£	1996 £	£
Current assets						
Cash	1,812		55		362	
Debtors	32,128		30,127		56,785	
Work in progress	5,811	39,751	21,000	51,182	31,000	88,147
Current liabilities						
Creditors	15,700		33,392		53,073	
Bank	17,122		40,499		40,642	
Hire purchase	4,611		14,746		13,046	
Directors' loans	7,457		18,971		1,009	
VAT and PAYE	3,133	(48,023)	21,698	(129,306)	28,082	(135,852)
Net current liabilities		(8,272)		(78,124)		(47,705)
Fixed assets						
Leasehold improvements	19,540		17,635		15,680	
Fixtures and fittings	23,848		24,914		22,833	
Motor vehicles	17,651		54,013		41,775	
Trade marks	1	61,040	5,898	102,460	6,331	86,619
Term liabilities						
Bank loan	–		–		17,320	
Hire purchase	15,188	(15,188)	29,797	(29,797)	16,751	(34,071)
Net assets		37,580		(5,461)		4,843
Financed by:						
Share capital		57,500		57,500		66,500
Profit and loss account		(19,920)		(62,961)		(61,657)
		37,580		(5,461)		4,843

Ashton Baker Marketing Ltd: Accounting Ratios

	1994	1995	1996	Budget 1997
Net gearing (%) (Directors' loans as capital)	78	629	1,493	-
Current ratio	0.83:1	0.40:1	0.65:1	-
Acid test	0.71:1	0.23:1	0.42:1	-
Credit given (days)	92	53	66	-
Credit taken (days)	242	243	219	-
Gross margin (%)	81.5	75.9	72.0	75.5
Net margin (%)	(15.5)	(20.7)	0.4	15.0

Suggested Answer: Ashton Baker Marketing Ltd

This question concerned an undercapitalized new venture which had hit problems.

The bank has seen the business through its difficult early stages and if possible will want to maintain the relationship into the good times if indeed they are coming. The directors have good experience of marketing and ought to complement each other well. However, they had little experience previously of running their own business.

The fact that they have been able to recruit some very high-profile top-name customers is a good indication of the professional quality of their work. However, having so much of their turnover in the hands of a very few customers is a significant risk. There could also be a temptation to underprice work for such high-profile customers.

The directors do not appear to have been good predictors of their performance in the past and the relationship has already been a bumpy ride for the bank – past arrangements have scarcely been honoured. The directors' problems with the Inland Revenue could be life-threatening and will be if a satisfactory arrangement is not now put in place and stuck to.

The current capital structure of the business is poor with almost total reliance on borrowed funds to provide finance. Despite the injection of capital and the profit made in 1996, the shareholders involvement is reduced because of withdrawal of directors loans! The directors appear to have been used to having a good life and not to be able to do without it. The directors' loan withdrawal in fact seems to equate to the cash shortfall in the business so the directors have been putting themselves before the needs of the business.

Liquidity is also poor, although it has shown an improvement in 1996 with both the current ratio and acid test getting better. The underlying problem is that there are more current assets to finance as turnover expands and with the bank facility fixed, the strain has been taken by the creditors who are clearly getting restless.

Profitability at the net level is extremely thin and in any event is heavily dependent on the directors' valuation of work in progress. With so much of the total cost base fixed, the gross margin is extremely healthy and suggests that if the business can indeed increase sales significantly then there should be a good result on the bottom line. This assumes that the overheads are indeed fixed which may be debatable in a business like this.

The sales target does not look unreasonable given recent performance although the directors should not be increasing their remuneration until the business is stable.

The bank needs to see detailed figures to verify that the proposed extra £20k is going to be enough. This information should include aged analysis of debtors and creditors together with a detailed cash flow forecast. Given the directors' lack of financial sophistication, outside accountants ought to be involved and there is a case for a really detailed investigation.

Increased personal guarantees are required and new valuations of the directors' homes should be considered. It is difficult to value the debenture – the debtors are good names but there could be counter claims for breach of contract given the small number of customers involved, which could have a major impact.

The request is clearly unwelcome but the bank is locked in. Provided an independent investigation is agreed and verifies the forecasts, the bank will probably he willing to stay in given the extent of the equities in the directors' houses. However, the business is basically undercapitalized and it would be best for all concerned if the directors found a new equity partner to ease the pressures.

Summary

After studying this chapter, you should be able to:

- Identify early problems with business lending;
- Define what actions to take;
- Know what action to take to minimize loss on problem advances;
- Understand the role of investigating accountants.

8

DIFFERENT TYPES OF BORROWER

Objectives

After studying this chapter, you should be able to:

● Assess lending approaches from a wide range of different industries and professions;

● Use appropriate techniques for evaluating and monitoring these types of proposals;

● Have an appreciation of the borrowing requirements and credit risks associated with different types of borrowers.

8.1   Builders and Property Developers

Introduction

This can be a complex area, with high dependence on good cash flows and careful monitoring by the banker. You will need to be very clear in your mind as to the type of proposal the examiner is presenting and then think carefully about the key risks in both the development and completion stages. In particular, the financing of development stages and control mechanics. Also this sector is particularly prone to economic cycles.

There are three main topic areas:

Contractors – A contractor is a person contracted to carry out building work on someone else's land. The bank is asked to lend money to the contractor to enable commencement of the building work, pending receipt of certified stage payments.

Estate Development – The builder will construct a property or properties on his own land for sale on completion. The bank could be asked to lend for the land purchase and the building costs, with repayment to come from sales, secured by a legal mortgage on the site. To control exposure, the bank will usually want the site developed in stages, so that the proceeds of one stage are coming in before the next stage starts.

Property Investment and Development Advances – The builder or developer buys a house or group of houses, vacant or tenanted. Some will be renovated for sale at a profit and others will provide rental income. As security, the bank takes mortgages over all the properties and looks to rent or sale proceeds for repayment of the advance.

Contract Building

Appraisal of the Proposition

The usual approach will be for the lender to investigate the details of the specific contracts. Reliance could be placed on the level of security available, but difficulties can arise as a result of inadequate capital resources or by inexperience. It is, therefore, vital that the borrower has the capacity and ability to complete the contract.

In evaluating the contract, the lender needs to examine carefully clauses that cover the following:

Variations – although the contract price will be open to adjustment in respect of variations, these could mean that additional finance is required.

Fluctuations in Cost – particularly in longer-term contracts where the builder can be vulnerable to increases in materials' costs and wages during the contractual period.

Penalties – these can be onerous, and the borrower must have the capability and ability to maintain a strict schedule.

Time extensions – to permit extensions due to extraordinary events, such as force majeure etc.

Interim payments – the intervals at which the work will be inspected by the architect and certificates issued in respect of completed work.

Retention funds – usually 5% or 10% of the contract price. This will build up from monies withheld from interim payments, although half of this fund could be released on completion.

Period of final measurement – frequently six months after completion of the work. During this period, the architect or quantity surveyor is required to inspect the work, verify the previous measurements and the amounts certified for payment.

Defects liability period – often six months, to allow latent defects to show through. Any defect must be rectified at the builder's expense.

Nominated sub-contractors and suppliers – these have the right to go to the employer if payment is not received from the builder when due. Where significant sums are involved, it is prudent to check that suppliers and sub-contractors are being paid regularly.

Amount – as previously seen in other units, the lender must be certain that the amount requested will, when added to the borrower's own capital, be sufficient for the contract to be completed.

The contractor should have his own plant and machinery and, therefore, should only need to borrow sufficient working capital to pay for labour and raw materials until payment is received. As security, an assignment of the contract monies could be taken. If the contract is not satisfactorily completed, then no monies will be forthcoming, so you would normally seek additional security.

Estate Development

Advances for estate development occur frequently, because considerable finance is necessarily tied up while the development work is in progress and before sales can occur. The developer's problem is basically that he produces a relatively small but expensive number of units with slow sales. If the builder does not provide all the finance himself, the bank may well wish a local agent to give his opinion whether a quick sale will be achieved, and it will also have to satisfy itself that the builder has sufficient experience to carry the transaction through in a satisfactory way. Finally, the bank will have to make sure that, should difficulties occur, the builder has a reserve of finance that he can use. This cushion of finance is very important.

Developments as Security

If no other security is available and the bank is to take as security the house or houses being built, it will be necessary to consider at what stage the building will be worth enough to be considered of some saleable value. The land is worth something just as a plot and lending 50% of its value should see the bank safe. Digging of foundations, laying footings and doing all the preliminary work is of value to the builder, but if it came to a sale at that point, little beyond site value would be realized.

Lending up to two-thirds of the cost of the work done is a reasonable basis, and if you take into account materials which the builder has provided but not yet used, and the delay in certifying the work done, then the finance provided by the builder for the project would probably be near to one-half of the total.

If the builder is experienced, has a good balance sheet, and adequate capital which can be called upon in emergencies, the bank might well agree to advances in four stages – i.e. plate (to top of walls), roofed, plastered, and finished. In every case, however, both the formula and the stages should be agreed dependent on your risk assessment of both the builder and the development.

The recommended approach for the examination is:

Stages of Development of House in Course of Erection

		Percentage of cost per stage	Percentage of total cost (cumulative)
1.	Damp-course high	8%	8%
2.	First-floor joists fixed	17%	25%
3.	Roofed-in	30%	55%
4.	Plastered (floors laid, door frames erected, etc.)	20%	75%
5.	Glazing and plumbing finished (primer coat of paint)	17.5%	92.5%
6.	Ready for occupation	7.5%	100%

Large-scale Developments

The principles involved above also apply to larger developments. Naturally, there are additional complications in dealing with big developments because when a number of houses are being built at once, the stage of construction of each house varies. It is cheaper to build a large number of houses simultaneously, because labour can be used to its best advantage without wasted time, and materials can be bought in bulk. However, a builder who does not have sufficient capital to build on a vast scale must tailor his development to his resources, with the bank agreeing to the number of houses to be built at one time or when it is reasonable to start another stage of development.

In present-day developments, it is often a condition of local authorities that service roads shall be built for estates. Often a developer asks a bank to advance up to 50% of the cost of service roads and, for an experienced developer, this is reasonable. Local councils often ask for indemnities concerning the construction of service roads. If a bank is asked to join in an indemnity for a builder, it must regard the liability as a real one, because local authorities are strict in seeing that their requirements are met.

Repayment

The final point which must be covered in initial discussions with the builder is the eventual repayment of the advance. A simple plan of the development will be necessary, or, alternatively, the builder can provide a copy of his own plan for the bank's use. For example, a plan such as the following should suffice:

Figure 8.1: Estate Plan

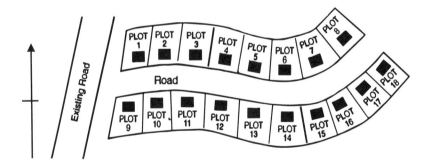

1st stage - plots 1-6. 2nd stage - plots 9-14. 3rd stage - plots 7&8, 15-18
Cost of land £108,000 - i.e. £6,000 per plot. Cost of Services - £18,000

Estate plan

The plan should be marked following regular inspections of the development, so that it can easily be seen how it is proceeding. It will also be necessary for a record sheet to be kept in order to calculate the lending figure in accordance with the formula agreed with the customer.

Sometimes, the individual houses will vary considerably in cost, but more usually the range will not be wide and an average cost per house can be applied.

Record Sheet

By using the following method, it will be seen that tight control can be exercised over the building finance and that, if bank money is being used for purposes other than the building of the estate or the costing has been wrong, this will be evident and quickly noticed. Examining the example record sheet you can observe the development costs of land and the number of houses together with the agreed lending values and formula per house. Also you can see the monitoring of the program in terms of sales agreed and deposits received etc.

A typical record sheet is shown over the page.

Property Advances

The property market tends to be cyclical, with periods of shortage and oversupply of certain types of buildings. In periods of excess supply, rents and property values fall before sufficient buyers or tenants can be found and equilibrium is restored. Property lending can be safe and remunerative to lenders, but lenders need to be very aware of market conditions and the likely prospects and changes.

There are two main types of property lending that are featured in the examination:

● Property investment where lending is provided to purchase an existing property or properties, with repayment coming from the rental income of the property or from the sales of some of the properties.

● Property development where bridging finance is agreed for the borrower to purchase and develop land or property, with repayment coming from the sale of the property or properties.

However, some proposals can be a combination of both.

Property Investment

Purchase of tenanted properties
If a customer wished to borrow to invest in tenanted properties, the loan repayment will come from rental income. The following points should be examined:

● **Margin** – The recommended margin should be at least 15% between rental income and out-goings for interest and capital repayments. A lower margin may be acceptable for a good customer if the tenants are first class and long-standing and there are other sources of income.

● **Tenancy/Lease Agreements** – Agreements should be for longer than the anticipated term of bank borrowing and the tenants should be good quality.

● **Security Cover** – The bank will seek full security cover. Tenanted properties may be

Ref: LS Dyer ISBN 085297 0560: Record Sheet

Yew Tree Estate Development of 18 houses.

Cost of Land: £108,000 (£6,000 per plot).
Cost of Services being paid by Company=£18,000

Building Cost: £11,500/£12,500 per house
Total Cost including plot: £17,500/£18,500 per house

Sale Price: £23,500/£24,500 per house

Lending Limit: £150,000 subject to formula of ½ cost of undeveloped plots plus ⅔ of development costs in three stages (1) Roofed (2) Plastered (3) Finished

Lending formula per house	Cost	Lending Value
½ cost of plots	£6,000	£3,000
⅔ of development costs		
(1) roofed	£9,800/£10,160	£6,520/£6,760
(2) plastered	£13,600/14,320	£9,060/£9,540
(3) finished	£17,500/£18,500	£11,660/£12,320

Reduction Terms £4,000 per house sold

No of Plot	10 April	10 May	10 June	12 July	11 Aug	Sale date	Sale amount £	Date deposit received	Deposit payment received	Date of final paym't	Amount of final paym't	How applied
1	6,000	9,800	13,600	17,500	-	25/5	23,500	28/5 / 14/6	6,000 / 3,800	20/7	13,700	£5,860 to Yew Tree account / £7,840 to current account
2	6,000	9,800	13,600	17,500	-	11/6	23,500	13/6	6,000	14/7	17,500	£9,660 to Yew Tree account / £7,840 to current account
3	6,000	9,800	13,600	17,500		14/7	23,500	19/7	12,000			
4	6,000	10,160	14,320	18,500		13/7	24,500	18/7	6,000			
5	6,000	6,000	10,160	14,320	18,500	13/7	24,500	18/7	6,000			
6	6,000	6,000	6,000	10,160	10,160							
7/8	72,000	72,000	72,000	72,000	72,000							

No of Plots	Costs and Land Value (as per agreed scale)					Sale arranged Date and Amount	Deposit Payment Received	Final Payment Received	How Applied
	10 April	10 May	10 June	12 July	11 August				
Totals Undeveloped Plots	108,000	84,000	78,000	72,000	72,000				
Developing Plots	39,650	65,280	95,480	64,660	79,100				
Lending Value	54,000	68,360	82,520	99,640					
Less:									
Amounts Received	-	-	6,000	15,800	24,000 *				
Sub-Total	54,000	68,360	76,520	83,840	55,100				
Less:									
Reduction on Houses sold	-	-	-	-	8,000 **				
Effective Limit	54,000	68,360	76,520	83,840	47,040				

* This figure is the total of payments received on plots 3, 4 & 5

** This is the agreed reduction of £4,000 per house on plots 1 & 2.

valued conservatively at three times annual rental. However, subject to professional advice and quality of tenants, this figure may be as high as six times annual rental. Vacant, immediately saleable properties could attract a security valuation of up to 80% of a recent professional valuation. If in doubt, seek independent professional valuations, and take additional security if you think it is necessary in the light of the valuation.

Where a borrower has an existing portfolio of tenanted residential properties, with surplus income or security value, the guidelines may be amended, subject to your risk assessment.

Property Development

Property development borrowings are, in effect, bridging loans, but the loan will usually be an open bridge, particularly where renovation is needed before resale. The following points must be satisfied:

- **Capability** – The developer must be capable of carrying out the work within budget and time. If the work is being contracted, the person(s) must be fully proficient and, preferably, doing the work on a fixed-price basis.

- **Planning permission** – May be required for the proposed renovations.

- **Amount** – The amount of the loan must not exceed 66% of the anticipated sale proceeds, to allow for interest, delays in completing renovations, market price changes, and selling costs. Reputable, independent advice is essential in this respect.

- **Security** – First-mortgage security is required, with a wide margin over the amount of the loan, even before renovations.

Case Study 12 – Zhin Nursing Home Project

The following case study features the development of a 72-bedroomed nursing home. Study the project carefully. How would you respond to this request?

Background

Mr Zhin is known to you as a property investor who banks with a competitor. He is said to own properties totalling around £1M. Details of outstanding loans are not known. Zhin calls to see you to advise that he has acquired a property, just outside the city, for £400,000. The site is substantial and he has obtained planning permission to demolish and rebuild as a 72-bedroomed nursing home.

With the help of his business consultant, he has prepared the following:

- projected profit and loss
- projected balance sheet
- notes to the balance sheet
- cash flow projection

● assumptions behind the projections.

The project costs, including a 6-month roll up of interest, total £1.68M. Mr Zhin has £324,000 that he can introduce. He requests a loan of £1.356M over 20 years together with a temporary overdraft of £60k for 12 months.

Projected Profit and Loss Account for the 2 Years Ending 30 June 1992

	1992	1991
	£	£
Fee Income Received	954.720	782.500
Less Expenses:		
Food and Medical Supplies (adjusted for stock)	57,280	46,950
Salaries and National Insurance	343,440	318,000
Water Rates and Insurance	9,288	8,600
Heat and Light	10,800	10,000
Telephone	4,320	4,000
Repairs and Renewals	6,480	6,000
Motor Expenses	3,240	3,000
Postage and Stationery	2,916	2,700
Advertising	6,480	13,500
Laundry and Cleaning	5,184	4,800
Bank Interest and Charges	1,728	6,342
Accountancy	2,700	2,960
Sundry Expenses	5,184	4,800
Depreciation	28,800	28,800
	487.840	460.452
Net Profit for the Year before Loan Interest	466,880	322,048
Loan Interest	(212,628)	(223,824)
Retained Profit for the Year before Taxation	254,252	98,224

Projected Balance Sheet as at 30 June 1991 and 1992

	Notes £	1992 £	1991
Fixed Assets	1	1,622,877	1,651,677
Current Assets:			
Stock of Medicines and Food		1,500	1,500
Cash at Bank		275,628	60,200
		277,128	61,700
Less Current Liabilities:			
Accruals		2,700	2,500
Net Current Assets		274,428	59,200
		1,897,305	1,710,877
Financed by:			
Capital Account	2	676,476	422,224
Long Term Loan	3	1,220,829	1,288,653
		1,897,305	1,710,877

Notes to the Projected Balance Sheet as at 30 June 1991 and 1992

1. Fixed Assets

	Land & Buildings	Fixtures & Fittings	Total
Land and Buildings			
Costs	1,480,000	–	1,480,000
Capitalized Interest	56,47	–	
	56,477		
Fixtures and Fittings at Cost	–	144,000	144,000
Cost at 30.06.91 & 30.06.92	1,536,477	144,000	1,680,477
Depreciation:			
Charge for the year ended 30.06.91	–	28,800	28,800
Charge for the year ended 30.06.92	–	–	28,800
	28,800		
At 30.06.92	–	57,600	57,600
Net Book Value:			
At 30.06.92	1,536,477	86,400	1,622,877
At 30.06.91	1,536,477	115,200	1,651,677

2. Capital Account	1992	1991
	£	£
Balance Brought Forward	422,224	–
Capital Introduced	–	324,000
Profit for the Year	254,252	98,224
Balance Carried Forward	676,476	422,224

3. Long-Term Loan	1992	1991
	£	£
Cost Brought Forward	1,288,653	–
Loans Advanced	–	1,356,477
Repayments in the Year	(67,824)	(67,824)
Cost Carried Forward	1,220,829	1,288,653

Major Assumptions Underlying the Cash Flow and Profit Projections for the Two Years Ended 30 June 1992

1. **Fee Income Received**

    1.1   An assumption has been made that each resident will pay £250 per week.

    1.2   The following levels of occupancy have been used in preparing the cash flow and profit projections.

	Nursing Care	Assumed Maximum
Month 1	25	72
Month 2	40	72
Month 3	50	72
Month 4	60	72
Month 5 – 24	68	72

    1.3   It is assumed that the business will not incur debtors in respect of nursing fees.

2. **Food and Medicine**

    Food and medicine has been included in the projections at £15 per resident per week. The costs for July 1990 includes £1,500 for the provision of a basic stock of food and medical supplies. It has been assumed that the business will not incur creditors for any purchases made.

3. **Salaries and Wages**

    Salaries and wages have been included in the projections based upon the size of the home and current levels of pay in the industry. PAYE and National Insurance is assumed to be paid during the same month as the salaries from which they have been deducted.

Cash Projections for the 12 months Ended 30 June 1991

	July 1990	Aug 1990	Sep 1990	Oct 1990	Nov 1990	Dec 1990	Jan 1991	Feb 1991	March 1991	April 1991	May 1991	June 1991	Total No.
Number of Residents	25	40	50	60	68	68	68	68	68	68	68	68	52
Number of Weeks	4	4	5	4	5	4	5	4	4	5	4	4	-
	£	£	£	£	£	£	£	£	£	£	£	£	£
Income													
Fees Received	25,000	40,000	62,500	60,000	85,000	68,000	85,000	68,000	68,000	85,000	68,000	68,000	782,500
Expenditure													
Food and Medicines	3,000	2,400	3,750	3,600	5,100	4,080	5,100	4,080	4,080	5,100	4,080	4,080	48,450
Salaries	26,500	26,500	26,500	26,500	26,500	26,500	26,500	26,500	26,500	26,500	26,500	26,500	318,000
Water Rates	300	300	300	300	300	300	300	300	300	300	300	300	3,600
Insurance	5,000	-	-	-	-	-	-	-	-	-	-	-	5,000
Heat and Light	-	-	2,000	-	-	3,000	-	-	3,000	-	-	2,000	10,000
Telephone	-	-	1,000	-	-	1,000	-	-	1,000	-	-	1,000	4,000
Repairs and Renewals	500	500	500	500	500	500	500	500	500	500	500	500	6,000
Motor Expenses	250	250	250	250	250	250	250	250	250	250	250	250	3,000
Stationery/Postage	500	200	200	200	200	200	200	200	200	200	200	200	2,700
Advertising	5,000	3,000	1,000	500	500	500	500	500	500	500	500	500	13,500
Laundry/Cleaning	400	400	400	400	400	400	400	400	400	400	400	400	4,800
Loan Interest	18,652	18,652	18,652	18,652	18,652	18,652	18,652	18,652	18,652	18,652	18,652	18,652	223,824
Loan Repayment	5,652	5,652	5,652	5,652	5,652	5,652	5,652	5,652	5,652	5,652	5,652	5,652	67,824
Bank Interest	-	-	2,432	-	-	2,310	-	-	-	-	-	-	4,742
Bank Charges	400	400	400	400	400	400	400	400	400	400	400	400	4,800
Sundry Expenses	-	-	400	-	-	400	-	-	400	-	-	400	1,600
Accountancy	460	-	-	-	-	-	-	-	-	-	-	-	460
Drawings	-	-	-	-	-	-	-	-	-	-	-	-	0
Total	66,614	58,254	63,436	56,954	58,454	64,144	58,454	57,434	61,834	58,454	57,434	60,834	722,300
Bank													
Opening Balance	0	(41,614)	(59,868)	(60,804)	(57,758)	(31,212)	(27,356)	(810)	9,756	15,922	42,468	53,034	0
Income	25,000	40,000	62,500	60,000	85,000	68,000	85,000	68,000	68,000	85,000	68,000	68,000	782,500
Expenditure	(66,614)	(58,254)	(63,436)	(56,954)	(58,454)	(64,144)	(58,454)	(57,434)	(61,834)	(58,454)	(57,434)	(60,834)	(722,300)
Closing Balance	(41,614)	(59,868)	(60,804)	(57,758)	(31,212)	(27,356)	(810)	9,756	15,922	42,468	53,034	60,200	60,200

Cash Projections for the 12 Months Ended 30 June 1992

	July 1991	Aug 1991	Sept 1991	Oct 1991	Nov 1991	Dec 1991	Jany 1992	Feby 1992	March 1992	April 1992	May 1992	June 1992	Total
	No.	No.	No.	No.	No.	No.	No.	No.	No.	No.	No.	No.	No.
Number of Residents	68	68	68	68	68	68	68	68	68	68	68	68	-
Number of Weeks	4	4	5	4	5	4	5	4	4	5	4	4	52
£	£	£	£	£	£	£	£	£	£	£	£	£	£
Income													
Fees Received	73,440	73,440	91,800	73,440	91,800	73,440	91,800	73,440	73,440	91,800	73,440	73,440	954,720
Expenditure													
Food and Medicines	4,406	4,406	5,508	4,406	5,508	4,406	5,508	4,406	4,406	5,508	4,406	4,406	57,280
Salaries	28,620	28,620	28,620	28,620	28,620	28,620	28,620	28,620	28,620	28,620	28,620	28,620	343,440
Water Rates	324	324	324	324	324	324	324	324	324	324	324	324	3,888
Insurance	5,400	-	-	-	-	-	-	-	-	-	-	-	5,400
Heat and Light	-	-	2,160	-	-	3,240	-	-	3,240	-	-	2,160	10,800
Telephone	-	-	1,080	-	-	1,080	-	-	1,080	-	-	1,080	4,320
Repairs and Renewals	540	540	540	540	540	540	540	540	540	540	540	540	6,480
Motor Expenses	270	270	270	270	270	270	270	270	270	270	270	270	3,240
Stationery and Postage	540	216	216	216	216	216	216	216	216	216	216	216	2,916
Advertising	540	540	540	540	540	540	540	540	540	540	540	540	6,480
Laundry and Cleaning	432	432	432	432	432	432	432	432	432	432	432	432	5,184
Loan Interest	17,719	17,719	17,719	17,719	17,719	17,719	17,719	17,719	17,719	17,719	17,719	17,719	212,628
Loan Repayment	5,652	5,652	5,652	5,652	5,652	5,652	5,652	5,652	5,652	5,652	5,652	5,652	67,824
Bank Interest	-	-	-	-	-	-	-	-	-	-	-	-	
Bank Charges	-	-	432	-	-	432	-	-	432	-	-	432	1,728
Sundry Expenses	432	432	432	432	432	432	432	432	432	432	432	432	5,148
Accountancy	-	-	2,500	-	-	-	-	-	-	-	-	-	2,500
Drawings	-	-	-	-	-	-	-	-	-	-	-	-	0
Total	64,875	59,151	66,425	59,151	60,253	63,903	60,253	59,151	63,903	60,253	59,151	62,823	739,292
Bank Account													
Opening Balance	60,200	68,765	83,054	108,429	122,718	154,265	163,802	195,349	209,638	219,175	250,722	265,011	60,200
Income	73,440	73,440	91,800	73,440	91,800	73,440	91,800	73,440	73,440	91,800	73,440	73,440	954,720
Expenditure	(64,875)	(59,151)	(66,425)	(59,151)	(60,253)	(63,903)	(60,253)	(59,151)	(63,903)	(60,253)	(59,151)	(62,823)	(739,292)
Closing Balance	68,765	83,054	108,429	122,718	154,265	163,802	195,349	209,638	219,175	250,722	265,011	275,628	275,628

Detailed Pre-Trading Long-Term Loan Account for the 6 Months Ended 30 June 1990

	Jan 1990	Feb 1990	March 1990	April 1990	May 1990	June 1990
Capital Expenditure						
Property Purchase	400,000	400,000				
Conversion Costs	216,000	216,000	108,000	108,000	216,000	216,000
	72,000	72,000	144,000			
Interest on Loan	3,696	6,477	7,926	9,394	13,158	15,826
	619,696	222,477	115,926	117,394	301,158	303,826
Long-Term Loan Account						
Opening Balance	0	295,696	518,173	634,099	751,493	1,052,651
Costs	619,696	222,477	115,926	117,394	301,158	303,826
Capital Introduced	(324,000)					
Closing Balance	295,696	518,173	634,099	751,493	1,052,651	1,356,477

4. Rates and Insurances

Insurance costs have been estimated at £5,000 per annum. It is assumed that the nursing home will be exempt for the purpose of general rates.

5. Loan Interest and Repayments

5.1 Loan repayments

It is proposed that the loan be repaid over 20 years on a straight-line basis.

5.2 Loan interest

Loan interest has been calculated using an annual percentage rate of 16.5% based upon the amounts outstanding at the commencement of the financial year.

6. Drawings

No provision has been made in the cash flow projections for the proprietor's drawings on the basis that he can derive sufficient income from his other established businesses.

7. Other Expenses

All other expenses have been included in the projections at a fixed monthly rate based upon the best estimate of the proposers.

8. Repairs and Renewals

It has been assumed that the business will not incur abnormal repair or rectification work other than the initial conversion during the first 2 years of trading.

Case Study - Zhin Nursing Home
Suggested Discussion Points

Do not be put off by all the detail!

Who is Mr Zhin? Why has he approached us and not his own bank? Is he really worth £1 million? What are his current loan commitments? What is his track record? What experience has he in running a nursing home?

Then the Project itself.

The initial debt looks very high, although payback from the cash flow is rapid. The payback is, of course, very dependent on the take up of residents, which is stated at 68 residents after only 4 months. It all looks just too good with a cash positive position of £275,628 at the end of the second year!

There are too many unanswered questions to make a decision at this stage.

Case Study 13 – Block Builders Ltd

David Block and his sister, Sally, are aged 36 and 34 respectively and have been customers at your branch for many years. They are both university graduates. David qualified as a building engineer and worked for major house builders for 8 years, planning and supervising site work. Sally qualified as an architect and worked in private practice for 6 years. Five years ago, David and Sally decided to form their own building business, Block Builders Limited.

The business has gone well, and the directors have proved that they can handle the practical problems involved in running a small building company. The work they have done includes both contracting – house extensions, alterations, office refurbishment etc. – and new house building, also largely on contract for private customers and small developers. In the last 12 months, they acquired a plot of land, obtained planning permission and built 4 small detached houses as a speculative development. The development is nearly complete, and 2 of the houses are contracted for sale at £60,000 each with considerable interest being shown in the remaining 2 at the same price.

The market for this type of house in the area is buoyant. The Blocks are aware that a small school near to their existing development has closed and is being sold by the local authority. There is land attached to the school on which they could build 4 further houses similar to the ones just completed. The local authority has indicated that it would look favourably on granting planning permission for building on the land. On the basis of this information, the Blocks have decided they must act quickly to buy the school and attached land and have exchanged contracts at a price of £100,000, paying a 10% deposit, with completion in a month's time.

They call to see you and request an increase of £200,000 in their overdraft limit. This increase is calculated as follows:

	£
Purchase of school and land	100,000
Building cost of 4 houses	120,000
Conversion of school into a house	25,000
Services	15,000
	260,000
Repayments from sales:	
Converted school	110,000
4 houses @ £65,000	260,000
	370,000

The current limit on the account is £75,000 and is fully drawn. It is secured by a debenture and unlimited directors' guarantees. The 10% deposits paid on the houses contracted for sale from the first development have already been credited to the account and completion is scheduled for 3 weeks' time.

Required:
Consider the Blocks' request and give, with reasons, your response.

Balance Sheet as at 31 December

	1991 £		1992 £		1993 £	
Fixed Assets:						
Plant and machinery	31,800	53,600	56,400			
Vehicles	10,000	41,800	18,000	71,600	19,000	75,400
Current Assets:						
Debtors	114,800		106,400		113,000	
Land held for development	–		–		36,200	
Work in progress	145,200	260,000	143,000	249,400	192,800	342,000
		301,800		321,000		417,400
Current Liabilities:						
Creditors	90,200		72,800		91,000	
Tax	9,400		23,800		24,600	
Hire purchase	6,400		13,800		9,000	
Bank	62,000	(168,000)	36,000	(146,400)	75,200	(199,800)
Net assets		133,800		174,600		217,600
Represented by:						
Share capital		2,000		2,000		2,000
Profit and loss account		131,800		172,600		215,600
		133,800		174,600		217,600

Profit and Loss Summary

	1991	1992	1993
Sales	620,000	834,000	780,000
Profit before tax	33,200	62,600	68,600

Accounting Ratios

	1991	1992	1993
Gearing	51%	29%	39%
Net margin	5.3	7.5	8.8

Block Builders Ltd Case Study – Suggested Key

A small building advance that is similar to the Supa Homes Limited case study iii *Applied Lending Techniques* by C.N. Rouse (Financial World Publishing).

This question *was* actually all about tracking cash flow, although a number of candidates became preoccupied with quoting building advance formulae that were not entirely appropriate in this case.

The Blocks are good customers whom we would wish to help. Unusually for the building business they are very well qualified, theoretically as well as practically.

However, they have been rather impetuous in contracting to buy the school before talking to the bank, and from the bank's point of view this is a *fait accompli* with an uncomfortable position for a good customer if the bank is unwilling to agree to provide development finance.

There are some positive signs though. The proposed development is very similar to one the Blocks have just carried out so they can handle it.

The marketplace is buoyant for this type of house – the company's own recent sales are evidence of this.

In financial terms the business has performed well to grow to a capital base of £218,000 in five years and gearing at around 40% is modest for a building company. suggesting conservative management. Profits have grown steadily in recent years indicating that the directors are particularly competent.

The amount being requested is unnecessarily high as a simple cash flow shows:

	£000s	
Present balance, say	(75)	
Sale of 2 houses	108	@£60,000 less 10%
	33	
Purchase of school	(90)	@ £100,000 less 10%57
Sale of next 2 houses	120	@ £60,000
	63	
Refurbish school	(25)	
Install services	(15)	
	23	
Build 4 houses	(120)	
	97	
Sale of school	110	
Sale of houses	260	
	273	

On this basis, the maximum borrowing requirement can be contained within £100,000.

The main problem would be if the sale of the remaining houses from the present development did not proceed quickly. In that case, it would be pointless to rush into construction of a further four houses. Blocks' workforce could still be kept occupied by allowing it to install services and carry out the school refurbishment until sufficient level of house sales have been achieved.

If the Blocks intend to continue with their existing contracting business, the working capital needs of this business will need to be taken into account when setting the limit.

On the security front, the current security position is very solid – 4 houses worth £240,000 and contract debtors to cover the £75,000 limit. The future position will be:

	£000
Land and school at cost	100
Maximum work-in-progress cost	160
	260

To cover £100,000, suggesting over 250% cover is available.

As the company is now going into speculative development, it is time to tighten up monitoring procedures – the lending should be on a loan account with drawdowns for work in progress made following site visits, etc. There will probably be a need for some sort of overdraft for the continuing contract business.

Overall, agreeing to a facility of around £100,000 – part loan, part overdraft – should not be a problem. A formal cash flow forecast ought to be drawn up to show the needs of house building and contracting, and to enable appropriate monitoring.

Case Study 14 – Milner Construction Ltd

Milner Construction Ltd is a firm of contracting builders. The company was established in 1977 and has banked with you since its formation. The founders of the company, Michael Milner and Patrick Greenwood, own all the shares. They are both now in their 40s. They were originally bricklayers and, at first, the company supplied bricklaying services to house builders. As the business grew, the company undertook a wider range of activities – supplying materials, scaffolding, etc. as well as labour. It now works mainly for large building companies as a subcontractor on major construction contracts, such as office blocks and shopping centres. Milner's normal minimum contract size is £300,000.

Although, at one stage, the company had 120 employees, most labour is now self-employed working on a subcontract basis for Milner. There are now only 10 full-time employees.

The company currently has the following facilities from the bank:

Overdraft	£500,000
Bonds/guarantees	£300,000

As security, the bank has a debenture that includes a first charge over the company's freehold office building, which was valued at £250,000 three years ago. There are also directors' unlimited guarantees, supported by the equities in their houses of £180,000 and £80,000. Six years ago, the company decided to expand into Europe and established a subsidiary in France. However, this venture was not a success and, earlier this year, the company closed the subsidiary down and wrote off its investment.

The 1995 audited accounts are now available. The directors call to see you to discuss their requirements for the next 12 months. The company has never produced management accounts or formal forecasts, although its 'back of the envelope' assessments have, in the past, been reasonably accurate.

The company currently has underway, or has won, contracts to the value of £1.6M which the directors believe will produce a net profit of £250,000 in the current financial year. In addition, they have a good chance of winning a contract worth £1M in the next 12 months as a subcontractor to one of the UK's largest building developers.

This contract will require a performance bond of 15% of the contract value. The company is utilizing fully the current £300,000 bonding facility, and is also making full use of the overdraft facility. The directors ask the bank to increase the overdraft limit to £600,000 and the bonds/guarantees limit to £450,000. (The company has never had a claim under any performance bond issued on its behalf.)

Required:
Analyse the current position of the company and give, with reasons, the response you would make to the request.

Profit and Loss Summary

Year to 31 July	1993	1994	1995
	£	£	£
Turnover	2,102,849	2,213,071	3,637,515
Gross profit	367,850	406,706	757,988
Depreciation	27,420	37,902	47,469
Directors' remuneration	96,487	130,350	222,160
Interest paid	51,320	63,815	78,682
Profit before tax	129,841	120,061	291,594
Extraordinary item (Write off of investment in subsidiary)	–	–	359,418
Tax paid	35,550	49,594	162,154
Retained profit (loss)	94,291	70,467	(229,978)

Balance Sheets as at 31 July

	1991 £		1992 £		1993 £	
Current assets:						
Cash	157		1,000		501	
Debtors	341,485		562,286		796,446	
Work in progress	132,050	473,692	188,624	751,910	411,913	1,208,860
Current liabilities:						
Creditors	226,802		232,323		457,266	
Hire purchase	22,008		17,810		24,748	
Bank overdraft	225,678		444,526		539,541	
Current taxation	82,686	(557,174)	100,722	(795,381)	117,659	1,139,214
		(83,482)		(43,471)		69,646
Net current assets/(liabilities):						
Fixed assets:						
Land and buildings	134,764		134,931		132,586	
Plant and machinery	135,009		110,116		130,776	
Investment in subsidiary	290,165	559,938	329,471	574,518		–263,362
Term liability:						
Hire purchase		(99,806)		(83,229)		(115,168)
Net assets		376,650		447,818		217,840
Financed by:						
Share capital		100		100		100
Profit and loss account		376,550		447,718		217,740
		376,650		447,818		217,840

Accounting Ratios

	1993	1994	1995
Gross margin (%)	17.5	18.4	20.8
Net margin (%)	6.2	5.4	8.0
Interest cover (times)	3.5	2.9	4.7
Net gearing (%)	92	122	312
Current ratio	0.85:1	0.95:1	1.06:1
Acid test	0.61:1	0.71:1	0.70:1
Credit given (days)	59	93	80
Credit taken (days)	48	47	58
Work-in-progress turnover (days)	28	38	52

Suggested Answer: Milner Construction Ltd.

The company is a long-standing customer of the bank which would want to help if possible. The management are experienced in the business but they do not have an unblemished track record. The French venture seems to have been a disaster. Despite this the core business has performed well recently The steady sales increase suggests the directors can get business from major builders so their reputation must be good, and in the absence of any claim on the bond indicates a high degree of technical competence.

The directors appear to be financially naive as indicated by the lack of management accounts and forecasts. However, they have proved that they can take hard decisions. for example the closure of the French business cannot have been very palatable.

Not least because of the French subsidiary write off, the capital structure of the business has weakened significantly. However when assessing the capital needs of the business it must be appreciated that the company has been living without the capital invested in the French venture for some time. The current liquidity pressure is more to do with the rapid expansion in turnover rather than the write off.

There is a hidden reserve in the property if the old valuation still holds good.

One of the problems for the business is that the directors have been taking too much cash out recently. They do need to be questioned about whether some of the cash previously taken out can be reinvested.

Given the nature of the debtors – large builders – the company may not have a great deal of control over the credit given.

There is also likely to be a significant element of 'retentions' in the debtor figure which will increase the locked-up cash as turnover expands. The bank needs to see a detailed breakdown of debtors, with retentions shown separately. There is probably some scope to squeeze creditors who are mainly the company's own subcontractors but it also needs to be recognized that these cannot be stretched too far because the subcontractors' own liquidity is likely to be tight. Fundamentally in this business there is a limited scope to improve liquidity if they want to undertake the desired level of turnover without a capital injection. They now need to produce a good detailed cash forecast and also a detailed forecast of bond movements. It seems likely that sonic bonds must be due to run off soon.

Underlying profitability is excellent as is shown in the impressive trend in the gross margin, and performance at the bottom line level is solid, especially in 1995 if the exceptional directors' remuneration is discounted. Basically this is a very good business which has made one serious error in France.

Looking at the security available, the freehold deeds need revaluing. However, assuming that there is little change from the balance sheet figures the main security is a second charge on the freehold office, in which there is an equity of £510,000. This has to cover over £1M of facilities. The debenture must have some value but this is a business engaged in large contracts and the debtors and work in progress would break up badly in a receivership. The bank's receiver would almost certainly have to trade on to complete contracts with the risks that it involves of further potential loss for the bank.

The decision is finely balanced with the fundamental strength of the business being matched against the thin security. The directors have already committed all their personal assets, although they should reinject any cash which is available from their large drawings. A detailed financial plan is needed and a good monitoring system put in place. This might be a situation where the bank would want to use a firm of accountants to design the monitoring package and to review the actuals. Provided this is done and is satisfactory, the previous good track record of the UK business and the good track record with previous bonds make a positive decision on balance the right one.

Case Study 15 – Lewis Willis

Lewis Willis is a successful property developer who, jointly with his brother, owns a group of private property companies which have an estimated net worth of around £25 million. Willis is 52 years old and has been a customer of your bank for 30 years in both a personal and business capacity.

Willis calls to see you. He wants to undertake a property development on his own and has set up a brand new company for the purpose. He has identified a site that has planning permission for 60,000 square feet of offices.

He has already found three large companies which have expressed keen interest in taking all the office space when built. He has also had discussions with a number of institutions (pension funds and insurance companies) which would be interested in buying the building from him once let.

Willis has produced a detailed feasibility study for the project which he leaves with you. He asks if you would be prepared to recommend that your bank lend him the £6.5M needed to complete the development.

Required:
Consider the proposition and give details of the risks involved. Indicate your response to the request made by Willis.

Lewis Willis – Project Appraisal (Feasibility Study)

	£	£
Sales		
Net useable space 60,000 sq. ft @ £12.50 per sq. ft rent		750,000 p.a.
Income capitalized at 9% yield		333,333
Less 2.75% purchasers' costs		229,167
Sales value		8,104,166
Costs		
Site cost	1,300,000	
Stamp duty on site @ 1%	13,000	
Legal fees on site @ 0.5%	6,500	
Agents' fees on site @ 1%	13,000	
Total site costs		1,332,500
Building 60,000 sq ft @ £47.50 per sq ft	2,850,000	
Access roads	750,000	
Site clearance	50,000	
Contingency @ 2.5%	91,250	
Professional fees @ 12%	438,000	
Total building costs		4,179,250
Interest at 12.5% compounded quarterly (13.1% APR)		
Site costs + fees 15 months to end of build	221,629	
Construction + fees 12 months (50% weighted)	265,284	
Void period (complete but empty) 9 months	589,369	
Total interest costs		1,076,282
Agents' letting fees @ 15% of rent	112,500	
Legal fees on letting @ 1%	7,500	
Agents' capital sale fees @ 0.5%	40,521	
Promotion	25,000	
Total disposal fees and end costs		185,521
Total costs		6,773,553
Sales value		8,104,166
Less total costs		6,773,553
Profit		1,330,613
Profit on cost		19.6%
Rent yield on cost		11.1%

Suggested Response: Lewis Willis

This was a question candidates strenuously avoided or, when they did do it, tended to do badly. This is a pity given all the banks' poor performance in property lending recently.

The question represented a fairly standard project feasibility study to which candidates simply had to apply their common sense.

Willis is a good customer and if possible the bank would want to help him. He has an excellent track record in the business (but then so did a number of property developers who have gone bust recently). This is a business where past track record is not necessarily a guide to future success if the marketplace fundamentals relating to property go against you.

Despite all the indications about future tenants, the development is not yet pre-let or sold, so it is open-ended and therefore speculative. Willis has deliberately avoided putting the project through one of his existing companies. Whatever the reason for this, it reduces the risk of loss to him and increases the risk to the bank. This is because the bank cannot look to assets outside the project if things go wrong. Moreover, Willis is putting in no stake and the bank will be lending 100%, including rolling up interest for two years.

Although there is an apparent 19.6% margin on the project, this is unlikely to be sufficient if things go significantly wrong.

8.2   So What are the Risks?

Letting risk – it might not be possible to let the building at all if the market is depressed or, if it could be let, it might have to be to tenants, which would not be attractive to an institution. It also might not be possible to achieve £12.50 per sq ft as rent and every £1 per sq ft off the rent reduces the profit in the project by £667,000. In fact, if rents were to reduce to £10.50 per sq ft. the project would be in loss. An independent view of the likely rents in the area is needed.

Construction risk – is there a fixed-price building contract? If not, there could be cost overruns. Is the builder financially strong? Cost will be significantly higher if the original builder goes bust and someone new has to be brought in. Although there is a 2½% contingency built into the project; this will cover only minor mishaps.

Disposal risk – institutions may decide to reduce/hold their property portfolios and not be in the market for this type of property. Alternatively they may require a higher yield than 9%. A 2% increase in yield requirement would wipe out the profit on the project. If the property was let but not sold, the rent yield on cost of 11.1% would clearly not be sufficient to meet bank interest at 13.1%.

In assessing the security value of the site, an independent valuation will be needed and also an independent view of its ultimate value. A charge over the site is needed and also a floating charge to enable the bank to obtain priority over any Law Property Act receiver, should one be appointed by another creditor. Any lending for construction would have to be against architects' certificates.

A significant number of candidates wanted to agree to this proposition but it is simply too speculative for a bank. Some re-engineering might be possible which would have to include a significant customer stake. This might then enable the bank to look at the proposition if it were pre-let. Ideally the bank would also expect the property to have been pre-sold and essentially to be financing a closed bridge.

8.3 Farming Finance

Farm financial planning has become even more important over recent years owing to the squeeze on profit margins. Farm input costs have been rising faster than the unit values received for the commodity sold. This has led to a greater awareness by the farmer of the necessity for improved planning to maximize the use of his resources in both land and finance.

The most widely used technique by both farm business advisers and more progressive farmers is the gross margin system.

Gross Margin System

A farm business will normally consist of several different enterprises. Each enterprise will have costs specifically related to that enterprise and also other costs which are shared over the total farm business. Allocation of a portion of all farming costs to a specific enterprise can be completely misleading when making planning decisions. For example, when an enterprise is expanded or contracted, or terminated, the variable costs for such an enterprise will vary roughly in proportion to the size of that enterprise, i.e. the variable costs tend to be volume orientated. Many fixed costs will stay the same.

Hence we have identified in farming two categories of costs:

(a) variable costs;

(b) fixed costs.

Variable costs are easy to allocate because they will change with the scale of enterprise (volume orientated). Fixed costs are not easy to allocate and do not necessarily change directly with the scale of the enterprise. Examples of variable costs are, for winter wheat, seed, fertilizers, and sprays; and for dairy cows, concentrate foods, veterinary fees and medicine, artificial insemination, straw, etc.

Examples of fixed costs are: rent, regular labour, machinery and motive power, miscellaneous farm costs.

Calculating the Gross Margin
The gross margin itself is the total in gross output of an enterprise less the variable costs. GROSS OUTPUT LESS VARIABLE COSTS = GROSS MARGIN, as in the following examples.

Gross Margin Calculation 1

	£/acre	£/acre
Winter Wheat		
Output 54 cwt per acre at £105 per ton		267
Less:		
Variable costs		
Seed	20	
Fertilizer	41	
Sprays	32	
Total costs per acre		93
Gross margin per acre		174

Gross Margin Calculation 2

	£/cow	£
Dairy Cows		
Milk sales per cow: 5,350 litres @ 17p		910
Less		
Cost of replacing cows		(140)
Plus: calf sale		85
Cull cows		90
		945 output
Less		
Variable Costs		
Concentrates	202	
Forage costs	71	
Bedding	8	
Veterinary and medicine	18	
AI and enterprise recording fees	18	
Consumable dairy stores, etc.	17	
Total variable costs		334
Gross margin per cow		£611

Having looked at gross margins for two enterprises, we now follow the same procedure for all the enterprises on the farm in question, and then deduct fixed costs to give a trading margin. This budget is similar to any industry profit budget based on contribution analysis from several products.

Having formulated a plan the farmer will then, using the gross margin techniques described earlier, calculate a farm budget for profitability (see below).

Farm Budget for Profitability (Example of Layout)

Assume a farm of 600 acres (cereal/dairy) rented at £26 per acre.

Enterprise	No. of Stock/Area Cropped	Gross Margin	Total £
Wheat	230 acres	£173 per acre	39,790
Dairy cows	120	£600 per cow	72,000
Dairy herd replacements	30	£200 per heifer	6,000
Spring barley	120 acres	£120 per acre	14,400
		Farm Gross Margin	132,190

Less:

Fixed costs

Labour	28,000
Power and machinery (costs and depreciation)	29,400
Rent and rates	15,600
Sundries	5,000
Trading Margin	£53,590

To meet commitments:

Personal drawings

Bank finance charges

HP/Leasing

Taxation

This budget must of course be based on realistic levels of expected technical performance. It must not be overoptimistic and should reflect past achievements on the farm. Then, as a footnote to the budget or alternatively as a separate budget, items of capital expenditure should be listed. These farm budgets then form the basis for the cash flow forecast which is similar to any other business in that it lists receipts and payments over 12 months, and the timing of those entries will affect the bank account balance.

To summarize:

- THE FARM BUDGET INDICATES PLANNED PROFITABILITY based on the stocking and cropping plan.

● A CASH FLOW FORECAST WILL INDICATE THE FEASIBILITY of the plan, in cash terms. We shall look in detail at this later.

Provided all looks well, the farmer can then put the plans into practice. If a negative position in the cash flow forecast occurs, then, unless the budget can be restructured, the help of his bank or other sources of credit will be needed.

Management Control and Monitoring

The farmer, having formulated plans and put them into practice, should monitor the farm process. It is not sufficient to organize the farm work daily. Performance levels should be checked regularly against budget, receipts and payments recorded on the cash flow forecast and compared with targets. Early indication of possible problems can then be seen and action taken.

Net Worth Movement

The success or failure of all the farmer's plans must at the end of each year be indicated in the resulting net worth (or capital) position. Many farmers seem to forget this! The net worth can be monitored effectively in two simple ways:

(a) **Audited Accounts**
Although probably out of date, these do indicate profits being earned and retentions in the farm business.

(b) **Farmer's Balance Sheet**
This is sometimes called the statement of assets and liabilities or the stock and crop form or the farmer's confidential statement. Net worth can be monitored by simply totalling assets less liabilities at a similar date annually. Most banks have a form for this and a typical example is illustrated in Figure 4.

In completing the form, the farmer should use estimated market values to give a true net worth position. Comparison with the previous year's statement will then indicate the net worth movement in the farm business. An increase in net worth should reflect profits earned and retained in the business, after allowing for any increased valuation in freehold land.

Farmer's Balance Sheet (Example of Layout)

Liabilities	£	Assets	£
Rent outstanding		Cash at bank	
Due to bank		Debtors	
– Current account		Grant due	
– Loan account		Stock	
Creditors		– Produce for sale	
Hire purchase		– Livestock	
Private loans (short-term)		– Produce for own consumption	
		- Fertilizer, feed, seed etc.	
		Valuation	
		– Growing crops	
		– Improvements*	
SUB TOTAL		**SUB TOTAL**	
Mortgages		Land and buildings acres @ £	
Dilapidations		Farm machinery	
Other liabilities		Tenant's improvements*	
		Other assets:	

LIABILITIES

Date

Net worth/balance

£   TOTAL £

Other Items:

1. Contingent liabilities

2. Leasing

3. Non-farming assets

*   The value of improvements made to the farmland, usually valued by a professional land agent, i.e. to fixed assets such as buildings, will affect the value of the tenancy and should only be made with the landlord's permission.

Assessing the Agricultural Lending Proposition

Basic Points to Consider

In looking at a lending proposition in farming you must take the same general starting points as with any business proposition. The first aspects to consider will be the farmer and the business. Then the amount of money requested – is it adequate? Can it be repaid? What if things go wrong? As with other lending, there is no mathematical formula to make life easy. Every farm is different – in structure, size, layout and facilities.

The financial resources of the business will also vary as between farms. It is a different proposition to lend £20,000 to a farm business with total assets of, say, £100,000, than to lend the same amount to one with total assets of £20,000. Also if you lend £20,000 to buy more dairy cows, then the cash return to the business will be different from £20,000 lent to buy a new tractor, which may only 'return' lower costs in fuel, repairs, etc.

The five basic points to consider once again are:

1. How much is required?

2. What is to be done with the money?

3. What are the plans for repayment?

4. What will be the bank's position if the plans for repayment go wrong?

5. What is the experience and track record of the borrower?

It should be possible to answer the five questions from the documents essential in farm financial planning.

(a) The cash flow forecast will tell us what is to be done with the money and how much is required.

(b) The plans for repayment will be illustrated in the cash flow forecast and the feasibility of any repayments shown by looking at any margin available in the farm budget together with the record of past profits in the accounts.

(c) If things go wrong, then the 'buffer' or net worth is illustrated in the past accounts and the up-to-date net worth position in the farmer's balance sheet.

Visiting the Farm

This is essential, as with any other business. You will gain a lot of information. Most farmers are very receptive and only too willing to show you around their farm. It is usually their pride and joy!

Observation and discussion will enable you to make a judgement as to the technical and management ability of the farmer. What is his experience? How long has he been at the farm? Does he use modern techniques? Is he in full control or does he spend a lot of time away from the farm? What is his depth of management ability and who is there to help him? Does he delegate routine tasks? Who keeps the farm records?

Also you will see the farm size and learn about the stocking and cropping of the farm, the land and soil types, the layout of the farm, the state of buildings and machinery. Does the place look well kept and well organized? Are the hedges trimmed, fences in good repair, ditches clear? Do the animals look healthy and well fed? Are the crops looking good or are they full of weeds and disease? Have the buildings and machinery the capacity to meet the farmer's plans? Look at the farmer's stocking and cropping plans and discuss them.

All this information will help you when going on to contemplate the financial picture of the farm business.

Financial Performance

The banker has all the usual bank records available. Examination of the bank statements will reveal the business turnover, the average bank balance, the range of the account, standing orders and direct debits and any unpaid cheques.

Comparison of these statistics with previous years will help to paint the financial picture, e.g. falling turnover coupled with an increasing debit balance will merit close investigation!

8.4   Looking at Asset Cover

Accounts

The accounts may well be historic but it is well worth looking at the balance sheet.

The following simplified farmer's balance sheet illustrates what can be revealed and whether certain items might require further investigation.

Liabilities	£	Assets	£
Rent Outstanding	3,500	Debtors	2,000
Bank	14,400	Stock	40,320
Creditors	3,150	Tenant right	5,000
	21,050 (b)		47,320 (d)
Capital/Net worth	30,070 (c)	Farm machinery	3,800
	51,120		51,120 (a)

1. Total assets (a) – are there any intangibles or fictitious assets?

2. Total liabilities (b) debt structure – long- /short-term

3. Total assets (a): total liabilities (b) – liabilities should be well covered.

4. Net worth (c) – the total assets minus total liabilities. This is the margin or buffer for the business. (This could well be understated.)

5. Total assets (a): current assets (d) – what is the proportion of quickly realizable assets?

6. Current assets (d): total liabilities (b) – This represents the liquidity of the business. Can current debts be repaid without resorting to sale of fixed assets?

Then, after examining the trading and profit and loss account record:

1. Stock: sales turnover – dependent on type of farm enterprises.

2. Debtors: sales – debtors figure in farming should be well covered.

3. Profits – are they being earned and retained? Look at the resulting profit and loss account balance.

Then, the bank lending:

1. Net worth: bank lending (this will be discussed in more detail later under the farmer's balance sheet).

2. Net worth: total liabilities – is the balance being maintained or deteriorating?

All of these ratios become more meaningful when you compare trends over several years' balance sheets. It is dangerous to make a judgement on the year's figures in isolation.

Limitations of Farming Accounts

Some of the limitations are:

(a) The accounts are often prepared with taxation in mind. They may therefore not give a true indication of the net worth of the business. Land, buildings and machinery may well be undervalued on a cost less depreciation basis. Stock may be undervalued and the accountant could accept the farmer's valuation without verifying this. Sales invoices could be carried forward into the next accounting period therefore reducing profits earned.

(b) There may be long delays between the date of publication and the date to which the accounts refer. They may well be 12 to 18 months out of date before the bank sees them!

(c) Individual firms of accountants may apply different interpretations to certain items in the accounts.

This brings us to the farmer's balance sheet.

The Farmer's Balance Sheet

As explained earlier, this management document is simply an up-to-date statement of assets and liabilities. It is designed to give an up-to-date assessment of the NET WORTH of the farm business based on realistic market valuations. It is important to take a consistent attitude to valuations. These can be checked against other information available such as other customers or journals.

Example 1: Farmer A

Take the farmer's balance sheet of Farmer A below. This provides considerably more management information about the farm business than the audited accounts.

Farmer's Balance Sheet

Name	Farmer A	Date	August 200X
Farm Address	West Sussex	Bank	A Bank

Farm Area	Owned	Tenanted	
Crops	-	62	Rent Payable: £6,400 p.a.
Grass	-	270	Landlord: Mr A Jones
Woodland and Roughland	–	13	
Total		**345**	

Estimated Effective Acreage: 320

Livestock	Cattle		Market Value	Total Value £
100	Dairy Cows	@	425	42,500
20	Heifers	@	400	8,000
60	Young Stock	@	250	15,000
	Pigs			
20	Sows	@	80	1,600
40	Weaners	@	20	800
	Sheep			
200	Ewes	@	40	8,000
180	Lambs	@	25	4,500
			Total £	80,400

Produce for Own Consumption

(Silage, Corn, Hay etc.)

30 tons	Hay	@	£40 per ton	1,200
200 tons	Silage	@	£10 per ton	2,000
			Total £	3,200

Growing Crops
(value usually at cost of variable inputs only)

Acres	Crop		£		Total value £
20	Winter Barley	@	65		1,300
12	Spring Barley	@	48		576
				TOTAL £	1,876

Stored Produce for Sale

Crop	Tons	Market value	£		Total value £
Barley	45t	@	90		4,050
				TOTAL £	4,050

Farm Machinery

Date of Purchase	Item	Cost £		Market value £
19X2	2 tractors	3,400		8,000
	Various Other Items			5,000
			TOTAL £	13,000

Summary

Liabilities	£	Assets	£
Rent outstanding	2,000	Cash at Bank	–
Due to Bank		Debtors	2,000
– Current Account	8,900	Grant Due	–
– Loan Account	5,000	Stock	
Creditors	2,150	– Produce for Sale	4,050
Hire Purchase	Nil	– Livestock	80,400
Private Loans (short-term)	Nil	– Produce for Own Consumption	3,200
		– Fertilizer/seed/feed, etc.	3,850
		Valuation	
		– Growing Crops	1,876
		– Tenant Right	5,000
SUB TOTAL	18,050	SUB TOTAL	100,376
Mortgages	–	Land and Buildings acres @ £	–
Dilapidations	–	Farm Machinery	13,000
Other liabilities	–	Improvements	–
LIABILITIES	18,050		
Net worth/balance	95,326		
	£113,376	TOTAL	£113,376

Other Items:

1. Contingent liabilities   Nil

2. Leasing   Nil

3. Non-farming assets – Life policies, surrender values   £8,000

4. Savings account   £5,000

The ownership of land is indicated (Farmer A is a tenant). The acreage is stated together with rent payable and the split between crops and grass. Then, the livestock are valued and it can be seen that this is mainly a dairy farm with sheep and pigs and a small corn acreage. Totalling livestock units at appropriate stocking rates and adding on the crops, the farm acreage being farmed can be roughly checked, depending on the time of the year.

The final summary shows a net worth of £95,326. This looks a healthy balance relative to the total debts at £18,050 and bank borrowing at £13,900. Looking at the assets the main item is the livestock at £80,400. There is little else other than farm machinery. From an asset cover viewpoint the bank borrowing is well covered, but this does not indicate business profitability. We shall look at this a little later.

Compare the farmer's balance sheet figures with the latest audited accounts (see below). What is the net worth difference? Why? Any other significant differences? Check creditors – this figure could be understated by the farmer!

BALANCE SHEET (FARMER A) (Audited on historic cost accounting basis)

Liabilities	£	Assets	£
Rent outstanding	3,500	Debtors	2,000
Bank	14,400	Stock	40,320
Creditors	3,150	Tenant right	5,000
		Farm machinery	3,800
	21,050		
Capital/Net worth	30,070		
	51,120	Total assets	51,120

The significant differences compared with the farmer's balance sheet are:

Total assets:	£51,120 compared with	£113,376
Net worth:	£30,070 compared with	£95,326
Stock:	£40,320 compared with	£91,500

This results from using market values in the farmer's balance sheet – the audited accounts will show the lower cost or market value.

Farm machinery: £3,800 compared with   £13,000

(The result, again, of using market values as opposed to the usual formula of cost less depreciation.)

Net Worth

Trends can be compared by looking at a series of farmer's balance sheets. No change can take place without some reason. Thus net worth is very important to monitor and changes should be investigated. A steady rise in net worth is most encouraging but still needs investigation.

Is a rising trend in net worth due to profit being earned and retained? It may be due to a revaluation of assets or a refund of taxation. Alternatively, there may have been a sale of machinery not previously included in the farm valuation in the balance sheet.

Asset Structure

In the UK farming scene, land values far outweigh earning capacity. For example, making Farmer A the owner of 345 acres rather than the tenant, the difference in the value of total assets is very large. Value 345 acres at say £1,500 per acre = £517,500. The total assets are then over £600,000. For this reason, freehold property in farming must be considered separately from the other assets being used. Hence we tend to look at farmers' balance sheets on a tenants' asset basis for comparative purposes. In our example Farmer A has total assets of £113,376. Dividing this by the effective farm acreage of 320 acres gives us a figure of £354 tenants' assets per acre.

This can be compared with standard farming statistical data*, or better still, you can build up your own file of tenants' assets/acre in your area. This is most useful when handling an approach by a farmer going in for a new farm or expanding his farm by taking on extra land.

Gearing

This is, as stated in earlier sections, the relationship between total borrowings and net worth. The business is said to be 'highly geared' when the proportion of borrowed money is high relative to the net worth of the business and 'low geared' when in the opposite situation. For total borrowings, all borrowed funds irrespective of length of credit allowed are included.

For tenant farmers experience shows that when the total borrowings approach the net worth, i.e. 1:1 gearing (or 100%), then the farmer has to be very good in technical and management ability to cope with this high level of gearing. There is however no 'proper' ratio – so much can depend on the individual farm business and effectiveness of management.

When you add the complication of freehold property values then, as stated earlier, the net worth will become far greater and the gearing will become meaningless. It is then that the banker must look again to the level of profits earned and to be earned, together with the cash flow generated, to determine the prudent gearing level.

*   Authors' Note – Most agricultural colleges collect data on a local basis and this can be very useful to the lending banker in judging the farmer's performance.

Looking at Serviceability

In assessing the farmer's capacity to meet his commitments and service his borrowing, as well as looking at the past profit records and trends in net worth, examination of farm enterprise recordings is useful to see more up-to-date progress. In our example, Farmer A could be recording his dairy herd on a government-run scheme. Figures will be available usually up to the end of the previous month in a very detailed analysis of input costs and output (per cow) for all the herds – identified by code number – in his area. Examination will indicate not only month-by-month costs and output, but also rolling averages, i.e. annual averages updated month by month.

Farmer A will thus be able to monitor his herd performance and compare it with that of other local farmers.

Quick Guidelines for Serviceability

There are two methods that will quickly identify the financial pressures that the farm business will face: rent and finance charges (rental equivalent) and rental equivalent as a percentage of gross output.

Rent and Finance Charges (rental equivalent)

This is useful as a guideline for tenants and owner–occupiers or a combination of both. It takes into account all financial commitments plus the rent payable and thereby removes the distinction between the tenant and owner. It is very useful to discuss this with the farmer who usually has a 'gut feeling' as to the level of rental equivalent per acre that he can manage successfully. The figure is calculated by including the following charges per annum:

(a) rent and rates

(b) bank overdraft interest

(c) bank loans – interest and capital repayments

(d) special agricultural loans – interest and capital repayments

(e) hire-purchase charges

(f) leasing charges

(g) credit charges

(h) private loans – interest and capital.

This total is then divided by the effective acreage.

Example

Using Farmer A's figures:

	£
Rent	6,400
Bank overdraft average balance – say £4,000 debit @ 15%	600
Loan capital and interest	1,400
	£8,400

Divided by 320 = £26 per acre.

The interpretation of this rental equivalent depends on the type of the farm and farming system. It is best, as with tenants' assets per acre, to build up your own file on rental equivalents. However, a charge of, say, less than £60 per acre would generally be considered low.

Rental Equivalent as a Percentage of Gross Output

The rental equivalent yardstick takes no account of the output of the business, but this new measurement looks at rental equivalent as a percentage of farm gross output. The farm gross output is the net of total farm returns plus the value of produce consumed in the farmhouse or supplied to workers, less purchases of livestock and other products bought for resale.

Guidelines in the UK are:

(a)   less than 10% – there should be little problem;

(b)   between 10% and 15% is the usual range;

(c)   15% to 20% is getting tighter and needs a closer look;

(d)   20% or more is considered high.

Example – Farmer A's rent and finance charges totalled £8,400. Let us assume for our purposes that his farm business gross output is £103,500 per annum. The rental equivalent as a percentage of gross output is therefore 8% (a low charge).

Farm Budgets

The guidelines we have looked at, i.e. rental equivalent and rental equivalent as a percentage of gross output, are only quick measurements. The total serviceability picture can be seen far more clearly when examining the total farm budget. Some farmers argue that budgets are a waste of time, but they are certainly essential in planning the profitability of the farm and the likely cash flow movements. If the farmer cannot prepare farm budgets himself there are many people prepared to assist, such as the local Ministry of Agriculture advisers.

Returning to our old friend Farmer A, it may help to refresh your memory on farm enterprises. Here is a farm budget which could be presented.

Gross Margin Budget

Enterprise			Gross Margin £	Total £
100	dairy cows	@	600	60,000
20	dairy replacements	@	271	5,420
60	sows	@	171	3,420
200	ewes	@	33	6,600
20	acres winter wheat	@	186	3,720
12	acres spring barley	@	136	1,632
30	acres winter barley	@	153	4,590
		Total Farm Gross Margin £		85,382

Less:

Fixed Costs

Labour	29,508	
Power and machinery:	9,688	
Running costs and		
replacement costs	(depreciation) 5,744	
Rent	6,400	
Other costs	4,224	55,564
Trading Margin £		27,818

Less:

Finance Costs

Overdraft interest	600	
Loan capital and interest	1,400	
		2,000
Net Margin £		27,818

Available for drawings, taxation and further items of capital expenditure:

New milking equipment	£12,000
Drawings	£10,000

The budget is based on existing information and expected yield levels to be obtained. The margin after finance costs of £29,818 should be compared with past performance detailed in the accounts. Also the individual gross margin levels stated can be checked against standard data.

Summary of Farmer A

Here it is worth restating some of the main points.

Farmer's Balance Sheet

	£
Total assets	113,376
Liabilities	18,050
Net worth	95,326
Bank borrowing	13,900
Budget margin:	27,818
Rental equivalent £26 per acre.	As a percentage of gross output = 8%

There should be no problem with this farmer, based on the assessments we have made.

Cash Flow Forecasts

The profitability of the farm business has been shown in the farm budget. The viability of the business in cash terms will be shown in the cash flow forecast. The basic principles of the cash flow forecast are exactly the same as with any other business. There are a few additional points to note:

- The timing of many items is tied to biological and physical factors which may well be fixed (e.g. milk production – lactation period 44 weeks).

- Some farm enterprises extend over more than a 12-month period (e.g. 18-month beef), and again, harvest proceeds may not be received before farm input costs are being incurred for the next year's harvest.

- The farmer's technical plan as to the stocking and cropping of the farm is useful alongside the cash flow forecast to make sense of crop sales figures, etc. (e.g. yield per acre multiplied by the product price anticipated).

- The farm business may well consist of several farm enterprises with differing cash flow forecast patterns, e.g:

  - An arable farm will have peak requirements probably August to November before receipt of harvest proceeds.

  - Dairy farms generally show a lower requirement during the summer grazing months.

  - Stock farms' bank balances tend to peak in spring and autumn, linking with livestock purchases and sales.

- If the maximum negative cash flow balance is unacceptable, can it be restructured?

  - Sell crops and livestock earlier?

  - Buy farm inputs later?

  - Phase capital expenditure?

  - Use leasing of expensive machinery, instead of purchasing?

  - Use other farm input credit plans?

As with other businesses, high profit will be useless if there is no cash available for working capital. There must be funds for the day-to-day running of the business.

An abridged example of a farmer's cash flow forecast form is given in the table below. The following are guidance notes for its completion.

Guidance Notes for the Farmer's Completion of the Cash Flow Forecast Form

1. Look at farming enterprise plans for the coming 12 months and from these plans estimate farm income and expenses (accepting that it is difficult to predict market prices and timing of sales).

2. It will probably be useful to group income under headings as follows: crops; livestock/milk sales; subsidies and any capital introduced.

3. Then group expenses under headings as follows: variable costs; fixed costs; livestock purchases; personal drawings; other expenditure.

Examples of Variable Costs	Fixed Costs	Other Expenditure
Feeds	Power and machinery	Bank charges
Fertilizers	Running costs	Mortgage repayment and interest
Spray	Regular labour	Taxation
Veterinary and medical etc.	Rent and rates	Capital expenditure (e.g. new tractor)
	Building repairs	
	Insurance – general	
	Other costs	

4. Now total income and expenses for each planned month and obtain a net inflow or outflow of cash.

5. Insert starting bank balance and then progress forward through the months. Predicted bank balances can now be seen clearly.

6. If the deficit in the predicted bank balance is unacceptably high, it may be possible to restructure by, say, altering the timing of product sales; altering planned capital expenditure; merchant credit; HP or leasing.

7. Finally as the year progresses enter actual income and expenses so that actual can be compared with predictions.

Farmer's Cash Flow Forecast

P = Planned

A = Actual

£'s

	Jan		Feb		Mar		And	Annual
Year	P	A	P	A	P	A	Subsequent	Summary
Income							months	
Livestock Sales							to the	
Milk Sales							end	
Subsidies							of the	
Other Income							year **	
Capital Introduced								
Total Income **(A)**								
Payments								
Variable Costs								
Fixed Costs								
Livestock Purchases								
Personal Drawings								
Other Expenditure								
Total Expenditure **(B)**								
Monthly Balance (A) - (B)								
Cumulative Balance								

** The complete form would have columns for 12 months plus the annual summary.

8.5   Security for Farm Lending

If the land is owner-occupied a first or second mortgage over the land can be taken. Some farms are operated by limited companies, in which case the usual fixed or floating charge may be taken. However, most farmers operate as sole traders or partnerships and, in addition to the usual forms of security, the following special type of security for farming advances should be considered.

An Agricultural (Floating) Charge

Such a charge covers all the farmer's farming assets, including crops, animals and farm machinery. It does not capture debts due to the farmer, or EC milk quotas, which are a personal asset of the farmer and are of particular value, nor does the charge cover the land.

Otherwise, similar rights to those under a limited company debenture are obtained, including the power to appoint a receiver to take over and realize assets.

The disadvantages of an agricultural charge are that farmers try to resist giving them, in the belief that registration will damage their standing in the farming community and that if a receiver is eventually appointed, the farm and stock will already be run down and landlords or bailiffs for other creditors may have seized stock already.

Case Study 16 – Grundy Farms

Jack Grundy is a farmer who has banked with you for over 20 years. He farms in partnership with his two sons who live in cottages on the farm; Jack Grundy owns all the farm property in his sole name. Grundy is in his 70s and the sons in their 40s; they have all been in farming throughout their lives. The farm currently consists of 497 acres which are held freehold by Grundy. It is an arable enterprise growing a mixture of wheat, oilseed rape and beans. You regard the Grundys as good, practical farmers who are lacking in financial acumen.

Over the years, the partnership borrowing has increased steadily. You have tolerated the situation partly because the bank has a charge over the farm and buildings (professionally valued at £850,000 two years ago) and partly because Grundy was involved in prolonged negotiations with a local builder to sell 10 acres of land for £250,000. This sale was completed a month ago and the overdraft now stands at £265,411.

Grundy has asked for an overdraft limit of £350,000 to see him through the next 12 months. In company with your bank's specialist farming manager for the area, you have recently visited the farm and have established that the enterprise's current financial position is as follows:

Growing Crops Value

	£
Ploughing – 280 acres x £12 per acre	3,360
Oilseed rape – 88 acres value x £42 per acre (including seed costs etc.)	3,696
	7,056
Stock – fertilizer, seed, etc.	6,900
Debtor – VAT refund	2,000
Plant and machinery	54,550
Farmland and buildings (Grundy's estimate)	750,000
Trade creditors	9,897
Tax creditor – PAYE/National Insurance contributions (estimated)	4,500
Hire purchase	10,777

The cropping plan for 1994/5 is as follows:

	Forecast Acres	Forecast Gross Income *	Margin *
Winter wheat	236	62,205	42,489
Winter oilseed rape	88	12,100	4,444
Winter beans	44	10,560	8,140
Set aside	52	4,427	4,427
Grassland/rough/buildings	77	–	–
Other government payments and income	-	48,768	48,768
	497	138,060	108,268

* Bank farming manager estimates

Required:

Set out in note form your analysis of the business and indicate the response you would make to Grundy's request.

J. Grundy and Sons: Balance Sheets as at 31 March

	1992			1993		1994	
Current Assets							
Debtors	6,002	2,747	2,533				
Stock	69,993	75,995	77,050	79,797	85,546	88,079	
Current Liabilities							
Creditors	46,589		24,457		36,976		
Hire purchase	–		16,898		6,064		
Bank	259,742	306,331	381,237	422,592	491,557	534,597	
Net current liabilities		(230,336)		(342,795)		(446,518)	
Fixed Assets							
Plant and machinery		29,783		54,735		47,014	
		(200,553)		(288,060)		(399,504)	
Financed By:							
Opening capital		(139,278)		(200,553)		(288,060)	
Add: Profit (loss)		(41,700)		(64,901)		(69,989)	
		(180,978)		(265,454)		(358,049)	
Less Drawings		(19,575)		(22,606)		(41,455)	
		(200,553)		(288,060)		(399,504)	

Profit and Loss Summary 12 months to 31 March			
	1992	1993	1994
	£	£	£
Sales	125,094	122,369	154,472
Gross profit	61,728	71,026	85,330
Overheads	103,428	135,927	155,319
including interest paid	39,441	59,543	77,169
Net profit (loss)	(41,700)	(64,901)	(69,989)

Accounting Ratios				
	1992	1993	1994	Forecast
Current ratio	0.24:1	0.19:1	0.16: 1	
Acid test	0.02:1	0.01:1	0.01:1	
Gearing %	–	–	–	
Interest cover	–	–	–	
Gross margin %	49.3	58.0	55.2	78.4
Net margin %	(33.3)	(53.0)	(45.3)	

Grundy - Suggested Response

The farmer is a long-standing customer who, effectively, the bank has stuck with. Although good practically, he does not seem to be able to make money in the business. If it had not been for the sale of land recently, the bank would probably have had no alternative but to call in the lending before now.

Given his age, Grundy is unlikely to change his way of operating and no comprehensive forecasts have been produced. In fact, the requested overdraft limit may not be sufficient and the bank needs detailed budgets and a cash flow forecast.

The absence of the deeds of the farm from the balance sheet makes a number of the accounting ratios worse than they really are. Even so, the ratios show that the business is highly illiquid, although the reduction in borrowing has improved the position since the year end. There is enough information to draw up a farmer's balance sheet:

	Liabilities		Assets
Trade creditors	9.897	Debtor – VAT	2,000
Tax	4,500	Growing crops	7,056
Bank	265,411	Stock	6,900
HP	10,777	Farmland etc.	750,000
Capital	<u>529,921</u>	Plant and machinery	<u>54,550</u>
	820,506		820,506

A new professional valuation is needed to confirm the farm value, but Grundy's figure may not be unreasonable and so prospective gearing is reasonable, with borrowing at around £360,000 against the capital base of £530,000.

The main issue is, therefore, whether the borrowing can be serviced. If the forecast growth in profit is right – and **it** is an independent estimate – the business is unlikely to be profitable. Overheads will reduce with the lower interest charge, but even with interest at, say, £30,000 per annum and other overheads remaining static, total overheads would still be around £108,000 compared to a gross margin also of £108,000– breakeven. Moreover, this takes no account of drawings which represent the labour costs of running the farm given the family involvement. So, unless overheads can be significantly reduced, the borrowing will steadily increase.

On the assumption that the hire purchase debt shown in the balance sheet has been repaid, the rental equivalent per effective acre can be assumed to be £30,000 acres to take account of set aside land, i.e. £81. The benchmark figure for arable land is £60 per effective acre, so the serviceability of the borrowing must be in doubt, especially when capital reductions are added to anticipated interest.

It looks highly unlikely that Grundy will be able to service the proposed level of borrowing. However, provided the security valuation stands up, the borrowing will be safe in the short term. Grundy will have to be pressed to sell more land if the borrowing is to be cut to acceptable levels, although this of course will reduce his income. While, therefore, it should be possible to agree the facility as a short-term measure, it can only be done on the basis that Grundy accepts professional advice on future planning and disposals.

8.6   Professionals

This implies someone with a professional qualification. A professional person is usually fee-earning and providing a service, rather than selling goods. He or she will usually hold a qualification from a professional body, e.g. accountants from the Institute of Chartered Accountants or similar body, solicitors from the Law Society. He or she may require a licence to practise from the professional body. The term 'professional' embraces a wide range of spheres and will include estate agents, in addition to doctors, dentists and architects.

Professionals are usually regarded by banks as key business influencers and may handle large sums of clients' money. These can be a good source of credit balances for banks.

Although some 'professionals' practise as sole traders, the more usual format is that of being a partner in a partnership.

Partners are jointly liable for partnership debts. Advances by banks to partners always embrace a joint and several mandate to ensure that each partner is both jointly and severally liable for partnership debts. This also means that personal assets are available for creditors.

Normally the workings of a partnership are covered by a partnership agreement in writing. If there isn't one, partners share profits and losses on an equal basis.

Partners are remunerated by drawings from the partnership. Although professional persons are highly regarded as potentially wealthy bank customers, the usual canons of lending need to be observed. Drawings may be anticipated before financial statements for the practice are published.

Having said this banks tend to be sympathetic to professionals in view of their usually high standing in the community and their often strong earnings potential.

Case Study 17 – John Tooth

John Tooth has had an account at your branch since he started his course at the dental school of a major university ten years ago. Since he graduated five years ago, he has worked as a full-time associate for a practice in your area. He currently earns around £36,000 per annum. The balances on his accounts are:

Current account	£1,000Cr.
Savings account	£3,000 Cr.
Car loan	£1,800 Dr. (repayable at £200 per month)

Tooth requests a meeting with you. At the meeting he explains that Alan Molar, the principal of another local practice, died suddenly in July. The practice was operated by Molar and two part-time associates who were paid 45% of their gross fees. For the past three months, the associates have continued to operate the practice but Mr Molar's widow wishes to sell it as soon as possible.

Molar's practice used the ground floor of his home, which Tooth has had valued at a figure of £106,000. Tooth has been negotiating with the executors of Molar's estate and they have agreed to sell the practice on the following basis:

House	£100,000
Equipment	£ 30,000
Goodwill	£ 30,000
	£160,000

Tooth has examined the equipment; it is in good order and in his opinion worth £40,000.

He is keen to purchase the practice. It is situated only two miles from where he works at present and he expects some of his existing patients to follow him. He hopes to be able to increase the income of Molar's practice by at least £20,000 per annum from this source.

Tooth explains that he bought his own house five years ago with the help of a building society endowment mortgage of £50,000. The house was valued last week at £90,000 and he has a number of potential buyers interested.

He has £12,000 saved in a building society account, although he has a tax demand of £6,000 to pay on 1 January 1998.

He has received copies of Molar's accounts which he gives to you. He asks you to help him to fund the purchase of the practice.

Required:

Set out, with reasons, the response you would make to Tooth's request.

Alan Molar, Dental Surgeon: Income and Expenditure Account for the year ending 31 March

	1995 £	£	1996 £	£	1997 £	£
Fees		133,400		143,600		152,600
Less:						
Materials, drugs etc.	14,400		15,800		17,000	
Salaries – associates	28,400		30,200		32,800	
staff	20,200		22,400		24,800	
Premises expenses	4,800		15,800		17,600	
Travel expenses	3,600		3,800		4,200	
Sundries	3,000		3,600		3,800	
Finance costs	4,000		3,600		4,200	
Depreciation	1,200		9,600		9,200	
Total expenses		99,600		104,800		113,600
Net income		33,800		38,800		39,000

Accounting Ratios

	1995	1996	1997
Current ratio	0.31:1	0.57:1	0.41:1
Acid test	0.27:1	0.52:1	0.36:1
Gearing (%)	183	137	111
Interest cover (times)	9.5	11.8	10.3
Credit given (days)	33	57	33
Credit taken (days)	106	111	120
Net margin (%)	25.3	27.0	25.6
(before drawings)			

Alan Molar, Dental Surgeon: Balance Sheet as at 31 March

	1995		1996		1997	
	£	£	£	£	£	£
Fixed Assets						
Equipment	40,800		37,200		35,000	
Motor vehicles	12,000		9,000		17,000	
	52,800		46,200		52,000	
Current Assets						
Debtors	12,200		22,600		13,800	
Stock	1,400		1,800		1,800	
	13,600		24,400		15,600	
Current Liabilities						
Creditors	4,200		4,800		5,600	
Bank	12,200		13,600		4,600	
Hire purchase	8,000		4,400		8,000	
Loan (father)	20,000		20,000		20,000	
	44,400		42,800		38,200	
Net current liabilities		(30,800)		(18,400)		(22,600)
Net tangible assets		22,000		27,800		29,400
Financed by:						
Capital b/f		19,200		22,000		27,800
Net income	33,800		38,800		39,000	
Less: drawings	(31,000)	2,800	(33,000)	5,800	(37,400)	(1,600)
		22,000		27,800		29,400

John Tooth – Suggested Answer

This question concerned the purchase of a professional practice for a dentist. Mr Tooth is a long-standing good customer. There is background evidence of an ability to save in the balances of his accounts, with both the bank and building society.

However, he has never run a business before and although it is natural that he should wish to have his own practice, the proposition needs to be approached with caution. Given Tooth's lack of business experience, ideally he should use an accountant to produce a business plan both for himself and the bank.

The proposition falls into two parts:

1. The house purchase

2. The purchase of the practice

Taking the house purchase first, the figures are:

	£	£
Purchase price		100,000
Sale of existing house	90,000	
Less mortgage	50,000	40,000
Requirement	=	60,000 + expenses

There should be no problem in agreeing a mortgage of say £65,000 (to include expenses) given Tooth's expected drawings.

There could be pressure for a bridging loan so that the purchase can be completed quickly. In all the circumstances, it would probably be unwise for Tooth to enter into an open-ended bridging loan because, if there were any difficulty in selling his own house, he would be starting up in business on his own with additional interest pressures which he will not need when trying to find his feet in the new venture. A bridging loan on a closed basis should not, however, pose any problem.

Turning to the purchase of the practice, the amount required is:

Equipment	£30,000
Goodwill	£30,000
	£60,000

Is the asking price reasonable?

Tooth ought to be reasonably competent in assessing the value of the equipment but, if there is any doubt, an independent outside valuation should probably be undertaken. The value of the goodwill is more problematical.

Essentially, this is what the business is worth to a purchaser because it assures him/her of a future income. The figures show that the business has been steadily profitable and at £30,000 the goodwill is less than one year's profit before drawings so the figures look reasonable or even cheap.

One problem could be that some of Molar's business may have a personal link to him and could go elsewhere. Some idea of the loyalty of the customer base would be helpful.

Tooth has cash available of around £16,000, but some of this may be needed to meet legal expenses and so on. Moreover, there will be a need for a working capital facility.

The 1997 balance sheet figures show current assets of £15,600, of which only £5,600 can be financed by creditors.

It would appear that there is a need for a working capital overdraft facility of around £10,000 to cover the gap, perhaps even more. This is where a business plan would be useful and in particular a detailed cash flow forecast. In any event, a budget is going to be needed to establish on reasonable assumptions that Tooth can afford the repayments on a loan of, say, £60,000, plus his mortgage.

As security, a charge over the house is needed/would be available. However, this will not cover the debt. Assuming an independent valuation confirms the £100,000 asking price, this amount of security will be set against debt totalling something around £130,000.

There will be a balance-sheet deficit at the outset, given the purchase of the goodwill, and the security position is weak. However, all the indications are that the cash flows to meet repayment should be strong and there is plenty of margin for error. A surprising number of candidates decided to decline the application on the back of the weak security position. Candidates have plenty of personal experience of dentists and their ability to maintain their cash flows provided they keep their clients happy. The stability of the cash flows ought to have swung things for them.

A detailed analysis of the existing balance sheet is not necessary given that Tooth is only acquiring the assets and not the business as a whole. This means the accounting ratios will change depending on Tooth's own financial position. The P&L account is different and the fact that there is already £4,200 of finance charges there indicates a figure available to meet future interest, assuming the existing customer base remains loyal. The extra £20,000 of business Tooth brings ought to be sufficient to cover the gap. Repayments on a £60,000 loan over 10 years should be less than £10,000 per annum, so the cash gap would look to be around £6,000.

One issue that ought to be considered is whether Tooth will indeed be able to bring the £20,000-worth of business because his existing employers are not going to like this and he may have a contract which restrains him from poaching customers.

8.7   High Technology Companies

A Definition

High technology is the conversion of recent scientific advances into commercial products or processes.

So What's so Different about Hi-Tech Companies?

One of the major problems in financing high technology companies is the complexity of the product or service.

The Features of a High Technology Company

Most high technology companies have products with short life cycles and a continuing need to allocate resources to research and development. Many companies find the cost and time taken up in bringing a new product or process to market to be far in excess of their original estimates. They need to have the resources available to bring their projects to fruition. The cost of research and development of new products and processes is such that most leading-edge development is undertaken by larger institutions – both private and public.

A feature in recent years has been the number of people who have left larger institutions to start up their own small companies. They are able to do this by virtue of the expertise that they have developed in their previous occupations. Considerable expertise is needed when lending to these new companies. Sometimes the capital required for technology start–ups comes from the venture capital sector.

There are two main types of company:

Those that seek to develop a product or process and take it to market through their own distribution channels. This can be very speculative with no guarantee of sales.

Those that shelter the risks by undertaking work on behalf of larger organizations on a consultancy/subcontract basis. By working on firm contracts these companies know the level of turnover that will be generated provided that performance is satisfactory.

Lending Considerations

Particular emphasis needs to be given to the following:

- Assessment of the business and its strategy.
- Tight monitoring of current profitability as well as future work/order book.
- Close monitoring of debtor security as regards worth, age and spread.
- It may be appropriate to take a charge over intellectual property rights which could have a residual value if things should go wrong.

Before lending, consideration should be given to the following areas:

It would not be usual to finance research and development expenditure. Where there is a need for such finance equity must be introduced.

Security Considerations

It may be appropriate when dealing with many smaller companies to lend only on a short-term basis against full debenture cover (a fixed and floating charge over the company's assets.) Lending would normally be against an agreed percentage of good book debts.

New Ventures

Care should be taken where principals leave an existing business to start up on their own. There could be disputes over the contracts of employment, the use of privileged information and the poaching of the customers of the previous company.

Nature of the Assets

Although debtors will be the most valuable asset of a high technology company, lenders need to be circumspect as to their worth. Stock can also be of dubious value as security, bearing in mind the short product life cycles involved. Care needs to be exercised regarding obsolescent stock.

The most important aspect of a high technology company may be the core technology itself. Intellectual property rights can be protected by registration of patents or trademarks. Some lending institutions have special forms covering a mortgage over intellectual property rights.

Monitoring

Advances to high technology companies require close monitoring. Fortunes can change rapidly in this sector and lenders need to stay close to ongoing situations. It is important to obtain detailed monthly management information. Too wide a diversification into the development of a wide number of products can be a drain on successful core income streams.

9

SPECIALIST SERVICES RELEVANT TO LENDING SITUATIONS

Objectives

After studying this chapter, you should be able to:

● Understand the risks involved in trade finance;

● Be aware of the various types of bank facility, specifically designed to assist importers and exporters;

● Have a working knowledge of some of the unique uncertainties facing your importing and exporting customers;

● Be aware of some of the specialist services available in lending situations;

● Understand the most commonly used risk management products;

● Describe the features of the main alternative forms of business finance;

● Analyse the needs of borrowing customers and recommend appropriate products.

9.1   Trade Finance

Introduction

Having studied international trade finance, you will already know there are a number of *ifs* recommended books available, which examine the technical aspects of international trade transactions.

The following pages will therefore concentrate on a summary for the assessment of credit risk in trade transactions. There will generally be higher risks for businesses engaged in overseas trading. For example, it will be more difficult to sue overseas debtors or suppliers should things go wrong and there are potential political and exchange-rate risks. Although the bulk of the finance for importing and exporting is still by means of bank overdrafts in the normal manner, there are several other ways of financing international trade.

9.2   Finance for Exporters

The terms and method of payment in international trade are agreed between the exporter and importer in their contract. The terms required by the seller will depend very much on previous experience, if any, of the market (including the degree of competition between other sellers for the business), the customer and the customer's financial standing. Due to the extra risks involved in international trade, the exporter will be even more concerned about the degree of security in the payment, the speed of its transmission and the costs involved in receiving it.

The main methods of obtaining payment, in increasing order of security from the exporter's viewpoint, are:

- Open Account;
- Bills of Exchange and Documents for Collection;
- Payment under a Letter of Credit;
- Payment in Advance.

Obviously, the order is reversed for importers, who will prefer open account and would wish to avoid payment in advance.

Open Account

Where an exporter is dealing with a first-class overseas buyer, goods are often despatched on an open-account basis. The exporter will send the documents of title for each shipment direct to the buyer and request settlement by a certain date. This is similar to the way in which credit sales are made between businesses within the same country, provided that the business's credit standing is seen as satisfactory. The only difference in international trade is that the distances involved are greater, the documentation is more involved and it is more difficult to pursue payment. The disadvantage for the exporter of open-account trading is that control is lost of the goods and the title to them. Therefore, it is advisable to establish the business integrity of overseas customers by obtaining a banker's opinion. Importers, however, prefer open-account trading, because it allows them to receive and inspect the goods (and perhaps even sell them) before making settlement.

Bills of Exchange

A bill of exchange is a means of payment used by companies to finance trade transactions. It represents an unconditional payment order for a fixed amount either at sight or at a fixed or determinable future date. The drawer of the bill (the exporter) is able to obtain monies in advance of payment by the drawee (the importer), through either discounting or negotiating.

Exporting with settlement by bills of exchange

An exporter can transact his business in several ways:

1.   He can export the goods and send all documents to the importer, together with a bill of exchange. The importer than accepts the bill of exchange and returns it to the exporter, who may then ask his bankers to collect the proceeds, or to discount or negotiate the bill of exchange.

2.   He can export the goods, but send all documents to his banker with instructions for the documents to be released against payment, or to be released against acceptance of a bill of exchange payable after a certain term. If the documents are complete and give a good title, the goods would provide additional security so long as the documents are to be released only against payment. If the documents are released against acceptance of a bill of exchange, the goods will then be obtained by the importer.

3.   He can ask the importer to arrange for a letter of credit to be established in this country whereby he can obtain payment or have a bill of exchange accepted by a banker upon presentation of stated documents.

Sometimes exporters consider that there is little risk to a banker in discounting bills of exchange, if the exporter holds a credit agency policy that is assigned to the bank. This can certainly strengthen the position, if the exporter is reliable and experienced, but if any of the conditions of the policy have not been observed, there will be no valid claim. This type of security falls far short of a bank guarantee.

Discounting and negotiating bills of exchange

There are differences between discounting and negotiating. If a bill of exchange in sterling is discounted, the resultant amount is also in sterling. If a bill of exchange in foreign currency is converted to sterling and then the sterling is discounted, the resultant amount will also be in sterling. However, an additional transaction will have taken place – i.e. the conversion into a different currency.

If in the second instance the bill of exchange is dishonoured (and recourse to a customer is invariably obtained by a banker), the banker will charge the customer with the sterling equivalent of the bill of exchange at the rate of exchange then ruling and not the rate ruling at the time the bill was negotiated. Except under the credit agency shorter-term schemes for bills and notes, bankers do not normally discount or negotiate bills of exchange of longer than six months' tenor.

A banker can discount or negotiate an unaccepted bill of exchange with recourse to the drawer. Once the bill of exchange has been accepted by a third party, a banker would have a claim on both the drawer and the acceptor. This could give the bill more substance, but a banker would prefer to rely upon his own customer of whom he has knowledge.

Bills of exchange can be drawn to be payable at sight or at a number of days after sight or date. It must always be kept in mind that bankers take the precaution of retaining recourse against their customers. This is the starting point when considering the liabilities that may have to be faced by a customer.

Advances against bills of exchange

An exporter with a bill of exchange, instead of asking his banker to discount or negotiate it, can ask for an advance to be made, prior to maturity, of less than the face value of the bill. The bill of exchange can be accepted or unaccepted, have documents attached or be clean. Similar considerations will apply as for discounting and negotiating. In the case of an advance, however, the liability of the customer on recourse would be less than when the full value is discounted or negotiated. The bills will be hypothecated to the bank as security. In addition, the bank will also take status reports on the drawees. Also it will make sure, if possible, that the goods involved are re-saleable, together with assignment of any credit insurance.

Documentary Credits

Bankers can lend to valued export customers, who are utilizing documentary credits. The bank must be certain that the customer can meet all the document criteria and will maintain full recourse to the customer.

Smaller Exports Scheme

Banks can provide 'non-recourse' finance, under an umbrella policy held by the bank, for customers with a low export turnover. The bank will, in effect, negotiate bills drawn by customers for exporters. If the customer has fully carried out the export transaction, the bank's policy will pay out if the bill is not paid. However, if the customer has not complied with the commercial contract or the policy rules, the bank will reserve the right of recourse to the customer. The main issuer of short-term exporter policies (up to two years), is NCM Ltd, which took over from the Export Credit Agency (ECGD) in this field.

Medium-Term Supplier Credit

For longer terms of supplier credit (usually for capital exports), between two and five years, the ECGD will guarantee to refund the bank up to 85% of the transaction if it provides finance. A 15% deposit from the buyer is taken in advance.

Forfaiting

Forfaiting is a facility available to exporters (although also being increasingly used for domestic transactions) who want to provide non-recourse credit to their overseas buyers. It is mainly used for capital goods transactions, but can also be used by exporters of raw materials and commodities. (Cross-reference to Chapter 9 for Specialist Services for Borrowers is recommended.)

Forfaiting works by the forfaiter purchasing, without recourse to the exporter, bills of exchange or promissory notes that represent the payment for the goods. The credit period is generally between one and five years, with the bills being drawn usually at six-month intervals. The forfaiter buys the bills at a discount and then relies totally on the overseas importer to obtain repayment. Because there is no recourse to the exporter the forfaiter will wish to be absolutely sure that the overseas buyer will pay. Thus, the ideal transaction is where the buyer is a 'blue chip' company or a government agency. Where this is not the case the forfaiter will normally look for the bills to be unconditionally guaranteed (avalized) by the buyer's bank.

Countertrade/Barter

Countertrade is the sale of goods or services to a country, where part or all of the settlement for the goods is in the form of an agreement to buy goods/services from that country. It is most commonly seen where exporters are dealing with countries that are short of foreign exchange, for example, Eastern Europe and the Third World. There is no generally accepted code of practice in respect of countertrade contracts, and there can be significant variations between one country and another.

International Leasing

This is identical to domestic leasing, where the leasing company purchases the asset and, for a regular leasing payment, allows the user full use of the asset. UK leasing companies, many being subsidiaries of banks, can provide this service direct to a foreign importer, or arrange for it to be done by a foreign associate. The exporter is paid in full by the leasing company without recourse (unless the goods are faulty).

Payment in Advance

For the exporter, this is undoubtedly the safest way to receive payment for goods. However, from an importer's viewpoint, it is the least acceptable. Buyers are seldom prepared to pay in full for goods in advance of shipment, unless for small consignments, e.g. spare parts, since the buyer is not only extending credit to the supplier, but relying on the integrity of the exporter to deliver the goods in a satisfactory condition on the agreed date. It is more common to find that the buyer is prepared to pay a cash deposit in advance, with the balance being settled by another method.

General Risk Considerations when Lending to Exporters

● What is the credit status of your customer?

● What is the status of the exporter's customer?

● Are there political risk implications?

● Are any credit insurances available?

● What is the spread of buyers?

● Are transit risks insured?

● Can security of goods be taken as fall-back position?

● Have exchange-rate risk management techniques been considered?

9.3　Finance for Importers

Documentary Credits

An importer can arrange for his banker to establish with a bank abroad a credit in favour of a third party upon which payment is to be made, when certain specified documents are presented. If a complete set of documents is insisted upon, a good title to the goods can be obtained and the bank will therefore have the goods as security.

If an importer is unable to get the goods shipped to him on open account, he may have to establish documentary credits, and these involve him in a liability to his banker. The importer has some protection, because the money is not paid away until documents showing shipment are produced. However, the documents purport to represent certain goods, and the goods have not been examined. An importer will, for his own protection, have to assure himself of the integrity of the exporter. Also, if a banker is relying upon the goods in any way as security, he will have to satisfy himself that the importer has ability and experience of the trade. If other security is not available, a banker would have to decide to what extent he would rely upon the goods and ask for any shortfall to be deposited in cash on a margin account, before the documentary credit is opened. By issuing an irrevocable letter of credit therefore, a bank is conditionally guaranteeing a customer's trade debt.

Acceptances

Just as an importer can arrange for his bank to tell a correspondent bank abroad to pay an overseas exporter, against the production of specified documents, so too can arrangements be made for a bill of exchange to be accepted when specified documents are produced.

As far as the importer's banker is concerned, he would be in the same position as with a documentary credit up to the time he released the goods to the importer. At that time, however, he would have given up the security of the goods, but would still be liable to the bank abroad on the bill of exchange, which would be presented for payment at the end of its tenor.

If other security was not available and a banker wished to retain the security in the goods he could either:

● warehouse the goods after having them pledged to him and release them against payment (or part of the goods against part payment), or

● in suitable cases, after the goods had been pledged to him, release them to the importer on a trust facility. The importer would then have to keep the goods separately, and account to the bank for all sales made. The proceeds of the sales would be credited to a separate banking account to meet the liability on the bill of exchange at maturity.

This type of facility should not be confused with the acceptance credits that are provided for exporters by merchant bankers. The exporter draws a bill of exchange on the merchant banker and produces the export documents. The merchant banker accepts the bill of exchange, which can be discounted immediately, and then collects payment against delivery of the documents.

Indemnities and Guarantees

Indemnities and guarantees are often encountered in importing and exporting. In order to assess the liability involved, every indemnity or guarantee has to be examined for amount, circumstances under which payment is to be made and period of time. Where importing is concerned, bankers are often asked to give indemnities because of missing bills of lading. A banker's liability will be the amount of the value of the goods, although this will be difficult to establish because the shipping documents are missing and he can only accept the importer's word. It is necessary, therefore, for the importer to have built up confidence with his banker and to have audited accounts sufficient to justify the banker accepting these liabilities on his behalf.

Avalizing

Avalizing involves adding the lender's name to a bill or promissory note on behalf of the drawee, giving the effect of 'guaranteeing' payment. An importer is therefore able to get his bank to guarantee a debt unconditionally to an overseas (or domestic) supplier.

As with finance for exporters, banks lending to importers must be fully aware of the risks involved. Again, do not overlook currency risk and make sure it is covered if appropriate.

Bonds and Guarantees Issued on Behalf of Customers

UK exporting customers, usually those dealing with large or capital goods, are often asked to provide various forms of bonds or guarantees to the purchasers of their goods or services. The bonds will be either conditional (requiring proof before calling) or unconditional (payable on call without proof being required). The bonds will be for varying percentages of the overall contract. As contingent liabilities, they need to be assessed against the customer's lending capacity. In all cases counterindemnities will be taken from the customer to enable the bank to debit the account immediately if a bond is called upon.

The recommended gradings of the various types of bonds and the associated risk are:

	Risk %
Tender or Bid Bond	20-100
Performance Bond	100
Advance Payment Bond	100
Progress/Retention Bond	100
Maintenance/Warranty Bond	100
Stand-by Credit	100

Before joining in a bond or issuing a guarantee, you must ensure that the customer is creditworthy and has a covering limit for the facility and that the document is in an acceptable format. If in doubt refer to the bank's legal department.

9.4   Specialist Services for Business Lending

Introduction

For the examination, you do need a working knowledge of banks' different methods of providing finance to mitigate or spread the various types of risks which may be present in any lending situation. For example, risks of non-repayment can often be minimized by offering the borrower insurance against the risks which might affect the earning capacity of the borrower or his business and reduce his ability to repay.

This whole area of risk management is a fast-moving sector and you will need to check on the availability of services from your own bank. Banks are frequently introducing new products and it is possible that your bank will have some very new products that are not mentioned below.

Risk management is a key area for all businesses and attention should be focused on all areas within the possible control of asset cover, insurance and transaction coverage.

Asset Cover

Any businesses can be vulnerable to loss of assets by fire, theft or accident. A lending bank could be affected by such a loss of assets through either:

(a)   charge over the assets as security for borrowing; or

(b)   income loss and subsequent failure of the business due to cash flow difficulties.

Other insurances need also to be considered:

- Keyman (loss of key directors, partners or employees);
- Interruption of business (in case of fire, flooding etc.);
- Public liability indemnity (against claims from staff or customers);
- Bad-debt insurance (against non-payment by debtors, both domestic and foreign);
- Employer's liability accident policy (for accident, injury etc.);
- Goods in transit;
- Loan payment protection;
- Credit insurance:
  - the provision of insurance policies to ensure that the seller of goods or services gets payment if the buyer defaults or fails to pay for reasons specified in the policy terms and conditions;

– Credit reference information to assist decisions and from which risk can be graded and assessed.

Insurance is available in the UK from commercial trade insurance companies such as Trade Indemnity, although some banks offer similar cover in-house.

Country and Political Risk Insurance

Risk insurance includes cover against income loss due to:

- Payment in foreign currency when payment should have been in sterling;

- Political, economic or legislative changes taking place overseas which delay or prevent the payment;

- An overseas government moratorium banning payments in general, or any specific loan by the foreign government;

- Force majeure.

Country-risk cover is available from specialist providers, mainly NCM Ltd for short-term payments or the Export Credit Guarantee Department (ECGD) for contracts with longer payment terms. ECGD also offer overseas investments insurance schemes covering political risks on British investment overseas.

Interest Rate Risk Management Products

Customers will be vulnerable to interest-rate risk if borrowing. For example, if borrowing at a floating rate, linked to base rate or LIBOR, the customer/borrower could face higher interest payments if interest rates generally increase. This is going to affect profitability and it could have severe impact in a heavily geared business. It must be remembered that investors are also vulnerable to a change in interest rates. For example, exposure to potentially lower return on investments due to a fall in rates.

Internal treasury techniques, which companies can use to minimize exposure, include:

- Smoothing – Process of distributing fixed- and variable-rate exposure in order to spread the risk. This maintains a degree of protection against increasing rates, while retaining the advantages of variable rate.

- Matching – Internal matching of liabilities and assets.

Banks are often prepared to offer fixed-rate loan accounts for business borrowing, but there are other mitigating techniques, which can either fix or reduce the interest rate risk, including:

- Interest rate swaps – A payer (or receiver) of floating-rate interest can agree to exchange or 'swap' his floating-rate commitment for a fixed rate of interest or vice versa. The underlying loan is not touched – only the interest-rate commitment changes.

- Caps and collars – Interest-rate caps can be arranged for a premium, where the seller will undertake to reimburse a borrower for any interest paid over an agreed limit for a certain period of time. A cap and collar is a cheaper way of doing this whereby the borrower purchases a cap, but agrees to pay over any interest saved if interest rates drop below a certain rate. With a cap alone, the borrower keeps the benefit of any fall in interest rates, however great, but he sacrifices some of this potential gain to benefit from a cap and collar.

- Interest-rate options – The buyer (borrower) has the right, but not the obligation, to a fixed rate of interest for a given borrowed sum for a certain period. This may be purchased in standardized form from futures exchanges such as LIFFE, or it can be tailor-made to meet the buyer's exact needs by way of an OTC (over-the-counter) contract, usually from a bank.

- Forward rate agreements – Forward rate agreements (FRAs) are a contract between two parties through which an interest rate is fixed to apply to a notional amount of borrowing for a specific period, commencing on a stated future date. This enables interest rates to be fixed on borrowed funds not yet drawn down.

- Interest rate futures – Interest rate futures are the main type of financial futures traded and are a special kind of forward contract. It is a binding agreement between two counterparties to buy/sell a stated notional amount of an interest-rate commitment on an agreed date in the future at a set price. Contracts have standardized terms and are linked to underlying financial instruments, such as long or short gilts.

Other interest-rates hedging tools, such as financial futures or 'forward forwards' are available through banks or specific future markets, but would usually be available for the higher levels of borrowing. For the examination, you need to know that such techniques are available and could be recommended to customers who may be interest-rates sensitive. It is particularly important to bear this in mind when interest-rates are low.

Exchange-Rate Risk Management Products

Overseas trade transactions involving foreign currency are subject to exchange risk. 'Hedging tools' can be used to protect your customers against such risks, but they need to be put in place at the time the contract is signed by your customer.

For example, when a contract for import or export is agreed, it will stipulate whether payment is to be made in the currency of the buyer, or of the seller, or in a third-party currency. If the currency of the deal is that of the buyer, the seller faces an exchange risk, because if the currency of the buyer falls in value, the seller will receive less of his own currency when the funds are received and converted. If the currency is that of the seller, the buyer takes the risk. If the currency is neither that of the buyer nor the seller, then both are at risk of adverse exchange-rate fluctuation.

Typical hedging tools available from most British banks would be:

Forward Foreign Exchange Contracts

These are irrevocable agreements between a bank and a customer for the purchase or sale of a fixed amount of a foreign currency at a specific rate of exchange agreed now. The contracts are traded in an over-the-counter (OTC) market in which most major banks participate. Dealers will make markets in different currencies and act as principal when taking customers' orders to purchase or sell currencies. Rates quoted for forwards are not speculative, they are quoted at a premium or discount to the spot rate. The forward rate is calculated from the differential between the interest rates prevailing in the two currencies that are being exchanged and the time of the maturity of the contract.

'Fixed' forward contracts can be used only on fixed future dates. Forward 'Option' contracts may be used at any time between two future dates. These contracts are still irrevocable and should not be confused with pure 'option' contracts. N.B. If the currency fluctuates in favour of your customer, he is obliged to deal at the agreed rate, and may miss out on an extra profit opportunity, but he is protected against any unexpected loss on the deal due to currency changes.

Currency Futures Contracts

A futures contract is a special kind of forward contract of sale. The most common type of financial futures contract traded are interest-rate futures. The main currency futures are for sterling, yen, Deutschmarks and Swiss francs, which are quoted against US dollars.

A futures contract enables the buyer to fix an exchange rate in the future. However, the terms of futures contracts are standardized, i.e. quantity and delivery date, and therefore it may not be possible to match a future commitment exactly. However, the standardized nature of the contracts and the centralized trading on regulated exchanges make most futures contracts liquid. The contract size is usually much smaller than the normal size of a forward foreign exchange contract. Currency futures are not widely used by corporates or investing institutions in the UK, who use the forward markets, which allow them to match exposures precisely.

Although contracts often require the delivery of a specified currency, in practice only a small percentage of contracts result in physical delivery. Instead they are closed out prior to the settlement date for the futures contract with settlement of any gain or loss. For contracts that are held until expiry, many are cash settled, i.e. one party pays the other party the cash difference between the price at which the contract was last revalued according to the margining process, and the exchange delivery settlement price. As with forwards, if futures contracts are used for hedging purposes, any potential profit from favourable movements, which may occur before maturity, will be foregone.

Currency Options

The customer has the right, but not the obligation, to deal in a certain amount of currency at an agreed rate at or between certain future dates. An option to purchase is called a call option and an option to sell is called a put option. The price at which the option is exercised is known as the strike or exercise price.

If the currency exchange rate moves in favour of the customer, he can choose to deal at the spot rate, and is not obliged to deal at the agreed option rate. Currency options (not to be confused with an 'option' forward contract) attract an up-front premium based on the rate, period and currency of the option. The higher the perceived risk to the bank in offering this option, the higher the premium. Banks do not normally charge for forward contracts. Both forward contracts and currency options are available for periods up to one year and often for longer periods, depending on the currency involved.

Foreign Exchange Accounts

Customers in the UK can hold bank accounts with their own banks in major foreign currencies. Overdraft, loan and other facilities may be made available in specific foreign currencies, or a cocktail of several, so that the customer can draw on his facility in the currency of his choice subject to the overall lending limit. For example, if a customer is expecting income in a foreign currency it may be worthwhile to borrow from his bank in that currency (particularly if the interest rates for borrowing in that currency are lower than those for sterling borrowing), and to repay it on receipt of the foreign income. Similarly, a customer may wish to purchase foreign currency now to cover an anticipated future debt, and invest it in a currency account (particularly if the interest rate is higher than sterling) until needed. In both the above cases the exchange rate for the foreign currency is fixed at an early stage for the customer, who can then budget accordingly.

9.5   Structured Financial Products

There are many products. For the purpose of the examination syllabus we will focus particularly on:

- Leasing
- Hire Purchase
- Factoring /Invoice Discounting
- Forfaiting
- Acceptance Credits
- Services to Farmers
- Venture Capital/Management Buy-outs and Buy-ins

Hire Purchase (or Lease Purchase)
- Utilized when a company does not wish to use cash to purchase new assets;
- Available from bank subsidiaries, or independent HP (hire purchase) companies;
- Repayments normally set at a fixed figure over periods up to 10 years;

- Interest rates fixed at the time the loan is agreed;

- Balance sheet treatment – Hire purchase appears on the balance sheet of the lessee. The equipment appears as an asset and the amount owed appears as a liability.

The customer is usually expected to make a payment of 10-20% of the cost of the asset. The remaining sum (plus interest) is budgeted for via fixed monthly, quarterly, half-yearly or annual repayments. With regard to tax, the interest part of the repayments is chargeable against profits and a writing-down allowance (WDA) on the capital sum is available as soon as the initial deposit or first repayment is made.

Leasing (or Contract Hire)

Leasing is the rental of an asset for a specified period of time during which the party having the benefit of the use of the asset pays a rental to the owner of the asset. The lessor is the owner of the asset, who receives a lease rental payment for the lease of the asset. The lessee is the user of the asset. A broker may act as an intermediary who may match the lessor and lessee. The two basic forms of leasing contract are operating lease and financial lease (or finance lease).

Operating lease

- Length of an asset's proposed usage is uncertain (it may be less than the life of the asset) or the expected use of the asset is limited. The lessee normally has the additional safeguard that should the equipment fail to function correctly during the agreed period, the lessor will replace or repair it at his own expense, or alternatively that the contract may be terminated.

- Documentation may also state that operating leases may be terminated by either party upon giving the required notice.

- Two common examples of an operating lease are for computers and industrial plant. Computer equipment leasing helps to protect the lessee from the effects of equipment obsolescence, because the contract may be easily terminated. With industrial plant, the lessor will often hire out the plant to, for example, a construction firm, for use on a specific project.

- Balance sheet treatment – Operating leases are not shown on the lessee's balance sheet. Hence operating leases do not affect gearing and are 'off balance sheet'.

Financial lease

- Covers the whole life of the asset and cannot usually be cancelled by either party.

- The two parties to the lease agree on an estimated lifespan for the asset, and the rental is fixed on this time period. If the lifespan of the asset exceeds the agreed period, the rental payments after that time will be reduced to a nominal sum. This sum remains in force until the asset eventually ceases to function, or until the asset is sold with the agreement of both parties.

It is a source of long-term finance because, to all intents and purposes, the lessee assumes all the benefits of ownership and thus uses the financial lease as an alternative to outright purchases.

● Balance sheet treatment – A financial lease appears on the balance sheet of the lessee. The equipment appears as an asset and the amount owed appears as a liability.

Pricing

The price of a lease is normally included as an amalgam of the interest, overheads, expected tax benefits and profit. Pricing is also linked to interest-rate expectations and the risk of the lessee. An operating lease gives potential for further profit because the asset may be re-leased. The lessor does, by contrast, face the risk that the resale value of the equipment is lower than the original estimate.

Taxation, capital allowances and leasing

A writing-down allowance (WDA) may be claimed, when an asset is purchased. The WDA effectively reduces the amount of tax paid by the owner of the asset. Clearly this is an important factor in the lease/buy decision, depending upon whether the company making the investment decision expects to pay corporation tax over the period for which the asset is required. WDAs, of course, change depending upon the latest government's budget directives.

If the company is liable for corporation tax, and it purchases the asset outright, it will claim the WDA, thereby reducing the amount of corporation tax actually paid. However, if there is little likelihood of the company paying corporation tax over the relevant future period, then the WDA would be of no use, and would not feature in its investment appraisal. Here it may be better for the company to lease the asset, and it may be presumed that the leasing company (the lessor) will claim the WDA to offset against its own corporation tax liability. This tax saving is then likely to be reflected in the lease payments agreed upon.

It may still, however, be cheaper for a company to lease equipment, rather than purchase outright, even if the company pays corporation tax. The decision to purchase or lease will be taken after a full investment appraisal, probably using discounted cash flow techniques.

Leasing Applicability Check List:

● Tax position – If your customer does not pay tax, leasing is probably the best method of acquiring plant and machinery.

● Type of machinery and usage – If usage is uncertain and if the machinery could soon become obsolete, operating leasing is the best method.

If neither of the above applies, ask your customer for details of expected net cash inflows to be generated by the machine over its life.

Finance Terms and Conditions for Leasing:

● The minimum amount must be £5,000. If the equipment costs less than this, it is not worthwhile, i.e. profitable, for the bank's subsidiary to arrange a deal.

● The client must be capable of meeting the rental payments. The leasing subsidiary will evaluate the proposition in a similar way to a bank's evaluation, but the leasing company can be more 'flexible' because (a) the lessor can repossess the leased asset in the event of default and (b) lessors have more expertise than banks in estimating the forced-sale value of machinery and finding buyers for repossessed machinery. In a 'marginal' case when a bank may not grant a medium-term loan, a leasing company may grant a leasing facility

Factoring and Invoice Discounting

Factoring involves the purchase from a company of some or all of its trade receivables with or without recourse to the company itself in the event that the receivables are unpaid. The factoring service may also involve the sales ledger administration for the company. Designed to aid a company's cash flow, it is mainly used by small companies where the ability to sell receivables immediately for cash can be vital.

Features of Factoring

● The customer gets immediate access to a cash injection which may otherwise not be received for some months. The factoring company can make available up to 80% of the invoice value to the seller. The balance will be paid over as soon as the factor receives payment from the buyer/debtor.

● Cash flow can be easily predicted.

● Finance available grows with turnover and therefore is available to fund rapid sales growth.

● The administrative burden of collecting debts can be lifted if the factor is running the sales ledger and chasing up payments.

● Even if advances are not drawn from the factor by the seller, debtors will usually pay promptly on invoice dates if they know they are dealing with a factoring company, thus speeding up cash flow.

● The customer enjoys the benefits of the factor's credit assessment techniques. The factor reserves the right to handle certain business. However, in general, it will wish to cover all a company's sales to get a good spread of risk because it guarantees the seller against buyer insolvency up to an agreed limit. The factor's customer can therefore trade safe in the knowledge that he will be free from bad debt losses. Factors normally expect to cover a minimum turnover of £100,000 per annum. Each debtor will be given a credit limit, which must be respected.

- Particularly when exporting, it enables the seller to offer open-account terms which increases his competitiveness in the local market and protects him against exchange risk if invoicing in foreign currency. Factoring can also aid the exporter by providing a service that allows credit checking and collection of overseas receivables, possibly in locations in which the exporter has no previous experience and few contacts.

- UK factors are able to provide factoring services also to overseas companies exporting to the UK. These services are usually provided through a correspondent factor based in the exporter's country. While UK factors can provide services directly to exporters selling into the UK market, it is normal that such factoring arrangements would relate to the 'service' element only, the financial facility not normally being available to overseas companies.

- UK importers also gain considerable benefit from overseas suppliers factoring their exports to the UK because they will receive open-account terms which save them the time and expense of arranging letters of credit or making payment on delivery. All accounting communication is taken care of within the UK, making payment for imports virtually as simple and straightforward as purchasing from a UK source.

Factoring Charges

- Interest on finance provided – comparable with most overdraft rates.

- Management fee for sales ledger administration, credit management and collection of payments. This will vary depending on the number of accounts, the number of invoices processed and the type of customers. The management fee, typically between 1-3% of turnover, has to be weighed against the time, resource and financial savings offered.

Invoice Discounting

Invoice discounting involves the discounter advancing the seller a proportion (usually 75% maximum) of a debt, upon receipt of a copy invoice. The seller issues his own invoices and receives the debtor's payments direct, thus not revealing to his customers that he is using a discounter/factor. The buyer pays the seller as per the invoice, and the seller then repays the advance to the factor. The administration fee for this service is much smaller than for factoring because sales ledger administration is not included, but bad debt insurance can be provided if necessary. The factor will wish to vet all debtors and the minimum turnover for an invoice discounting agreement is normally £500,000. The service is particularly popular with exporters.

Comparisons between factoring and invoice discounting

Factoring	Invoice Discounting
Invoices sent to the factor	Invoices sent directly to the buyer. Copy invoice sent to the factor/discounter
Up to 80% advanced. Factor collects the debt	Up to 75% advanced. Seller/client collects the debt
Debtor pays the factor	Debtor pays the seller
Factor settles the balance to the seller, less interest and charges on receipt of payment	Seller/client settles with factor/discounter when payment received
Sales ledger administration can be taken over by factor administration	Seller/client responsible for sales ledger
Factoring disclosed to the debtor	Discounting usually undisclosed
Charges between 1% and 3% of turnover, plus interest on any advances	Interest charged on amounts advanced.
Factor will handle all turnover	Factor discounts invoices as required.
Usually bad debt insurance included as part of the package	Usually bad debt insurance included as part of the package

N.B. The bank overdraft facility will need to be reviewed because it is currently being cleared by receipts from debtors. As cheques are received from the factor, the overdraft limit should be reduced. If the bank holds security, it will be asked to postpone its charge over debts to the factor/invoice discounter.

Forfaiting

Forfaiting is the purchase and trading of fixed medium-term debt obligations arising from the export of goods and/or services, as evidenced by fully negotiable promissory notes or bills of exchange guaranteed by a bank in the importer's country. Purchase is from the exporter and without recourse at a discounted rate.

Characteristics

- Transactions appropriate for forfaiting are normally for capital goods. Bills must relate to trade, and cannot be merely a means of raising finance.

- Normal transaction period is up to 5 years.

- The financial documents used are 'guaranteed', either because they are promissory notes of a reputable financial institution, or if bills of exchange because they are 'avalized', i.e. signed by a bank undertaking primary responsibility for payment (rather stronger than merely endorsing a bill, which makes the bank liable alongside any other endorsers).

Pricing is based on a discount in the relevant currency, representing LIBOR (or appropriate cost of funds), the tenor of the transaction and a risk weighting for the particular country and the bank that has given its guarantee or aval to the notes or bills.

- The bills or promissory notes are usually in a series with maturity dates at regular intervals, e.g. every six months, except where the full term of the arrangement is very short.

Advantages for the customer

- Improves liquidity and aids cash flow management, thereby reducing need for other forms of credit.

- Reduces administrative work and the cost of collecting debts over a period of years.

- Exchange risk transferred to the forfaiter as soon as paper is discounted.

- Avoids credit risk because payment is guaranteed as soon as paper is discounted. In the event of default by the buyer, there is no recourse to the customer.

- Enables indication rates to be obtained if required.

- Enables finance costs to be accurately included in the contract price a business quotes.

- Can eliminate interest-rate risk (which is helpful if rates are volatile) because firm quotes on rates are usually held for 48 hours.

- Encourages investing banks to take paper because there is a secondary market between forfaitors to some extent.

- Wide range of currencies (forfaiting is suitable where ECGD cover is available).

- Entails less documentation than for ECGD.

Acceptance Credits

An acceptance loan or acceptance bill facility can be arranged for suitable customers. The customers are allowed to draw bills of exchange on the bank, up to an agreed total amount at any one time. Bills are usually drawn at three-month terms, and the maximum for each bill is currently £10 million, although more than one bill may be drawn if within the overall limit.

The bank will accept the bills, which may then be discounted at very fine rates in the money market, and pay the customer the face value of the bill(s) less discount interest. The bank does not normally lend the money itself but will need to be satisfied that the customer will be creditworthy enough to stand the amount of the bill when it falls due. Interest is at money market discount rates, but if the acceptor is an eligible bank and the bill is drawn in connection with an underlying trade debt, claused to that effect, then interest at 'eligible bill rate' will be charged. It is common for one bill to be repaid by discounting another (rolling over). Bills are normally identified with a particular transaction, usually between £300,000 and £50M, with a maximum period of six months.

Services for Farmers

Trade credit

Trade credit in agriculture is basically the same as trade credit in any other industry. Suppliers give customers time to pay for goods supplied and, in doing so, help to finance their customers' businesses. In farming, the main source of trade credit comes from agricultural merchants who sell feed, fertilizer, seed, spray etc.

Trade credit in the past has tended to be rather generous, and merchants have allowed some farmers to carry forward unpaid amounts if their income from the harvest is not enough to pay their bills in full. Trade credit is not entirely satisfactory, however, for either the farmer or the merchant. The farmer will not be able to take advantage of bulk purchase discounts on offer from merchants if he takes too much credit. The merchant, on the other hand, has to wait for his money and so must obtain more finance himself for his working capital. Concern by merchants at the increasing cost of providing trade credit led to the development of point of sale credit schemes.

Point-of-sale credit schemes

Credit is offered by the agricultural merchant/supplier at the point of sale (i.e. when the customer makes his purchase). Normally as part of an agricultural merchant scheme, the merchant acts on behalf of a bank's subsidiary company and it is the banking subsidiary that provides the credit. Loans are available to the customer at a fixed or floating interest rate option to purchase 'inputs' such as fertilizer, feed and seed.

Similar point-of-sale credit schemes linked to machinery dealer schemes have been set up to provide farmers with loans to purchase machinery. Additionally, leasing may be arranged, via the merchant, by a leasing company.

Point-of-sale credit has been increasingly used in recent years because:

● Manufacturers and distributors have been increasingly aware of the marketing advantages of offering a 'financial package' to customers. Farmers are more likely to purchase their goods if such a package is offered. Some sales-aid schemes have been subsidized by manufacturers and distributors as a part of their marketing campaign, with the result that credit has been offered to farmers in these cases at low interest rates.

● Farmers were affected by high rates of inflation in the 1970s and then by the economic recession in the early 1980s and may have found themselves wanting to take advantage of credit more than in the past.

● Point-of-sale credit is readily available, without having to make a direct approach to the bank.

Leasing and hire purchase

There are three types of leasing arrangement in the agricultural industry: plant hire; financial lease; and contract hire. Financial leasing is the most common type.

Plant Hire

Plant hire involves the hiring of large items of machinery usually for a very short period of time, and paying a hire charge. (At the end of the hire period, the machinery is returned to the owner who then hires it out to another customer.)

Financial Lease

Under a financial lease, the machinery is sold by the supplier to a leasing company or finance house, which is often a subsidiary company of a bank. The leasing company does not take physical possession of the machinery because it will immediately make a lease agreement with the farmer. The leasing company is the lessor and the farmer is the lessee. The supplier delivers the machinery to the lessee.

Leasing Arrangement Terms:

- The lessor owns the machinery or equipment;

- The lessee makes regular payments to the lessor throughout the primary period of the lease, which will be a number of years. (Leasing is a form of medium-term credit);

- The lessee is responsible for repairs and maintenance of the machinery;

- The lessee's payments to the lessor are all 'allowable' expenses for tax purposes;

- At the end of the primary lease period, the lessee/farmer will be given an option to continue to use the machinery at a very low 'rent'. If the machinery is sold instead, the lessee will be allowed to keep most of the proceeds of the sale. (In effect, the lessor allows the lessee to keep most of the money as a rebate on previous lease payments.)

Farming cooperatives

A group of farmers might purchase an expensive piece of machinery and share its use. The purchase may qualify for government grant and a syndicate organized by the NFU will be favourably treated by a bank, if it applies for a bank loan.

A machinery syndicate is not strictly a cooperative, because a cooperative must be registered under the Industrial and Provident Societies Act 1945, or as a company under the relevant Companies Act. The government has given the task of encouraging cooperatives in agriculture to the Co-operative Development Board, which reports to the council of an organization called Food From Britain.

There are three broad types of cooperative:

- Marketing cooperatives – Associations formed to market and sell jointly the produce (outputs) of the group of farmers.

- Requisite cooperative – Association formed to obtain supplies or requisitions jointly, e.g. sprays, fertilizers etc. Cooperative buying should be successful in reducing purchase costs through bulk discounts.

- Service cooperative – Association that makes joint use of certain 'back-up' or administrative services, such as a secretarial office.

Government grants are available under certain EC schemes and the Agricultural and Horticultural Co-operation Scheme. Grants are available, for example, to assist storage/marketing cooperatives, fruit and vegetable producers' organizations, and 'mutual aid' production groups. A bank manager might find occasion to refer a customer in a cooperative to The Ministry of Agriculture for the possibility of applying for such a grant.

Provision of loans to a cooperative is governed by the normal canons of lending. The feasibility of the project, the ability of the cooperative to service the loan and security must be considered. In particular, you must be satisfied that the members' agreement includes safeguards that commit every member to the cooperative, i.e. there must be no scope for members to pull out, leaving the cooperative as a dwindling organization unable to operate at a sufficient volume of activity to service the loan adequately.

Banks may also be asked for bridging finance to cover the period between incurring expenditure and the receipt of grant money from the EC, which will inevitably take time to come through. EC grants are known as FEOGA grants, because the money comes from a fund with these initials.

In assessing a bridging finance proposition, you need to be satisfied that the cooperative members will:

- Qualify for the grant for which they have claimed;

- Spend a certain amount of their money on the project before they make use of the bank's facilities; and that

- When the grant money is received, it is used to repay the bank and does not go into the pockets of the cooperative members.

The Agricultural Mortgage Corporation Plc (AMC)

The AMC lends money to landowners and owner-occupiers of agricultural property for any agricultural purpose. This includes not only capital improvements and working capital, but also the purchase of agricultural property or the repayment of other borrowing. As security the AMC requires a first mortgage on the land.

Two basic types of loan are available over periods of five to 40 years:

- Repayment loans – Provide for repayment of capital during the life of the loan. (Half-yearly payments include both interest and capital.) With repayment loans, the maximum advance from the AMC is two-thirds of the value of the land offered as security.

- Interest-only loans – Interest only is paid during the loan period, and the capital is repaid at the end of the period. This method can be used effectively with life assurance policies or personal pension plans. With these types of loan, the maximum advance from the AMC is 50% of the value of the land offered as security.

AMC Lending Criteria:

- The AMC argues that 'it makes good sense to approach AMC for medium- and long-term loans and to use your bank for short-term lending and overdrafts'.

- The AMC recognizes that many investments in farming take a long time to pay back and so provides loans from five to 40 years (up to 60 years in the case of forestry loans).

- AMC loans are secured by mortgages on the farm property and it will normally advance up to 50% of the mortgage value of the property offered as security

- Interest rates are fixed or variable, depending on the borrower's choice. The borrower can also convert from fixed to variable interest rate, or vice versa, at no service charge cost.

- Interest is payable half-yearly in arrears. Borrowers can, if they wish, also opt to pay interest only and repay the capital amount of the loan at the end of the term of the loan. (Ordinary annuity repayment terms are also offered.)

- The AMC offers highly competitive interest rates, and most farmers are unlikely to be able to borrow more cheaply elsewhere.

- The AMC, like a bank, will vet loan applications and look for the same things that a banker looks for, i.e. ability of the borrower to repay out of the profits of the farm. The ability to service loans is of prime importance. Viability is assessed on the total area farmed, and not just on the land offered as security.

Venture Capital, MBOs and MBIs

In its formative stages the sector invested capital into new ventures (i.e. start up businesses), hence the term venture capital. This type of financing will typically be offered by specialist financial institutions. Terms vary enormously but will usually incorporate equity participation and exit options. However, as the sector was established focus shifted to lower-risk transactions involving mature businesses, where the equity returns required were obtained by leveraging the initial transaction so as to produce high levels of equity return for comparatively low levels of absolute growth. These transactions are mainly known today as management buy-outs (or MBOs) and management buy-ins (MBIs).

Management Buy-out (MBO)

The opportunity for such a transaction arises, for example, when a group decides to sell one or more subsidiary businesses. The management then make an offer to purchase, in conjunction with a venture capital fund/bank, or from their own resources, all the equity in the business with the majority of the consideration being raised by the MBO team and the venture fund as debt of various types. These highly-leveraged structures can work for debt providers because the businesses themselves can be well established and operating in mature markets. The existing management should already understand the business and are therefore best placed to know what unrealized potential actually exists within the business and exploit it. In addition, they should already understand and should have adequate controls to mitigate the specific risks within the business itself.

Although not the original plan, in many large transactions MBO companies have often remained as continuing investors. These continuations fall into three distinct subgroups:

● Those companies that are still active buy-outs as such, which may or may not be proceeding in accordance with the original business plan and where the final outcome is not known.

● Buy-outs that have run for the period anticipated in the original plan but for whom no appropriate exit has been achieved, often for reasons beyond the control of management or other equity providers.

● Businesses that have failed to deliver the growth in returns and capital value promised in the original buy-out but which continue to generate sufficient cash flow to survive at their existing level of activity and service most or all of their repayment obligations.

Exits of Management Buyouts in the UK by Year of Buy-out

Year of MBO	Float	Trade Sale	MBO MBI	Receiver-ship	No Exit	Total
1981	17	24	4	14	84	143
1982	23	36	7	17	154	237
1983	26	35	4	18	152	235
1984	20	53	8	18	140	239
1985	24	42	7	23	166	262
1986	17	46	7	22	223	315

Source: CMBRO/BDCL/Touche Ross.

Management Buy-in (MBI)

The emergence of the management buy-in (or MBI) has occurred more recently. In this situation, a group of managers within a sector identifies a business which they believe has growth potential in their hands. They persuade a venture capital fund of the merit of their strategy and the two parties then make an approach to the existing owners of the business to acquire it. Again a majority of debt is used in the financing structure to leverage (or increase) the potential equity returns when the growth is achieved.

Management buy-outs from the perspective of the venture capital fund

Venture capital funds raise their capital from pension funds and insurance companies who wish to diversify their investment portfolios as much as possible. They will have a returns expectation (or benchmark) for such an investment a few points higher than the long-term return available from a portfolio of equities. This is because, unlike equities, the investment in the venture capital fund will be illiquid for the duration of the fund, typically seven to ten years. A higher return is therefore required to compensate the investor for the lack of liquidity.

Having secured the funds the investment management team will then seek to invest the funds in a variety of venture capital situations, typically buy-outs of medium sized manufacturing companies. Ideally they will seek a wide variety of investments. A small fund, having say £20 million to invest, might seek to place between £1 million and £2 million at a time in about 15 investments. A large fund with £100 million might seek to invest £4 million to £8 million in about 20 investments, the object being to diversify the specific risk faced by the portfolio. This is very important because until all the funds are invested and at risk, the fund will be very lumpy and have high specific business risk. Venture capital funds may also participate in syndications of larger projects in order to improve the diversification of specific business risk in the portfolio.

Management buy-outs from the perspective of the buy-out management team

In the past, business performance could have been restricted by:

- Lack of new capital available stunting growth prospects, perhaps due to the diversion of funds into other businesses with greater growth prospects, or other larger parts of the business which are sustaining losses. This has the effect of preventing management from taking advantage of cheap opportunities to add value.

- Lack of vision for the company leading to acceptance of average industry returns when significant growth opportunities actually exist.

- Poorly structured remuneration arrangements for the key managers, offering them no incentive to take additional risks in order to add value to the business.

The business plan must be credible and the forecasts that derive from it believable. Developing the plan is probably the most difficult exercise for the MBO team as this will be rigorously evaluated and criticized by both the venture capital group and other investors in the buy-out.

Management buy-outs from the perspective of the lending banker

Generally, the prudent banker will look for the following:

- Primary and secondary sources of liquidity, the primary source being the cash flow of the business and any built-in cash safety margins. The secondary sources are the sale of the business, or in the last resort the sale of the assets to obtain debt repayment.

- A cash flow offering repayment of debt as soon as cash is generated.

In respect of security the lender will consider:

- The existing and likely future value of security in a recession.

- The pure asset value of all assets pledged as security in a liquidation situation.

- The vulnerability of the business to recession.

- What sources of additional liquidity may be available.

9.6   Franchising

Definition

Franchising is an operation whereby an organization (the franchisor) with a market-tested product or service enters into contracts with individuals (franchisees) to set up and finance their own business to operate under the franchisor's trade name to market the product or service. The franchisee is the potential entrepreneur. The franchisor charges an initial fee for use of the name and backup facilities, plus an ongoing annual charge usually based on the turnover or a loading on costs of supplies from the franchisor.

Some Advantages of Franchising

- Support of Large Organization – The principal advantage of franchising is that it allows the franchisee to start his own business with the support of a large organization.

- Reduced Risk – The risks involved in setting up your own business are significantly reduced, because the franchisor should have tried and tested the operation and established a business format that works.

- Access to Finance – Raising finance to get started may be made easier through the franchisor's arrangements with sources of finance, including specific clearing banks.

- Training – The franchisee with no experience in the business gets the training necessary to get started.

- Continuing Assistance – Continuing assistance is provided by the franchisor in, for example, advertising, training, research and development.

- Purchasing Power – Bulk purchasing power is obtained by the franchisor to the benefit of the franchisee.

Some Disadvantages of Franchising

- Restrictions – There may be contractual restrictions placed on the franchisee which he finds unreasonable covering the standard and quality of service provided, for example, or on the ultimate sale or transfer of the business.

- Payment of Fees – If he believes the success of his outlet results primarily from his own efforts, the franchisee may begin to regard the payment of continuing fees as a disincentive.

- Action of the Franchisor – The franchisor may not operate the franchise as the franchisee had expected. For example:

- Support may not be provided by the franchisor.
- The franchisor's policies may change to the disadvantage of the franchisee.
- The name of the franchise may not be promoted to best effect.

Example Questions on the Franchise Aspect by Potential Franchisees

- How strong is the market for this service? What information can the franchisor provide on this matter?

- Is the franchise a member of the British Franchise Association, which lays down a strict code of conduct, and, if so, is the franchisor a member of its arbitration scheme?

- How long has the franchisor been established?

- Is there any competition, either independent or under a different franchise?

- Has the franchisor prepared any projections, i.e. operating and cash budgets? Do these seem reasonable?

- How is the franchisor to be paid? Is it by way of royalty, a levy on profits, a levy on turnover, or by fixed payment regardless of results?

- Are there restrictions on the disposal of the business, if the franchisee wants to sell? Consult a solicitor about the terms of the franchise agreement.

- What assistance will the franchisor offer with the book-keeping and VAT aspects of the business?

Conclusion

Banks are developing new products aimed at borrowers, both personal and business, on an ongoing basis, and many of these include ways of reducing risk, both for the customer and the bank. You must keep up to date.

Case Study 18 – Wagstaff

Ken and Mary Wagstaff have maintained a satisfactory joint account at your branch for a number of years. Mr Wagstaff is 41 years old and has been the manager of a newsagent's shop in your local shopping centre for five years. Mr Wagstaff calls to see you. The company he works for is a national chain. It has decided to dispose of a number of its shops and he has the opportunity to buy the unit he manages. He tells you the following:

He believes that he will have to offer £67,000 to purchase the business.

- The shop is leasehold. A 20-year lease was granted in December 1990 at a rent of £10,000 p.a. subject to reviews every five years. The landlord is a national insurance company.

- He has arrived at the purchase price as follows:

  Fixtures and fittings £15,000

  Goodwill   £52,000

  Stock will be acquired at an agreed valuation. The current stock figure is around £30,000.

- He has extracted the following figures for the shop from the accounts he submits to head office:

£s	Actuals			Budget	
	12 months ending 30.6.93	12 months ending 30.6.94	12 months ending 30.6.95	3 months 30.9.95	12 months to 30.6.96
Sales	415,000	450,000	487,000	133,000	584,000
Gross Profit	73,500	82,500	92,100	24,000	110,000
Gross Profit %	17.7%	18.3%	18.9%	18.0%	18.8%
Salaries (inc. Manager)	31,700	34,400	37,100	9,500	38,000
Rent	10,000	10,000	10,000	2,500	16,000
Other Expenses	15,300	17,100	18,300	4,700	20,000
Net Profit	16,500	21,000	26,700	7,300	36,000
Net Profit %	4.0%	4.7%	5.5%	5.5%	6.2%
Credit Taken (Days)	36	41	35	42	35
Stock Turnover (Days)	22	20	21	25	21

- Mr and Mrs Wagstaff have £30,000 in building society accounts which they inherited from Mrs Wagstaff's mother, who died last year.

- The Wagstaffs jointly own their house. which they believe is worth £75,000 (subject to a £30,000 endowment mortgage). They also own a two-year-old van.

- Mr Wagstaff's current salary from the shop is £18,000 p.a. His wife, who has not worked recently, would assist him in the shop and this would enable him to save wages of £8,000 p.a. currently paid to other staff.

Wagstaff asks for your assistance to purchase the business.

Required:

Set out in note form your analysis of the business and its requirements, and indicate how you would respond to the request.

Suggested Answer

This question was a very small-scale management buy out of a newsagent shop owned by a large chain.

The Wagstaffs have been good customers of the bank and can provide a substantial capital stake from their own resources. Mr Wagstaff has a good knowledge of the business, having run it for 5 years, and under his stewardship it has apparently been successful. All the indications therefore are that management will be good, but it is still necessary to question why the national chain has decided to sell and what the competition is and how it might develop. For example, newsagents are facing increasing competition from large supermarkets.

A particularly important issue will be the price being paid. No value is being put on the lease, which is probably sensible, but a view needs to be taken as to whether the fixtures and fittings are in good condition and are indeed worth £15,000. The bigger issue is the value of goodwill. At just under 2 times last year's net profit it does not seem unreasonable and an alternative assessment would be on the basis of average sales – goodwill amounts to 5½ weeks sales, which again looks not unreasonable.

The amount Wagstaff needs to borrow is ostensibly £67,000 less the £30,000 he and his wife have in the building society, i.e. £37,000. Legal expenses etc. need to be added and, more importantly, a view has to be taken as to what sort of working capital facility is needed to finance ongoing trading. £30,000 or thereabouts will have to be paid for the stock immediately but the business ought to be able to have the capacity to finance some of this on credit as replacement items are bought. Comparing the historical credit taken and stock turnover figures suggest long term that it may be possible to finance virtually all the stock on credit. However, it has to be recognized that the current credit terms are for a national chain and may not be available to a small shop. The issue has to be pursued with Wagstaff and a simple cash flow forecast drawn up in the light of whatever credit terms he can obtain. However, it does look as though an overdraft limit of £10,000/£15,000 ought to be enough.

A term loan of say £40,000 over 5-10 years should be well within the business's capacity to repay given the strong historical track record and net profits. Repayments over 5 years will be around £10,000 against last year's net profit of £26,700. Some caution is needed because both the historical and budgeted profits are for the current owners and may not reflect the new situation. Also the rent is budgeted to jump by £12,000 in a full year, although wage costs should be £8,000 lower. Wagstaff needs to produce a proper budget reflecting how he sees the situation.

A charge over the lease is required as security and a second charge over the Wagstaffs' house will also be appropriate.

Overall the request is straightforward and is capable of agreement subject to a satisfactory budget and cash flow forecast.

Term Lending

In 1971 the U.K. Clearing Banks began to expand the period over which loans were granted following the abandonment of the deposit cartel, which allowed them to obtain a wider range of deposit maturities.

The granting of medium- and long-term finance, usually for the acquisition of fixed assets, requires the lending banker to look further into the future, thus increasing the uncertainty of repayment, particularly where he only has access to short-term projections for the future.

The financing of fixed assets requires the banker to match the length of credit granted with the expected life of the asset. It is usual for loans to be granted for periods up to 20 years for the finance of fixed assets, with support for working capital requirements usually for a shorter period of, say, 5 years maximum.

It is usual for a borrower to have a choice of interest rates, either fixed or variable. The variable interest rate may be linked the bank's base rate or LIBOR. The customer may seek an option to switch between fixed and variable interest rates during the life of a loan. With longer-term loans the interest rate is often reviewed after a period of 2 or 3 years.

Such loans are usually the subject of a facility letter setting out the terms and conditions upon which the loan is granted.

Repayment can be structured to suit the borrower with either monthly or quarterly repayments, or sometimes a bullet repayment at the end of the loan period. If requested a capital repayment holiday is sometimes agreed for a period of 2 or 3 years at the commencement of the loan to improve the business's cash flow.

In addition to the interest-rate formula agreed the customer will often pay a negotiation fee to cover the cost of setting up the facility.

Commercial Mortgages

Some bank lenders will provide commercial mortgages to finance the purchase or renovation of commercial premises. The amount advanced would normally be 75%/80% of the cost or value of the property, whichever is lower. Such lendings normally are for a maximum period of 25 years.

Interest rates may be either variable or fixed by arrangement, with an interest review held periodically. Drawdown may usually be made as a lump sum or in tranches to suit customer requirements.

The borrower often has the option of a capital repayment holiday at the commencement of the loan, with repayments made either monthly or quarterly, by arrangement. A negotiation fee is usually payable for the setting up of the commercial mortgage.

Pension Loans for Professional Persons

Such loans are provided for members of recognized professions for business purposes and are usually repaid from the proceeds of an Inland Revenue approved pension plan.

A professional is defined as someone who is in partnership and self-employed and has undergone the training required to become a practitioner in a profession and is the holder of a current and acceptable qualification awarded by the recognized body or institute of the profession. He or she must be deemed a good credit risk and hold or be in the process of arranging an appropriate self-employed pension policy or personal pension plan.

Normally such a loan is used for investment in a professional's business, by the purchase of a share in a professional firm or membership of a group practice. It may also be used by the partner or partners concerned of long-term fixed assets for the development of the business.

There is usually a maximum sum that may be borrowed, depending on the lender's criteria. The actual amount lent may be related to the maximum lump sum available on the maturity of the policy, the size of disposable income, the amount of premiums paid annually, or the value of premiums paid to the date of the loan request. A tax-free lump sum is normally available, subject to Inland Revenue guidelines.

Loans can often be made for a term of up to 35 years. The length of the loan will depend on the age of the applicant and the applicant's anticipated retirement age. The loan is repaid upon the retirement of the policyholder, usually between the ages of 50 and 70, or a sale of the practice, or maturity of the policy.

Loans will normally be separately secured. Pension plan policies are not assignable and cannot be offered as security. A negotiation fee is usually payable for facilities of this type.

Asset Finance

Customers often find that capital is better used expanding the business, buying raw materials, or developing sales rather than purchasing fixed assets. Some alternate asset finance facilities improve cash flow and allow customers greater flexibility in running their businesses.

One of the most common facilities is that of leasing. A lease is a transaction where the owner of an asset (the lessor) agrees to let someone else (the lessee) have the use of it for a specified period for a rental payment. The leasing company provides up to 100% of the purchase price of the asset in return a fixed monthly sum which is agreed from the outset. Most commercial lease arrangements run for between 3 and 5 years. Shorter or longer periods can be arranged.

All major U.K. banks have leasing subsidiaries, as do most foreign banks operating in the U.K. There are also specialist leasing companies and some manufacturers have their own in-house leasing facilities. Virtually all assets can be leased. There is normally a minimum lease amount but no maximum.

The terms of financing can be matched to the anticipated useful life of the asset. Customers are able to retain assets for as long as it is economic to do so, because although the lease is for a fixed period it is possible to terminate the agreement early or extend it into a secondary lease period. Lease rentals can often be paid from the revenue generated by the asset.

Leases are commonly divided into two types: finance leases and operating leases.

Finance Leases

In a finance lease, the minimum rentals to which the lessee is committed cover the full cost of the asset plus financing costs. A finance lease is therefore one that transfers most of the risks and rewards of ownership to the lessee.

A finance lease generally has the following features:

- The lease period will usually be for between three and five years but not longer than the estimated useful life of the asset.

- The lease period and payments due may not normally be altered and neither the lessee nor the lessor has the right to early termination, although in the event of default or by mutual agreement the lease may be terminated and the asset sold to cover remaining payments.

- The lessee chooses the equipment to be purchased by the lessor and negotiates the purchase terms with the supplier. Any discounts obtained are reflected in the rentals charged, but the lessor takes no responsibility for it being fit for the intended purpose. The lessor will provide up to 100% of the purchase price of the asset in return for a fixed monthly sum which is agreed from the outset.

- The lessor requires the lessee to maintain and insure the asset.

- Rentals are normally tax deductible.

- Payments can be matched to the depreciation of the asset.

- Additional security is not normally required.

- In the U.K., if the asset has a residual value at the end of the lease period, the lessee has the option of extending the lease (often for a small rental) or, if he no longer requires the asset, selling it on behalf of the lessor. The lessee can then usually retain a portion of the proceeds of the sale (technically, as a refund of rentals). However, the lessee may not become the owner of the asset at any stage. In many other countries this restriction does not apply, and the lessee may buy the asset.

A leasing arrangement is a means of financing an asset, directly competing with other means of finance such as bank lending.

Operating Lease

The distinction between a finance lease and an operating lease is essentially one of degree. The main difference lies in the treatment of the asset's residual value. In an operating lease the lessee foregoes his right to the asset's residual value. An estimate of the asset's residual value is built into the rental structure and the risk inherent in this estimate is borne by the lessor. This gives the lessee greater certainty over the cost of using the asset.

Operating leases generally have the following features:

- The lease period is normally somewhat shorter than the primary period for a finance lease of a similar asset but still usually falls within the same three- to five-year range.

- Total lease rentals payable will usually be lower than for a finance lease, reflecting the fact that the asset is expected to have some material residual value after the end of the lease.

- Periodic lease payments are likely to be higher than for a finance lease, reflecting the increased risk and closer involvement of the lessor (i.e. an operating lease will cost more per month, but for fewer months, than a finance lease for the same asset).

- The lessee can sometimes terminate the lease early. However, unless this is in order to replace the asset, usually a computer, with another lease of a newer model, there may be a cancellation charge.

- Rentals are fully tax deductible, except in the case of cars.

- An operating lease is not usually repayable upon demand.

- Because insurance and maintenance are important in maintaining the asset's residual value, they are more important to the lessor in an operating lease than in a finance lease. The lessors may therefore carry out maintenance themselves, or verify that the lessee has done so, and ensure that adequate insurance cover has been taken out.

- There will be an option to extend the agreement at the end of the initial lease period, or if the customer wishes, he simply returns the asset.

Operating leases are used for assets that the user requires only for a specific period and which are likely to be saleable at the end of that period. Vehicles, computers, and aircraft are examples of items for which a reasonably active second-hand market exists and for which an operating lease might be appropriate.

Hire Purchase

Commercial hire purchase is similar to finance leasing. The critical difference between a hire purchase agreement and a finance lease is that in a hire purchase agreement, provided the conditions of the contract have been met, ownership of the asset passes to the user at the end of the hire period.

This has important tax implications and a hire purchase arrangement has none of the tax advantages of a leasing contract, but in all other respects it makes very little difference. The hirer, like the finance lessee, has substantially all the risks and rewards of ownership and views hire purchase as a way of financing fixed assets. It is sometimes referred to as 'lease purchase' or 'lease with option to purchase'.

Many U.K. customers prefer hire purchase to leasing for the somewhat irrational reason that at the end of a hire purchase contract they own the asset. In a finance lease title remains with the lessor but this has no effect on the lessee's right to usage and possession compared to outright ownership.

Hire purchase is probably most familiar as a means of financing major items of consumer expenditure. Carpets, domestic appliances and furniture are often sold under hire purchase agreements. Cars are also often sold to the personal sector via hire purchase agreements.

Benefits to a business include:

● Budgeting is made easier because the payment structure is agreed at the outset.

● Payments can be matched to the depreciation of the asset.

● You can claim immediate capital allowances on the asset.

● The interest element of the payments is tax deductible.

● In the U.K. VAT is immediately recoverable on the whole purchase price (except in the case of cars).

● Additional security is not normally required.

● A lease purchase agreement is not usually repayable upon demand.

● Funding is on balance sheet and there may be a choice of fixed or variable interest-rate agreements.

However, hire purchase is also common outside the personal sector and can be used for a wide range of assets. Customers for hire purchase tend to come from the manufacturing sector and to use HP to finance items of plant and machinery with a relatively long expected life.

Advantages of Leasing

Convenience

A lease spares the customer the necessity of finding a large sum of cash to buy an asset outright. In addition, the documentation for all but the largest leases is very straightforward, and most leases are quick to set up. Lease payments can be structured to suit the customer, and the major leasing companies compete actively to find new variations.

In an operating lease the lessor takes care of aspects of the ownership of the asset, such as ultimate resale, which might be bothersome to a user wanting the asset for only a limited period. The lessor's security is the leased asset, which avoids the necessity for a floating charge over assets, which many customers perceive as complicated and restricting.

Lower Cost

Leasing can often use a combination of tax and cash-flow advantages to reduce the overall cost of acquiring an asset, particularly in large-value leases. Its attractiveness to the lessee depends a great deal on his tax situation, as well as on the alternative financing opportunities available and the other advantages of leasing. In particular, lease rentals are generally fully tax deductible, and usually allow a faster write off than the combination of interest and depreciation deductible for an owned asset.

Developing Technology

Items of rapidly developing technology, such as computers and office equipment, make up a growing proportion of leased assets. Leasing offers the customer a convenient way of staying abreast of technology while introducing greater certainty into the cost of doing so.

Alternate Source of Finance

Leasing is an alternative source of medium-term finance. By leasing, a customer may keep open lines of bank credit or overdraft facilities which he would prefer to use for working capital requirements.

Off Balance Sheet Finance

In some countries (principally the U.S.A. and the U.K.), assets used under finance leases must be treated as if they were purchased assets and capitalized (i.e. included in the company's balance sheet as if the company owned them), but assets used under operating leases can be excluded from the balance sheet.

Advantages of Hire Purchase Finance

The advantages of hire purchase are in almost all respects identical to those for finance leases. However, because the asset ultimately becomes the property of the hirer, he is entitled to capital allowances as if he had purchased it.

Summary

After having studied this chapter, you should be able to:

- Understand the risks involved in trade finance;
- Be aware of the various types of bank facility, specifically designed to assist importers and exporters;
- Have a working knowledge of some of the unique uncertainties facing your importing and exporting customers;
- Be aware of some of the specialist services available in lending situations;
- Understand the most commonly used risk management products;
- Describe the features of the main alternative forms of business finance;
- Analyse the needs of borrowing customers and recommend appropriate products.

GLOSSARY

Accrual Accounting
The reporting of income and expense at the time they are earned or incurred, not when they are received or paid.

Asset
Item of value, which is owned by a company or person and is expected to be of economic benefit. Assets may be divided into fixed assets (e.g. buildings), current assets (e.g. stock) or intangible assets (e.g. patents).

Balance Sheet
Periodic (usually annual) statement of a company's financial position, which summarizes what is owned (assets) and owed (liabilities) by the business.

Capital
Money invested in a business by its owners in order to earn income.

Cash Flow
The inflow and outflow of cash though a business.

Cash Flow Forecast
Estimation of expected cash flow used to alert management to future cash shortages or surpluses.

Corporate Strategy
Assessment of the relationship between an organization and its environment, resulting in a plan to achieve the business objectives.

Current Assets
Assets of a company that are likely to be converted into cash (e.g. debtors, work in progress) within 12 months.

Depreciation
The amount by which a fixed asset is diminished in a particular year though its use in the business. This amount is charged against profits.

Equity
The capital invested in a company by its owners, together with profits from previous years that have not been distributed as dividend.

Fixed Assets

The assets of a company (e.g. equipment, land and plant) that are held not for conversion into cash, but over long periods to further the main trading activities.

Fixed Costs

Costs that are unaffected by changes in volume, but tend to change over time (e.g. rent, rates).

Gearing

Relationship between the amounts invested in a business by its owners (equity) and by outsiders (debt).

Indirect Cost (or Overhead)

Cost not directly associated with a unit of production and which will be apportioned across a number of activities or products(e.g. the cost of running a canteen in a car factory).

Intangible Assets

Assets that are neither physical nor financial (e.g. goodwill, trademarks, licences etc.)

Inventory

List detailing stock that is kept for use as required – particularly raw materials, work in progress, supplies and finished goods.

Liability

Obligation of a company to make payment in the foreseeable future for goods or services already received.

Limited Company

Company in which the shareholders' liability is limited by shares or guarantee.

Liquidity

The pool of accessible funds, either in cash or in assets that may be transformed rapidly into cash, to meet immediate debts.

Long-term Debt

Loan repayable one year or more from date of transaction.

Net Realizable Value

The price at which assets could be sold minus all the cost of selling them.

Overtrading

Trading that exceeds the financial capacity of a business and may lead the company into financial distress.

Payback Period
Time taken for the initial investment in an asset or project to be repaid from profits.

Preference Shares
Form of share capital whereby the holders have a preferential right to receive a dividend out of profits of a certain percentage of the share capital before the owners of ordinary shares get any dividend.

Price Earnings Ratio (PE)
The relationship that a company's profits bear to the publicly quoted value of its shares, usually expressed as market value of share/earnings per share.

Profit
What remains when costs (of producing, selling etc.) have been deducted from revenues.

Sale and Leaseback
Form of financing by which a business sells an asset that it owns and then leases it back at an annual rent from the purchaser.

Share Capital
The amount of money invested in a company by its risk-taking shareholders.

Share Premium
Money received by a company for a share issue that is in excess of its nominal value.

Solvency
Maintenance of a sufficient level of liquid assets by a company to meet its short-term obligations.

Statement of Source and Application Funds (SSAF)
Analysis of the sources of funds (financial resources) and how of they have been used, showing how and why a company's cash position has changed.

SWOT
Acronym for strengths, weaknesses, opportunities and threats relating to a company. These are investigated as part of strategic analysis.

Turnover
The gross revenue earned from providing goods/services to customers.

Variable Costs
Costs that vary directly with the level of output.

Working Capital
The amount of short-term funds available to a business to perform its normal trading operations. Usually defined as the difference between current assets and current liabilities.

Index

Index

Index